GHOSTS IN THE MACHINE

GHOSTS IN THE MACHINE

SPECULATING ON THE DARK HEART OF POP CINEMA

BY **MICHAEL ATKINSON**

LIMELIGHT EDITIONS

These essays were originally published, in sometimes different form, in *Film Comment, Sight & Sound, The Village Voice, Detour, Bright Lights Film Journal* and *Baltimore City Paper*. "Long Black Limousine: Rock Biopics" originally appeared in *Celluloid Jukebox*, ed. Jonathan Romney and Adrian Wootton (British Film Institute, 1995).

First Limelight Edition November 1999

Published by Proscenium Publishers Inc., New York.

Cover and interior design by Orlando Adiao

Manufactured in the United States of America.

Library of Congress Cataloging-in-Publication Data

Atkinson, Michael, 1962-
    Ghosts in the machine : the dark heart of pop cinema / by Michael
    Atkinson.
        p.   cm.
    ISBN 0-87910-285-3
    1. Motion pictures.   I. Title.
    PN1995.A775 1999
    791.43—dc21   99-39871
                                                    CIP

For Riley

CONTENTS

INTRODUCTION

You're sitting in the dark, waiting for that moment of lambent awe when your conscious mind may willfully and with immense satisfaction recede into its own shadows and surrender your eyes and id to the image on the rectangular screen. The waiting is half the pleasure, because it's not merely an image when it comes (although it is in reality less than even that); it's an endless corridor into a separate but instantly intelligible world, a world that threatens to extend out beyond the colonnade afforded us but never does, a world in fact that seems controlled by our vision, our act of watching. As long as we're watching, it's *our* film, our experience. If we don't watch, could the world of a film's alley be said to exist in any significant way? For others, perhaps; for us, decidedly not — an unseen film is as real to us as a forgotten dream. At best a movie sits in the can or on the videostore shelf, coiled inaccessibly like a snail in its shell, waiting for us to unfurl it and then enter its phantasia. Of course, film culture began in earnest in the '50s when movieheads began to realize in important ways that a film's corridor of vision was not under their control but that of the film's director — it was his or her will that dictated in what direction the cinematic hallway would aim, what would clutter its corners and who would walk its mile. This epiphany didn't ruin the dream; on the contrary, it compounded it.

Ever since, we witness the film with one eye as a construct, as the other crosses the veil-like interface between worlds and scans the illusory horizon. Cinephilia, as well as serious film criticism and its readership, was born.

We do not truly participate in the movie regardless of who's in control, but because we take the corridor as ours, we are so close we can smell the rain steam rising off the street, the villagers' torches, the unicorn dung. We are so close that we can, if we listen, hear the lawless chant of the troglodyte that is our cultural crucible and has been since mass culture began. If movies are this century's conscious/subconscious, then the Conradian struggle with our darker selves can be seen, simply put, as their neurosis — except that the struggle is anything but simple, or anywhere near its match point. Pop cinema is fraught with the ambiguous damnation inherent in the civilized attempt at spackling over our primal mechanisms, at characterizing the 20th century's ascension into world technocommunity as a circumstance that somehow makes us spiritually, emotionally, viscerally different than our star-worshiping forbears. Take Griffith's *The Birth of a Nation,* described by Woodrow Wilson as "writing history with lightning"; how prescient and immense that description of Griffith's scorchingly immodest testament to ethnocentrism seems today. Wilson meant it as an endorsement of the depiction of history, but what he said pegged the movie *as* history, as a monument to human viciousness. Griffith's immersion into racist mythopoeia wasn't a mistake, as we tend to consider it now; it was and is an inevitable tragedy, the failure of the culture as well as the man to fulfill their own claims of enlightenment. Name a "better" film about racism — perhaps anti-Semitic Nazi melodramas like *Jud Suss* are its only rivals. Because it's a movie, Griffith's tragedy lives on today as that of no book, play or artwork ever could. It is history that has no end. *Birth* still happens to us anew each time someone watches it, and its bitter angels will always haunt us.

Nothing else we've ever created as a culture, except perhaps automobiles and nuclear warfare, has been as clear a window on our own worst instincts as cinema. Complex entities born of the labor, ideas and prejudices of often hundreds of individuals, movies (like cathedrals) cannot help but display the subconscious impulses of their society. Continually, what are conceived and consumed as innocent pop movies — from Feuillade to the Marx Brothers to film noir to *I Married a Monster from Outer Space* and beyond — are in fact manifestations of wild horror, superstitious ignorance, fatalistic dread and bigoted savagery. The machine in question, then, is the irreducible, quasi-cosmic apparatus of the movies — the mechanical/chemical/plastic gadgetry from the zoetrope to perishable nitrate celluloid to pure digital imaging; the self-apprehended movie history of entrancing faces, hypnotic body motion, cataclysmic events, seductive landscapes, moving fables and unforgettable utterances; and the entire "media culture" (including everyone's individualized brain bank of cinematic memories) born of its first century; all of it as fantastic and divine in scope as any medieval sorcerer's grand design for a stairway to Heaven. The ghosts are you and me.

I was first drawn to movies through what is now tentatively labeled "monster culture," the mudslide of youthful fascination with old and not-so-old horror and science fiction films that began once those absurd but subtext-packed movies began showing up regularly on TV in the late 50s and early 60s. The obsession was perhaps epitomized by the Universal horror cycle of the 30s and 40s, the only great roar of pure Gothic spirit in American film, stretching from 1931, with *Frankenstein* and *Dracula,* into the war years. These chilly, rotting-on-the-vine antiquities wore their expressionism lightly, and any child who watched them on television in the 60s knows the imagery in his or her bones: the dark gray heavens of fake forest, ground fog, decaying castles, cobwebs thick as paste, Tudor villages, gypsy caravans, walking corpses, Dwight Frye bulging his eyes out like an electrified kinkajou. A hidden, faux Euro hinterland where wolves roam free, the Universal horror landscape must have provided some kind of antiquey succor for Depression-era moviegoers, but for the Aurora monster model generation, the films felt more like sleepy, corroded dreams of violation (sexual, communal and otherwise), pubertal shock and deathlessness. Responsible for more specific cultural touchstones than the era's westerns, musicals and gangster films combined (Jack Pierce's flatheaded Frankenstein monster makeup, Lugosi's accent, the hunchback lab assistant, the mad scientist, the throbbing electrical hardware of the lab itself, crowds of townspeople with torches, the details of werewolf myth, etc.), these "vintage" photoplays did shudder regularly with conflicting accents, locales and the viral manner by which modern anachronisms (suits, slang, cars) softened their menace. But watching them alone in your living room as a child because no one else could be bothered with the damn things, there was still the nervous sense of glimpsing a forgotten edge-world struggle with its own, seemingly ceaseless metaphysical ruptures.

But that was just the beginning. What were on the face of it absurd and childish exercises in genre exploitation and post-atomic hyperbole seemed to the preadolescent yahoo I was then to be expressions of anxiety so deep the movies themselves couldn't quite fathom it all. The fear of flesh inherent in Boris Karloff's lost, mewling patchwork corpse in *Frankenstein* (1931); the grotesque parody of painful biophysical transformation — sexual maturation, aging or disease, take your pick — in *The Wolfman* (1941); the profound distrust of modern middle-class living spaces and accouterments in *The Incredible Shrinking Man* (1957); the surreal, entomophobic visions of natural chaos in *Tarantula* (1958), among scores of other Brobdignagian bug movies of the Eisenhower era; the startlingly overt portrait of psychological struggle in the perambulating brains' attack on the house of the scientist who foolishly manufactured them in *Fiend Without a Face* (1958) — if I didn't as a child quite understand what was profoundly upsetting about these movies, I nevertheless loved them for the mysteries they held like monstrous sideshow jars. Of course, such films helplessly invoke the diminutive and bombarded outlook of childhood, but nevertheless the subterranean sense of aboriginal unease they possessed is, I discovered later as I began to ingest film noir in Mike Mazursky-sized quantities, essentially ubiquitous. Little more than hardboiled formula pictures, film noir emerged from its postwar cave as a worldview whose singular cohesiveness and darkling spirit had little or nothing to do with the filmmakers' conscious intentions. The films simply stood knee-deep in their society's current, absorbing its repressed rage and terror and then spitting it back at us in shocking, shadowy, bite-sized hunks of flatout nihilism. What began as merely crime melodramas became a living document of our collective doubt. Just like *Birth of a Nation*, noir (real noir, which for me had its last cackle with Sam Fuller's *Underworld U.S.A.* in 1960) was a taking of the cultural pulse, and the diagnosis, as usual, wasn't hopeful.

Movies — particularly horror films, noir, conspiracy thrillers, war movies, animations, exploitation toss-offs, experimental films, rock movies and weepies, but really any movie at all, from *Le Voyage a Travers L'Impossible* to *It's a Wonderful Life* to *Titanic* — are the modern equivalent of folktales, insofar as they externally dominate our consciousness the way precivilized mythologies used to, and insofar as they render the same psychosocial service, whether it be in the end actual Aristotelian *katharsis* or simply taking the mad dogs cornered in our blood — by language, civility and social enforcement — out for a wee stretch of the legs. Viewed this way, cinema has an essentially pagan cast, tremendously dependent as it is on the primacy of events, on icons, imagery, symbology, ritual, cause, effect. Even the movies about Christ describe an untamed universe demanding sacrifice, idolatry and benighted fear. (Perhaps *especially* they do.) If a movie could be called realistic, then so could the belief in having angered the harvest god and caused a famine. Both are fatally, ineluctably human. We are able to take the movies' subtextual nightfall for granted because, although we are the same beasts, we are somehow different than we were just a century ago: we've all grown into adult consciousness together gazing down that corridor, all movies becoming one infinite "universal movie" (in Bruce Conner's phrase) in our united forebrain, a single alleyway as seductive, frightening and tragic as any real experience, and sometimes more so. The corridor has become a permanent attachment to our lives, an additional hallway in our homes we can step down at any time. These essays, all written on the edge of the millennium and within spitting distance either way of movies' centennial, have been my way of attempting to understand that corridor, why it never disappears and why it still frightens me. More vital than regarding film as an aesthetic, anaesthetic or economic force is regarding it as a soil sample of our aggregate psyche, especially once all of the landscaping and sculpted bushes have been shunted aside and only the worms remain. Then, suddenly, our truth hits open air and, as H.G. Wells said, we go in fear.

Michael Atkinson
New York
1999

YOU MAY NOT LIKE WHAT YOU FIND: THE *PLANET OF THE APES* CYCLE

Midst the unflagging 90s epidemic of post-Boom, slack-fueled, Tarantino-inflected Seventies cyber-nostalgia, it's a shock to realize that arguably the era's most complex and outrageous popcult entity has been all but ignored: the *Planet of the Apes* cycle. To cast a cold eye back on the infamous SF pentalogy is to revisit, for me, a preadolescent compulsion and state of feverish Saturday-matinee geek-worship. Largely regarded then as the *Nightmare on Elm Street* and *Friday the 13th* movies were in the 80s — a seemingly neverending series of lurid fantasies meant exclusively for "monster culture" aficionados and the 5th grade readers of *X-Men*, *Creepy* and *The Monster Times* — the *Apes* films were hugely popular with their target audience. The phenomena didn't even end with the release of the final film, *Battle for the Planet of the Apes* (1973); that summer, the notorious *Go Ape!* festivals ran amok, during which theaters would run all five films in sequence, starting at 11 AM. The series spawned two television shows and a kudzu jungle of spinoff merchandising, including models, action figures, masks, novels, comics, plates, bubble-gum cards, etc. That three out of the five films were simply wretched, directed by hacks J. Lee Thompson and Don

Taylor, only further justified their exile to the dodge-ball demographic.

For ten-year-olds (of which I consider myself then an archetype), the *Apes* movies were a snowballing, nightmarish spectacle of disorder and madness, in which the apes were convincing enough to disquiet us with realizing that, while not looking much like actors, they didn't quite look like real apes either, and whose collected narrative fucked with both temporal logic and racial subversion in ways that could shock anybody weaned on post-Reagan-era Hollywood culture. (Each of the five films ends with a narrative Nagasaki.) Few adults, then or since, seem to have recognized the cycle as the radical pop culture apocalypse it still is, formally and thematically. It's one of the few science fiction movie texts that rivals in sophistication the best SF literature, and it's the only cinematic experiment with time travel that completes its own hopeless cycle on a planetary scale, an elaborate scheme worked out in the four sequels by screenwriter Paul Dehn. Most of all, especially when viewed today and in light of Hollywood's still frustrated efforts to remake the first film (Oliver Stone and Arnold Schwarzenegger were both attached to the project for some time), the *Apes* films stand as the scariest, ballsiest, most breathtaking essay on racial conflict in film history.

Think about it: where but in film #4, *Conquest of the Planet of the Apes* (1972), has a movie ever dared to climax in a successful, implicitly *global* armed slave revolt? From the get-go, the series was a broad and hysterical parable on race relations; the first film emerged in 1968, knee-deep in civil rights dialogue and hippie-era liberalism. Directed by Franklin J. Schaffner, co-scripted by Rod Serling and Michael Wilson (from the otherwise trifling, and erroneously titled, Pierre Boulle novel *Monkey Planet*), *Planet of the Apes* (1968) was packed with glib *Twilight Zon*isms (the orangutan tribunal doing see-no-evil, hear-no-evil, speak-no-evil; a gorilla guard muttering "Human see, human do") and roughshod potshots at apartheid-think: an elder ape maintaining that only apes have souls, the observation that being clean-shaven makes a man "look less intelligent," the Darwinian dread implicit in every ape's reaction to stranger-in-a-strange-land astronaut Taylor (Charlton Heston), who, as chimp Zira (Kim Hunter) boldly asserts at one point, "must have sprang from our own." (Remember the first word spoken by an ape, over a stack of human corpses: "Smile.") She doesn't know how right she is — neither do we, until the end — and every supremacist's deepest qualm rears its head: of being the progeny of an inferior, less "divinely inspired" breed of creature, of having "other" blood run in your veins.

The movie laughed at every tribal instinct we've got, which may be another reason why, in an adult world where tribes are taken very seriously indeed, especially in the 90s, they remain cinema non grata. (The vacant phenomena of 80s slasher films have garnered more homages and academic consideration.) Recognizable American authority icons are routinely defiled: the Statue of Liberty; NASA (the nexus of anti-ape hysteria in *Escape from the Planet of the Apes* (1971, film #3); human scientists, presidents and governors portrayed as bigoted scum. Even John Ford's Monument Valley stands in for a nuclear wasteland — in a film about racial rancor, yet. (There's no ignoring HUAC-roadkill Lew Ayres' appearance in the last film as an orangutan who deems himself "the keeper of his own conscience.") Still, what as children gave us the heebie-jeebies seems, in retrospect, relatively less fantastic. The apes, after all, were only a few hundred years behind the human civilization that Taylor left behind, and with their slave hunts, superstitions, medieval admixture of science and religion, and Nazi-like racial theories, seemed hardly any stranger or crueller than man at his most modern. Perhaps what remains most disturbing, and what may have been a larger part of our juvenile fascination with the films than we ever suspected, was the recognition of our de-evolved selves in the apes' xenophobia, righteous ignorance and mythmaking. Both *Planet of the Apes* and the first sequel, *Beneath the Planet of the Apes* (1969), were intended as crude we've-seen-the-enemy-and-it's-us metaphor; what doesn't seem as intentional is the primal unease over *otherness* it musters within ourselves, regardless of race. Somewhere under the skin the central ordeal of Heston's missing link is one we face only in our darkest dreams.

But, as a text, is it inherently racist? (Note, queasily, the implicit IQ caste system stretching from the light-skinned heads-of-state orangutans to the pitch-black, thug-like gorillas.) What begins as a evolutionary switcheroo turns, as the series progresses, into a civil rights conundrum; can apes be equated with African Americans without setting off a sociopolitical H-bomb? Even if the apes themselves become oppressed, violently oppose their oppressors, and succeed in acquiring a social stasis (in *Battle*) at least temporarily just and peaceful? In 1968, perhaps not; today, most certainly — anyone remaking the first film today has his work cut out for him. Identity politics being the ethical quicksand they are, however, the *Apes* films read today like koans: contradictory, equivocal, cryptic. Within every deliberate liberalism lurks a reactionary instinct; every racist misstep is steeped in radical good intentions. They may be, when the smoke clears, the ideal film text for the coming century, the ultimate cross-country track on which to run the principles of political correctness against one another.

In the first two of the five films, the apes represent white Western Civ a few Galileos short of a Renaissance; it was with *Escape* that the tables began to slowly turn. Suddenly, the free-thinking chimpanzees Zira, Cornelius and Milo (Kim Hunter, Roddy McDowell and, briefly, Sal Mineo) are caged, victimized, characterized as freaks, and eventually as threats, by 1970s America. As was clear from the start, the *Apes* movies are a study in the hunger for, and transferral of, political power: within minutes of glimpsing the primitive humans in the first film, Taylor asserts that in a month "we'll be running this planet." Of course, the power is divided along special lines. In *Escape*, the weasely white-men-in-charge Eric Braeden and William Windom are ostensibly out to prevent the planetary decimation that ends *Beneath* (recounted by Zira as seen through Taylor's resurrected ship's window — the cycle's only serious lapse of reason), but there's an acute sense of irrational lynchmob fever right under the surface. There's more than a whiff of Johannesburg in the final helicopter shot of Zira and Cornelius shot dead in an empty California naval yard, and perhaps a hint of Malcolm Little in the penultimate scene of the orphaned baby chimp burbling "Mommy," suggesting an inevitable moment when the future will have its revenge on the past, thus creating itself.

Conquest of the Planet of the Apes is the cycle's Götterdämmerung, a shrill, anarchic pulp prophecy of social mayhem, and without it the series would have remained merely a baby-boomer guilty pleasure. It's also the most incendiary: we're introduced into a near-future ("North

America — 1991" says a title) where "normal," present-day yet still oddly unapelike apes are kept as slaves, after being cultivated years earlier as pets. It's the B-side of the world as it's seen three films ago and many thousands of years hence. *Escape's* milieu was recognizably here-and-now; in *Conquest*, set a few decades later, suddenly we're in Harriet Tubman territory. Indeed, Cornelius and Zira's grown son Caesar (also McDowell) watchfully enters the modern, ape-serviced metropolis with revolution running hotly in his veins. The slaves have serial numbers, cannot gather together or communicate (their masters are fined if they do), are routinely administered electroshock, and are trained for everything from waiting tables to factory work, a cold-blooded service economy so mercenary we glimpse at one point out-of-work humans protesting the shortage of jobs — a scalding prediction of the affirmative action issue. (Evil governor Don Murray does little else besides agonize over ape disobedience stats.) The humiliations and atrocities — including subduing gorillas by flamethrower — are both futuristically hyperbolic and ringing with memories of Eisenhower-era Alabama. (Caesar refers unironically to his ape army as "my people" at several points.) We are never meant to ponder the fate of the planet as Braeden and Windom did; indeed, concern for the outcome of the human race is a moot issue. Right here, right now, the apes *must* revolt, and if it means the end of human civilization, or eventually the Earth itself, so be it.

Conquest's only sympathetic human (beyond liberal circus-owner Ricardo Montalban) is MacDonald (Hari Rhodes), the governor's black assistant and the film's sole voice of conscience. "What's with that guy, he an ape lover or something?" says one stormtrooper-ish cop when MacDonald stops him from beating an ape. "Yeah, don't it figure?" is his partner's reply. Though in a position of power, MacDonald bitterly weathers with tight lips and heady glower the reverb of a slave society, and even the governor is wary of his token staff member, calling him a "bleeding heart," and proclaiming confidently, "All of us were slaves once, in one sense of the word or another." Neither Caesar or MacDonald would agree, of course, and yet once the hellish revolt gets rolling (the imagery of gorillas swarming through the city's nighttime streets is shuddery and wild), MacDonald is forced onto the MLK-like high ground. "By what *right* are you spilling blood?" he demands indignantly after

Caesar's ape forces have succeeded in conquering the city. "By the slave's right to punish his persecutors," the messianic Caesar replies, and though *Conquest* makes a feeble, last-ditch effort to be pacifist (in a sorely unbelievable, tacked-on speech dubbed over close-ups of Caesar's eyes), the film supports him right down to the brickbats. We do, too; the panicky sops to flower power notwithstanding, the Apes movies are nothing if not a raw acknowledgment of racial antagonism. The facile lessons about the evils of race hate fall away in the face of a five-film-long exploration of the hopelessness of racial fraternization. In fact, the whole cyclical structure of the series, in which the roles of oppressor and oppressed are perpetually exchanged, suggests the circular motion of human history in grim detail. There's no small cynicism in portraying a rabid social dynamic that must and will lead to Armageddon over and over again.

The last film, *Battle for the Planet of the Apes*, affects a manageable degree of interspecies cooperation, but it's hardly a socialist-minded triumph: Caesar has established himself as no-questions-asked autocrat (with a son to continue the bloodline), and the Lawgiver (John Huston) regales us with a version of ape-human history that sounds objectionably mythic and revisionist. We're assured by this "greatest of all apes" that ape and man can live side by side in peace and harmony, but we remember the crazed future of the first film, and the uses to which the Lawgiver's teachings are eventually put, and we know it's all a lie. (If Caesar is Christ, then the Lawgiver is his collective Apostle, even to the extent of having his work corrupted centuries later.) Cheap B-movies meant for kids, the *Apes* movies knew then what many earnest, high-profile films about injustice and race relations don't today: that intelligence cannot housebreak our inner homunculi, seething with pigheaded pride and raw jungle hate; that intelligence will inevitably breed war and waste given half a chance. *Battle*'s paramount tenet is that no ape shall kill ape — is it so much better that they kill men? Along which measurement do the moral lines get drawn, xenophobic separatism or quality of intelligence? Clearly, the former; as evil white man Don Murray puts it in *Conquest*, under a splay of gorilla gunbutts, "Man was born of the ape, there's still an ape curled up inside every man, the beast who must be whipped into submission, the savage that has to be shackled in chains. *You* are that beast, Caesar." By the time the world ends, with a Charlton Heston-instigated bang and not a whimper, the apes could say the same of men. In fact, orangutan zealot Zaius (Maurice Evans) *does* say it, in several different ways. And they're both right.

As films, roughly four-fifths of the *Apes* phenomena is pure dross, fashioned in different degrees of hackhood but maintaining the creepy cheapness that has empowered pop cult apocalypses from *Metropolis* to *The Ten Commandments* to *Invaders from Mars* to *Night of the Living Dead*. The first film is the most fluent and original work Franklin J. Schaffner ever did (compare the leaden *Patton*); the sequels were somewhat carelessly chaperoned by Ted Post (on his way to low-rent 70s beauts like *Magnum Force* and *Go Tell the Spartans*), Don Taylor (as an actor, one of the gregarious POWs in *Stalag 17*, and style-vacuum behind *Damien: Omen II* and 1977's *The Island of Dr. Moreau*) and J. Lee Thompson, who has become a paradigm for promising directors crash-landing into hack landfill, arcing from the early 60s with the stalwart *The Guns of Navarone* and the genuinely frightening *Cape Fear* to the post-*Ape* rockbottom of Charles Bronson jalopies. If an individual, and not simply the entire operandi of media libido in the early 70s, must be credited with the distinctively wacko wallop of the Apes cycle, credit instead screenwriter Dehn, whose grand, nasty vision supports the whole cycle, and the plethora of design craftsman (including mask engineer John Chambers, for his subtle adjustments between human and ape physiology) who dared to make the much-loathed differences and even-more-loathed similarities between ape and human uncomfortably intimate and skin-deep. Try to imagine coming up with the visual and thematic conception of the cycle from scratch, and suddenly even the crudely-made last entries seem formidable.

Perhaps most formidable is the claustrophobic bedlam that the time discontinuum creates, a process we see on a millennial scale but which few of the characters ever grasp at all. It's time travel as no-exit extinction, creating a resonant context for racial nihilism and man's mad sense of significance and destiny as well. There's no escaping the global whorl of cause and effect once it's put into motion. The first film merely leaves Charlton Heston, and us, on the beach with nowhere left to go, while the second drove its combat-driven narrative (throwing nuke-worshiping mutants into the mix) right to Doomsday. The third, however, made ersatz sense out of what merely seemed an atomic scrambling of evolutionary logic by making Taylor's initial plunge through the time warp the event that changes everything — once his ship, on its *preprogrammed* course (!), enters the future, it opens the possibility of retreating into the past. Which it does, carrying Cornelius & Co., who proceed to inspire a revolution and the ape sovereignty that literally creates the scarred, "upside down" world Taylor finds thousands of years later. Chronologically, the "first" moment in real time is Heston chewing on a cigar in the first film's precredit sequence; the "last" is Heston setting off the bomb in the final moments of *Beneath*. Everything else happens somewhere in between. (Even the casting of Heston seems in hindsight like brilliantly triple-edged swordstroke.) It conforms to the films' sense of merciless irony that Taylor and his crew are sound asleep when the time stream is violated; the earth's future history is set on a permanently self-destructive course and no one knows what happened until it's too late. Even we don't fully understand the fatalistic ramifications until the fourth film. Intimations of damnation haunt every step of the films' timeline — however ignorant of the shape of history, nearly every character is helplessly overcome with panic. Just as the orangutans in the first film knew Taylor was trouble on a scale they couldn't comprehend, the jittery humans of both *Conquest* and *Escape* (including Natalie Trundy, who, as Mrs. Arthur P. Jacobs, holds the dubious honor of having played a human, an ape *and* a mutant at different points in the series) were dead-on in their cosmic paranoia. The signs were everywhere, even if we didn't notice them the first time around: the slave apes of *Conquest* even wear color-coded uniforms that subtly prefigure the ape fashions of Cornelius' day, first glimpsed four movies earlier. Mull that over: the weird, half-Egyptian, half-Mao earth-tone dress styles of the distant simian future began as totalitarian jumpsuits for the service population, circa 1991. Talk about "chickens coming home to roost," in Malcolm X's words. The manner by which the films are narratively constructed forces you to discount any respite from the relentless dialectic of oppression because it all leads to a genocidal auto-da-fé we've already witnessed.

The miracle of the *Apes* films is that such complex and dour textual issues dominate an otherwise preposterous manifestation of cheap trash culture, one that was from the outset unashamed and unfettered by art or conscience or responsibility. This is, of course, the gutsy, low-rent glory of authentic pulp. It's not a quality that can be recaptured in expensive remakes, no matter how strenuous the effort; if *Planet of the Apes* is indeed reincarnated, the brute nerve and chilling disorientation of the thing will surely be lost amid the acres of trod-upon eggshells. Of course, the remaining films will never be remade — they're too disreputable, too berserk. America prefers nerveless anodynes like *Forrest Gump* as prescriptive psychic histories of itself. Ruefully, raw visions of everlasting heat-death seem to be a thing of the past.

(*Film Comment*, September – October 1995)

CORNEL WILDE
AT WORK IN THE BADLANDS

Somewhere within the panicky, popluxe chopshop of Cornel Wilde's berserk movies lie the raw urges of personal, and "primitive," cinema, and within that beats the adrenalinized heart of pulp culture, its essential tenets, and the secret reasons why our style cosmos is ruled by brute trash. *The Naked Prey*, *Beach Red* and *No Blade of Grass* are gashouse fables, rude odysseys of survival whose visual argot is as abrupt, savage, churlish and, finally, infantile as any the movies have ever seen. Wilde's a cave painter, a filmmaker born straight out of primeval ooze with the ideas and beliefs of a rogue hyena deranged by drought. Watching the films, you may certainly get the sense, as David Thomson memorably suggests, of "watching the first films ever made," but what's more, you may sense that an untamed id is being stoked, and you can get a reawakened sense of how deep in our reptile brains the fears, hatreds and needs of being alive still lurk unappeased by the narcotics of technology, fame, ritual and entertainment.

For pulp matters. It matters in ways the workaday, incessant discourse about pop culture can never understand. Wilde uses brute pop strategies to manifest the elemental horror of animateness, and what matters is that in the end they're the same nervous beast. Contrary to Raymond Durgnat's presumptions in his famous essay on sci-fi cheese, "The Wedding of Poetry and Pulp: Can They Live Happily Ever After and Have Many Beautiful Children?", pulp is hardly the less authentic aesthetic argument (and so must be seen as awkwardly mating with "art"), but merely the more ruthless, the more aboriginal. Its down-your-throat tropes and assertions are a hair's breadth away from expressionism, futurism, surrealism and cubism, not to mention religious icon art, and if its subjectivism is less schematicized, that's because it simply obeys the more commanding voice of the viscera. It therefore resonates with suggestions of a Jungian "collective" in ways high art cannot by its very aspirant nature.

Today, pulp has been sanctified as the lingua franca of modern culture: we all shiver in the discreet taboo-ness of the lowbrow and base; nostalgically yearning for less sophisticated selves, we convert Jim Thompson and Jack Hill and Jack Kirby and the Ramones into artistes-after-the-fact; we recycle the then-disposable totems of yesteryear trash into today's supercool postmodernity. It's the ultimate art democracy — those who cannot fathom Umberto Eco or Frank Stella bond instead via Clive Barker and Moebius. Those who can enjoy a good slum. A self-consuming vogue machine set in perpetual motion, the popular ardor for pulp shall never wane; rather, the question is are we ardent for the right reasons?

Somewhere deep inside our skulls, maybe. Wilde's films, like Sam Fuller's but many times more delirious and archetypal, may hold the key — the truths that explode from them like launched grenades are the truths of pre-intellect, pre-reason, pagan terror, the truth of the hellkites. The best pulp preaches from the ratpit, presenting to us in varying degrees of rank hyperbole the world, looming monstrously, as absorbed by a child, and, by extension, the world as confronted by all of us at our most ignorant, selfish and superstitious. The generosity and restraint of an Ozu or a Renoir appeals to our hyper-civilized idea of ourselves, personas we carefully cultivate through a lifetime of acquiring cultural standards and opinions we may still secretly only half-believe on our deathbeds; pulp is our common art straight out of the womb, an expression of our first horror and excitement. It's with us from the beginning, like our incisors. Are we ever really above it, even as we condescend to being in its thrall? What American film of the 60s is more terminally profound than *Night of the Living Dead*? Aren't Feuillade, Lang, Hitchcock, Sirk and Melville all masters by the pure grace of pulp? Unfettered by decorum and traditional aesthetic judgments, pulp is nevertheless unconcerned with truth but with getting our attention, slapping us awake and then pushing a gun barrel through our lips — like it or not, truth is what happens next. Our own fear, our own wounds, our own conflicted instincts.

Wilde's brand of pulp has the cruel simplicity of folk art. His sensibility occupies the distant outskirts of low art, in that the semi-barbaric, moralized conventions of genre were generally still too rarefied for the man; Wilde's war film, *Beach Red*, is a hopeless tableau of severed limbs and ruined lives, dressed in the earnest seersucker of 'Nam-era anti-war homily while the naked ape of idiot terror frantically rips its way out into the sunlight. These aren't merely films about lawlessness, they're lawless themselves. And while Fuller may subliminally acknowledge that underneath the fatalism creeps the newsstand/comic book glow of remembered childhood fiction, Wilde's vision entertains no hardboiled quaintness or respite from doom. Blunt, cartoony pulpness is employed because it is passion without affect, not because of nostalgia. The implicit child in Wilde's films is scared, utterly alone and compelled into blind survival.

Throughout Wilde's normative career as a mild Hollywood leading man, lasting nearly 40 years and including Jean Negulesco's *Road House*, Charles Vidor's *A Song to Remember* (in which Wilde played Chopin), John M. Stahl's *Leave Her to Heaven*, Joseph H. Lewis's *The Big Combo* (the first film from Theodora Productions, Wilde's production company) and scads of grade-B swashbucklers, only his reliance on brawn and anxiety gave any indication of his future filmmaking M.O. (He was an Olympic fencer but reportedly opted out of the 1936 Games to pursue acting, and ended up being the fencing instructor for, as well as playing Tybalt in, the 1940 Laurence Olivier Broadway production of *Romeo and Juliet*.) Perhaps his bland presence as an actor has meddled with his films' legacy, but with one glimpse of him reduced to animal angst in *The Naked Prey* or grimly approaching the formidable beachfront in *Beach Red*, you sense a cohesiveness between man and vision heretofore only available in Welles.

Still, he remains an unexhumed master today, a longlost renegade in search of a cult — 40 years since his first film, he still awaits critical reappraisal. He didn't warrant inclusion in Richard Roud's 1980 *Cinema: A Critical Dictionary*, although with characteristic acumen, David Thomson provides Wilde a short but amazed entry in *A Biographical Dictionary of Film*. In *The American Cinema*, Andrew Sarris half-heartedly commended *Storm Fear* for its "half-baked intensity," while Stuart Kaminsky went on the record as saying that Wilde "deserves a vote as the most neglected creator in film of the last quarter century." Otherwise, Wilde's career as a startlingly bold and brutal image-maker has been all but forgotten.

His first films — *Storm Fear* (1956, with a screenplay by Horton Foote), *The Devil's Hairpin* (1957), *Maracaibo* (1958) and *Sword of Lancelot* (1963) — are gently overwrought genre pieces, each in its own way bearing the claw marks of Wilde's nihilism and obsession with physical trial. It wasn't until *The Naked Prey* (1966), still the most fondly remembered of Wilde's films, that his fauvist, scorched-earth visual syntax began to crystallize, and his bloodthirsty ethos found unmitigated expression. Its plot is primitive like a Shaker chair: Wilde (identified as "Man" in the credits), on a colonial-era ivory safari, gets captured by a tribe of cannibal bushmen; when they arrange to hunt him for sport, he kills their pointman and keeps on running. The film is stripped of non-essentials (it has the least English or subtitled dialogue of any Hollywood movie since *Modern Times*), and the essentials boil down to a dry-eyed seminar in natural violence, from the tribal executions to the parade of veldt atrocities — it was surely the first film in which we saw a tribesman casually step into the carcass of a butchered elephant, drag out an armful of innards and hang them over the campfire to dry. Here is the hemorrhaging heart under the darkest-Africa safari romance, the thorn-spearfight-&-starvation bones beneath the chest-pounding adventure saga.

Purified of character, dramatics and language, *The Naked Prey* has the force of a campfire myth, a story of the hunt told not to assuage our fears but to contextualize them, and to prove that we are not in the end so very different from the cro-magnon tribes waiting out a thunderstorm in fear of an irrational god's aimless rage. For all that, however, the movie is scrupulously unManichean and villainless (the "pursuers" grieve, bicker, joke, grow despondent, etc. — is this the only film to read cannibals as complex human beings?), a quality shared by *Beach Red* and *No Blade of Grass*, films just as exhaustingly combative in nature. Somewhere in Wilde's otherwise eolithic topos is the democratic, almost cosmic notion that everyone is equally lost on the plain, and equally apt to feel the teeth of the others' hunger.

But *The Naked Prey* would seem today merely as a stripped-down riff on *The Most Dangerous Game*, or a roller-derby alternative to Peter Brook's pretentious *Lord of the Flies*, if its shot-arrow adventure tale was all there was to see. Simply, it's because of Wilde's damned-on-holiday visual approach that his thematic thrust has the weight it does — in nearly every frame, you smell the sulfur of his conviction. His framing and cutting have an amateur's faith in totemic meaning, and a warrior's impatience with ambiguity and trickery. The tribe's pig-sticking of one of the safari party is shot by Wilde from on high and foregrounded by a wreath of blood-red flowers. A tense shot of Wilde listening to the wilderness is so intimate that his ear fills one end of the Panavision frame and his eye fills the other. The fights are fast, merciless and full of jump-cuts — Wilde would cut from somebody throwing a spear to an already impaled body for lack of expensive opticals or prosthetics, but the effect is that the camera just couldn't keep up.

With its skeleton of a text and its what-you-see-is-what-you-get formal agenda, it's hardly surprising that *The Naked Prey* was and still is today Wilde's most popular and easily digestible movie, and that *Beach Red* (1967) has been radically neglected by comparison. (Both, incidentally, were co-written by Clint Johnston.) *Beach Red* is Wilde's masterwork in much the same manner that Fuller's talky, tough-guy war movies — *Merrill's Marauders, Fixed Bayonets, China Gate, The Big Red One* — aren't his. To my mind, the experiential, apolitical *Beach Red* is superior as well to *The Steel Helmet*; there may never be or have been a less sentimental American war film. (Fuller's own description of war as "body parts everywhere" graphically evokes Wilde's film, not any of his own.) At the same time, *Beach Red* is saturated with cheap pathos, iconic spasms of empathy for nearly every character, American or Japanese, as they stumble into the slaughterhouse. No one talks when Wilde can instead thumbnail-sketch the scenario's emotional contexts with unpredictable metafictive splats: feverish slo-mo close-ups, step-printed hallucinations, freeze-framed memories, distorted POVs, soft-focused home movie flashbacks, overlapping streams-of-consciousness, Pudovkinian montages, etc. It's the war film as assaulted consciousness.

Beach Red isn't entirely *maudit*, insofar as the opening shot of exploding palm trees was stolen for *Apocalypse Now*. (At the same time, both entries in the 1998 WWII bonanza, *Saving Private Ryan* and *The Thin Red Line*, owe more to *Beach Red* than to any other film.) The film's title sequence, however, hasn't been robbed by anybody: a series of lurid, heavy-brushstroke battle paintings, half 60s Ace paperback cover, half Saturday Evening Post; Wilde pans slowly to the right across the final image of soldiers heading into a holocaust, and we discern a few real soldiers blending into the image. One (Rip Torn) looks at us, bites a chaw of tobacco and turns quickly to the right, the camera following him to a *real* beach, with real soldiers. It's one stunning shot, requiring only a large-scale painting on-location and a full measure of chutzpah, but it's also an ideogram of Wilde's worldview — there's no chasm between realism and crude expressionistic hyperbole because in extremis our subjective experience is chaotic and vulgar, and there's nothing less "real" about subjective experience. It's a venerably Freudian dichotomy, ego and id — why does it still seem to require defending? After all, James Ellroy, hardly canon fodder, is surely the manifested id of Dostoyevsky, *Watchmen* the bastard grandson of Rabelais, an entire songbook of teary Irish tavern anthems the dirty blood of *Ulysses*..., just as surely a philosophical consideration of ethical action essentially requires the violation of crime and its attendant fear and loathing.

At any rate, *Beach Red* is every inch a cinematic Guernica — painting *and* killing field — down to the shipboard crushing of a roach that a terrified soldier relives in freeze-framed close-up and sobs helplessly over under fire. The film's first section is a simple beach assault, the nerve-wracked American forces maimed in waves like locust heading into a helicopter blade, the living freely vomiting or jabbering or glancing over a single foot floating in the brine or wondering where in hell their arms went. "I've got to move faster, I can't move," says one grunt's Beckettian interior monologue, and no sooner does the battalion's obnoxious cameraman tell a soldier to "get out of my way!" that the soldier is shot dead. The colors are jaundiced, the music is a canned patriotic drone, the smoking bodies pile up too quickly to count. Again, the editing can't keep up: by the time Wilde cuts from a gun firing, the body is already cold. And when the film cuts to the Japanese camp, it's to a sitcom-like two-shot accompanied by a punctuative soundtrack gong.

Not even Fuller would dare zoom-pan from a spider devouring a moth to a jungle firefight. *Beach Red* is equal parts eye-roasting mayhem and free-associative snippets of the emotion-flushed mini-movies running forever in every character's head, Yank or Jap — memories of wives, children, gardens, girlfriends, all seen for only a few seconds, most often as still photographs. (A notable exception is the *La Jetée*-like moment when Wilde's sleeping wife — Jean Wallace, the real Mrs. Wilde — suddenly opens her eyes.) Wilde's uncultured, jumbled visual vocabulary could give a semiotician a migraine — some dying characters' lives literally flash before our eyes, and a Japanese officer's memory snapshot of bathing with his family even gets blood optically syruped over it once he commits seppuku.

Perhaps too neatly, *The Naked Prey*, *Beach Red*, and *No Blade of Grass* comprise a triptych of human self-destruction at three evolutionary stages: primal, "civilized," and post-civilized, and it may very well have been Wilde's point that there's precious little difference between them. For *No Blade of Grass* (1970) is an apocalyptic dogfight, based on a John Christopher novel about a pollution-triggered world famine, and although it begins in (a badly dated) 1970s England, the story quickly de-evolves into a Year Zero journey to the end of night. Although like the other films *Grass* begins more or less in the middle, with the protagonist's bags already packed for escape into the hills once London becomes a lynch-law basin, Wilde is afforded the opportunity of observing the shanty walls of civilized (and *British*) conduct slowly collapse under the pressure of scavenger rule. As Nigel Davenport and Jean Wallace again (swollen and vulnerable like a queen ant) are fleeing north to a farm we're already sure is no sanctuary, the movie undergoes red-filtered, sometimes solarized flashback/flash-forward seizures, of suburban gardeners torching their tulip gardens and of devil-horned motorcycle gangs raping and pillaging the countryside. The landscape is all refuse and muck and barricaded manor houses; at times, the traffic jam carnage suggests a penny dreadful edition of *Weekend*. "Cannibalism is already widespread," a radio announcer intones, not long after Davenport breezily shotguns a housewife in the belly (producing a strange swash of optical blood), the eighth or ninth body left in his matter-of-fact wake. En route, Wilde is never shy about panning from corpses to a pond thick with chemical scum; as with *Beach Red*'s raving pacifism, *No Blade of Grass*'s eco-hysteria provides Wilde with limitless opportunities for comic-book frisson and vigilante sang-froid. Though the characters are quickly reduced to two categories, survivor and carcass-to-be, they're all on a road to nowhere. Wilde doesn't waste a frame on self-acknowledgment, comedy or thrill; you sense the movie was meant as a bludgeon, and yet it feels like one long, thin, desperate sob finding no echo in the abyss.

True to their nature as primitive creations, Wilde's movies resisted the marketplace as thoroughly as they resisted sophisticated filmic conventions. He went on to make only *Sharks' Treasure* (1975), a tame post-*Jaws* saga nitroed up with uncut sequences of a robust 60-year-old Wilde and his cast battling with real sharks, and died in 1989. It may not be possible any longer for a filmmaker to approach the innocence and ferocity of Wilde's unblinking armageddons — try to imagine a work of true pulp that doesn't feast on, or "deconstruct," what the filmmaker in question remembers enjoying as a young, closeted trash glutton a la Burton, Tarantino, etc. But who would have thought it possible in 1966? Perhaps more than any other one filmmaker, Wilde came close to making movies seem like a force of nature — as simple, fated and fearsome as a rolling boulder. His auctorial dominion, after all, seems haplessly inbred with received wisdom from the collective unconscious — who else could so extemporaneously capture the eruptive warp of our everyday nightmares?

(*Film Comment*, November – December 1996)

UNSILENT NIGHTS: THE BROTHERS QUAY

To watch, indeed to enter the impossible, ghosted night of a Quay Brothers film is to become complicitous in one of the most perverse and obsessive acts of cinema. We're suspended in our own need to see (as we were meant to be at, say, Cocteau's falling chimney) as random, tiny, decaying objects and relationships are fetishized beyond the point of simple imagery and into alchemy. *Street of Crocodiles*, *The Cabinet of Jan Svankmajer*, *Nocturna Artificialia*, *This Unnameable Little Broom*, *Rehearsals for Extinct Anatomies*, *The Comb from the Museums of Sleep* and the *Stille Nacht* pieces are all ferociously hermetic films whose interface with everyday culture is both undeniable and nearly impossible to articulate. Flamboyantly ambiguous, retroactively archaic, obeying only the natural forces of a purely occult consciousness, Quay films are secret, individuated knowledge for each and every viewer. (Try and discuss them with other enthusiasts — the conversation is usually reduced to thoughtful nodding.) To immerse oneself in their chthonic cadences, their sacred sense of the hidden lives of dust, shadow and broken toys, is to glimpse the infinite within the finite, the ghost in the machine.

A headful of horsefeathers, you may be thinking, but Quay films inspire fanatical allegiance and intense superlatives, due in no small measure to the strangely private connections they make with attentive viewers. (It wouldn't matter if every man, woman and child on Earth saw *Street of Crocodiles*, only I would truly understand it — which is not to say I literally understand it *at all*.) Any attempt to invoke and articulate the experience of a Quay film becomes a mad wandering through a dense forest of metaphor, an effort that is inevitably doomed — they're all sublimely textural, possessed of an arcane inner law that is, in the end, only seeable. We become dazzled agnostics. We surrender to ignorant awe.

Much has been made of their evocative choices of thematic imagery — the pervasive lint, insect wings, rusted screws, threadbare fabrics, moldy dolls, antiquated typography, a veritable curiosity shop of self-entwining string, meat watches, stray wire and the household scraps of a buried yesteryear — but just as vital to the films' creepy mystery is the Quays' protean mise-en-scene, which no sooner confronts a spatial impossibility within the confines of an animated film than surmounts it. Their arsenal of visual tropes are in fact what clearly differentiates a Quay piece from seemingly countless imitators (MTV is fairly awash with Quayesque apes, most shamelessly Fred Stuhr's video for Tool's "Sober"). Look carefully at the later films' use of camera movement: the juxtaposition of slow dollies (often *around* moving figures) with sudden, vision-straining sweeps, the point-of-view moving through its miniature universe like the sightline of a cat hearing a floorboard creak, often finally focusing on a minuscule detail of random movement shot within a microscopic depth of field. That the film image is animated millimeter by millimeter along with its content is an obsessive degree of creative authority that rhymes with the films' subcellar ambience. Thus the "subject" of a Quay film — characteristically, a weathered puppet constructed from common, discarded materials — shares its frame-by-frame life-movement with the "object" — namely, the frame, the film, the camera itself (referred to by the Quays as "the third puppet."). The seamless animated manipulation of the camera's position, *and* its focal setting, is perhaps the Quays' trump card, a degree of fanatical precision no other animator would, or could, sanely co-opt. Like a gifted magician, a Quay film often prompts us to wonder how in hell certain images are achieved, all of them completely in-camera — the reconstitution (natural collapse printed backwards) of a dissipated dandelion, shot in looming closeup and within a *moving* focal plane, and the blurred frenzy of the toy monkey in the same frame as ordinarily animated figures, in *Street of Crocodiles*; the nervous mid-air suspension (and focal flux) of the pearls in *Rehearsals for Extinct Anatomies*, the ping pong ball in *Stille Nacht II*, the fired bullet in *Stille Nacht III*. A Quay film is the closest anyone has come to authentically gnostic cinema; it fascinates and confounds in equal measure on every level: narratively, thematically, technically, even authorially (the creepy image of the reclusive twins secretively tinkering like deranged watchmakers with the subconscious detritus of forgotten Euroculture is one the brothers have never tried to dispel).

Indeed, though Timothy and Stephen Quay were born and raised in Philadelphia's suburban working class, they have come to seem positively exotic, as their twinness (they commonly finish each other's sentences and sign collective correspondence "Q."), expatriation and hobbyists-gone-monastically-insane working methods become an inevitable subtext for their films — a circumstance they are quite conscious of. Think of them as the squared cinematic equivalent to Walter Benjamin with his paperweights or Swiss author Robert Walser on a semi-surreal stroll. (The Quays' first feature, *Institute Benjamenta*, is a live-action take on Walser's first novel, *Jakob Von Gunten*.) Check out a bio excerpted from a letter to poet J.D. McClatchy for a *Connoisseur* magazine profile: "What if we said we [were] born of a heavily tainted family, neurasthenic, microcephalic, each with one atrophied testicle, a sly liking for geese, chickens, etc., pigtails in pillow cases... No, we grew up sweating with obedience. Our Father was a 2nd class machinist for Philadelphia Electric, our mother your impeccable housewife... On our Father's side there were two grandfathers, one a tailor from Berlin who had a shop in South Philly, and the other, who was apparently a cabinetmaker and we were told that the 5th floor of Lit Brother [department store] in Philly has cabinets by the Quays. Our Mother's father was excellent at carpentry and was also a chauffeur when Philly only had 5 automobiles to its name. So! In terms of puppetry it's surprisingly all there — carpentry, mechanisms and tailoring and figure skating to music to score any of our aberrant tracking shots. Big deal, will this help you dear fellow?" There's little extra-cinematic oddness we can imagine about the Quays that they don't seem happy to confirm, with the exception of parental dementia a la Bruno Schulz, whose father conversed with tailors' dummies. Here's another typical flush of correspondence, in answer to my question about their short *Stille Nacht* pieces: "They're all linked by the common theme of Black & White and the belief in oblique salesmanship. *Stille Nacht I* was selling steel wool. *Stille Nacht II* was selling ping pong balls or socks with one vocation in life. *Stille Nacht III* was trying to sell pre-anamorphisized reindeer dining tables with a bullet already fixed in one testicle (which even more accurately & obliquely explains the deformed antlers)(documentary hyperbole). Of course none of all this is really apparent, but it gives us the sublime belief that no one is ever looking. And it's the premise we're most comfortable in starting from."

They're a striking enough public persona to have inspired the twin mortomanic zoologists in Peter Greenaway's *A Zed and Two Noughts* (after having appeared in Greenaway's earlier, obsessive epic *The Falls*) and it's hard to feel as a viewer of their films that you're not trudging around in their shared cortex — their co-created Hotel Subterranea, where the corridors are piled high with moldering, century-old trash and where a submerged, animistic life-force throbs within the walls, under the floorboards and inside every morsel of inanimate dross. It is, after all, the second-hand, rust-never-sleeps iconography of their films that grips the imagination most acutely, and while Quay films can often seem closed up in their own independent dimension dynamically, their textual interface with modernist history is palpable and evocative, "adapting" the work or sometimes simply the aura of Kafka, Schulz, Walser, Arcimboldo, Fragonard, Lewis Carroll, Janáček and Stravinsky, and indirectly invoking the spirits of Bosch, Munch, Ernst, Bacon, Escher, Beckett, the original Surrealists, Joseph Cornell, Arthur Rackham, Lorenz Stoer, Karl Korab and countless others. More than that, Quay films are largely unspoken sleepwalks through environments crushed by the torque of industrial progress, and as such reference the central material drama of the last century — the abandonment of a society constructed around manual labor, around the power of the simple man, a crucial drama that mirrors, not incidentally, the history of movies. (Though Quay films, if they take place anywhere, take place in a fever-dream vision of *Mitteleuropa*, their blanket of uncomfortably indefinable dead-factory dust is just as appropriate for Philadelphia and the Ohio valley, where empty industries litter the landscape like churches during the Renaissance.) Though scarcely proletariat in any other way, films like *Street of Crocodiles* are dramas of lostness, of man dumbly wandering the dusty cloisters of his own wrecked sense of self.

Most of what is normally thought of as Quayesque is epitomized in *Street of Crocodiles*, the first of their films to be shot in 35mm: the ubiquitous decrepitude and proto-totalitarian menace; the Schulzian characterization of Poland as a moth-eaten stage for existentialist dread; the rusty, perambulating screws and gears; the multi-planed images and bottomless shadows; the amber-mud hues; the pointless contraptions performing rote activities on the verge of entropic breakdown; the spindly, shabbily suited protagonist stalking through the soft machinery of a psychic warehouse in a startled state of paranoid worry. *Crocodiles* is arguably still their crowning achievement, the film in which they surpassed contemporaries like Czech animator Jan Svankmajer in creating a curious and original visual syntax, and the film in which that syntax was best expressive of a cultural mood. The design of the film's central figurine exemplifies this: pallid, desiccated, hyper-aware of his surroundings yet lost in delirious shock at some unexplained horror, he's the perfect modernist hero, a version of Beckett's Lost Ones, Kafka's *Der Verschollene* — the Disappearance Man — as well as Bartleby, Gogol's Akaky and the Underground Man. That he belongs to Schulz, possibly the saddest literary loss to Nazism, imbues him with an added poignancy. His eyes haunted by hopeless fear, the puppet's wary lurch and puzzled regard for the film's shopworn decor brings both Groucho Marx and Caligari's somnambulist to mind, all the while being nakedly a contraption cobbled together from scraps. Like most of the Quay figures, he is a ball-and-socket construction a la Ray Harryhausen, and sometimes the joints show — the Quays never try to disguise the scale or makeshift nature of their films, down to building characters out of drafting compasses, wire tangles and tattered stuffed animals. This is as much an aesthetic of *detournement* as it is economic necessity — the brothers tell of British animator Barry Purves's puppet armature for his film *Next* costing 5,000 pounds, compared to the *Crocodiles* model, which cost a thousandth of that for the metal hardware underneath the desultory surface.

All Quay films celebrate their own exploding miniatureness in similar fashion, by locating within their tabletop cosmos unsounded depths of image, allusion and atmosphere. The hallways of *Street of Crocodiles* go on forever, though we never see to where, and we know on the right side of our brain that it's a matter of inches to the table edge. It's endless in the sense of a Borgesian maze, removed from Borges' cool ironies by the autumnal rot and post-Great War era melancholia. In one fabulous scene the scarecrow-ish hero is led to a small window (not unlike a projection booth portal — *Crocodiles* is rife with cinematic symbols) by a gaggle of half-headed dolls, and through it he observes a plastic infant sitting alone behind dirty glass, playing with a giant light bulb and watching a stream of ant-like screws dislodge themselves from the crud-covered floor and scramble away, all accompanied by the morose dead-soul-of-Europe strings of the Quays' composer, Leszek Jankowski. (Only a handful of cinematic moments match for me this scene's visceral, enigmatic woe: the husband's underwater search for the image of his lost wife in *L'Atalante*, the quiet raft-ride up the nighttime Beatrix Potter river in *The Night of the Hunter*, the final self-fetalizing in the rain and in the middle of the road, after three lifetimes' worth of trauma, of the little boy searching for a father that doesn't exist in *Landscape in the Mist*.) The Quays' camera seems to be on a perpetual hunt for tableaux and textures that pierce the skin of an ancestral unconscious bruised by failure and fear — at one point, and quite incidentally, one among many screws busy unthreading themselves from the floor suddenly pauses and rotates the other way, back into the floor, for a moment, as if it's unsure of where it's going, unsure of freedom and purpose. Watching *Street of Crocodiles* you could easily miss it, but in a world assembled frame by frame, there are no accidents. Even the screws are plagued with lostness.

Of course, the implementation of such common and therefore meaning-loaded objects could lend Quay films an overt Freudian-ness that they neither deserve nor altogether deny. *Crocodiles* even has a few outright genital representations formed from organ meats and gloves, and indeed all of the Quay films bear undeniable kinship to surrealist impulses, and therefore, technically, to dreams. But saying they're dreamlike is not the same as saying they're Freudian, as the filmmakers rather peevishly pointed out themselves in another letter re: the dreamer and the dream in *The Comb*: "For us it was *more* a 'troubled sleep' (based on a Walser short story) and as in all troubled sleeps it was a restless half-wakened state which produces the possibility of dream material, and a dream syntax, but to say that anything relating to dream is therefore Freudianizing seems a bit too glib and would disqualify a great amount of film... We wanted to keep the live action scenes resolutely separate from the animation *and yet* integrated in the overall flow and at hopefully an uncanny level, and this was done thru analogic gestures and cutting." Clearly, Freud is a troublesome figure, because little of the Quays' dreamish imagery pertains to wish fulfillment at any rate, but all of it seems scooped from a dark cultural id. Insofar as the Quays have also managed to make so much mundaneness virtually archetypal, the films seem caught somewhere between Freud and Jung, all the while tripping down their own cryptic yet endlessly signifying paths.

This tension is not nearly so much an issue in their earlier, relatively less cunning 16mm films — *Nocturna Artificialia, This Unnameable Little Broom, The Cabinet of Jan Svankmajer*, and, presumably (because unavailable, even from the Quays), *Michel de Ghelderode, Igor: The Paris Years chez Pleyel* and *Leoš Janáček: Intimate Excursions* — which are all more overt about their parabolic narratives and more Arcimboldoesque about their designs. But nowhere is the tension between psychological translation of any stripe and the Quays' ferocious hermetism more tangible than in *Rehearsals for Extinct Anatomies*, their starkest and most oblique film, free as it is of any (discernible) relationship with outside source material — a surprising move, coming on the heels of the attention-getting *Crocodiles*. Of all Quays, it's a film governed by superego — albeit a superego twisted into knots by disease and technology. It trades in the previous films' antiquey gloom for the clean lines of bar codes gone berserk and a cool black-&-white biohorror that could make David Cronenberg sweat in his sleep. The central cyclopean figure aside, not much in it looks handmade, and this time even the milieu is a neurotic puzzle. By way of explanation, a typically Quayesque title card appears: "These decors have been engraved with great modesty and dedicated to London Underground as part of its present evangelical rampage, and to an anonymous anatomical specimen — to the single still dreaming hair in his head with its desire to disturb the wallpaper. O Inevitable Fatum." Actually the set design is an enlarged etching detail based on Fragonard, which the roaming bar codes mesh with seamlessly, and the film can be read as an abstracted meditation on AIDS, with its physiologically devastated central figure, the shadowed sickbed it presides over, and the occasional glimpse of hypodermics amid the refuse. Sterile and gruesome both, *Rehearsals* chills like a sick ward, and is the only one of their films truly scented with end-time. Formally, it's repetitious and cyclical and directionless (by virtue of going in every direction) — it's the Quays' *Last of England*, their *Salo*.

In terms of set pieces, it's also the only wholly "modern" film in the Quay corpus, inasmuch as it dwells not within a rotten past but in a rotting present. In sharp contrast, *The Comb from the Museums of Sleep* explores new tonal territory while further expanding the brothers' visual patois. After the washed-out linearity of *Rehearsals*, *The Comb* positively glows with fairy tale peaches and salmons, resembling a Bosch painting where the sun's come out. If *Crocodiles* is the Quays' journey to the end of night — literally and allusively — then this is their Grimm Brothers morning, complete with sun-saturated hills and trees (albeit with cartographic lettering). Intercut with an anonymous woman's "troubled sleep," a blistered doll journeys through a skyless, uterine-red maze/forest by way of a ladder, which often leaves him in a narcoleptic daze and carries on itself, the doll's detached hands fluttering around it like gnats. Freud would have had a field day. Essentially a drama of frustrated desire, *The Comb* is not merely a dream, but the portrait of a (semi-)subconscious moment — which is still several steps further toward understandable daylight than the Quays have ever been before. In this they may have been subject to the same serendipity as Dali and Bunuel, who worked hard at making *Un Chien Andalou* incomprehensible but ended up filling it with easily deciphered Freudian symbols all the same. What's more interesting about *The Comb* is its place in the Quay style trajectory, which graduates from tarnished existentialism to gray technodread to auroral phantasia.

The *Stille Nacht* shorts are purposefully incidental in this process, affording the brothers the opportunity to explore possibly neglected backstreets of imagery within a commercial context — one of the myriad of ways the Quays fund their work and themselves, in addition to shooting commercials, documentaries and TV trailers, and designing book jackets and theater sets. Whatever else the Quays themselves say they are, these shorts seem to function as working junk drawers, using up whatever the brothers couldn't squeeze into their larger films. (Notably the shorts' signature valentine — by most reports the Quays' studio in London is stacked floor to ceiling with moldy tea bags, fish bones and other sundry garbage waiting to be included in a future film.) *Stille Nacht I* was a 60-second MTV "art break" predominated by metal filings and the weathered homunculus later used in *The Comb. Stille Nacht II* is an appropriately quizzical video for "Are We Still Married?" by the group His Name Is Alive, a Brit pop group whose dirgey melodies play like nursery rhymes on warped vinyl. *Stille Nacht III*, subtitled *Tales of the Vienna Woods*, follows the haphazard meanderings of a pair of severed hands and a single bullet through an environment that suggests the monochromatic mildew of *Eraserhead. Stille Nacht IV* is the video for His Name Is Alive's "Can't Go Wrong Without You," and may be one of the Quays' most disturbing pieces, a bizarre Easter suite with the resourceful stuffed rabbit from *Stille Nacht II* battling the forces of evil (a pixilated human in horns and skullface) for the possession of an egg. Like all Quays, plot synopsis is seriously deficient in capturing the film's thrust, and leaves out the film's extraordinary, ashy visual texture and soundtrack song, which is a childish and creepy nightmare of distorted guitar wails. (In fact, Quay soundtracks, most often engineered by Larry Sider, are their own masterpieces of muffled background noise and suggestive portents.)

Like all artists working in "found," nontraditional imagery, the Quays have too often been dubbed surrealist, most often by people who have little idea what that means. True, they have been compared most often to quasi-mentor Svankmajer, who regards himself as a "card-carrying militant surrealist," but films like *Alice*, Svankmajer's Lewis Carroll feature, rely too little on ambience and too much on gastrointestinal distress for the comparison to hold. From *Crocodiles* on, what distinguishes the Quays is their carefully wrought sense of otherworldliness, of relationships ruled by incomprehensible needs; Svankmajer, and most serious surrealists, are too busy politicizing (*The Death of Stalinism in Bohemia*), burlesquing traditional forms (*Punch and Judy*) or using outrageous imagery for social commentary, or, often, for the imagery's own sake (*Dimensions in Dialogue, Food*). The Quays cross paths with the world outside their films in a much more sophisticated manner, opening the forgotten corners of existence to the strangest, quietest, most unpredictable traffic — they have us questioning the meanings things have for each other every 1/24 of a second, which all film would do if we were to look at it more closely. Whereas traditional surrealism regards reality as a weapon best used to beat itself, the Quays summon a latent breed of audiovisual cabbala, a new, hoodoo way of understanding space, gravity, connectedness. Quantum physics' Butterfly Effect says that a butterfly beating its wings in China means it will rain in Cleveland; for the Quays a butterfly means rain even, or especially, if the butterfly and the rain are inches apart.

In this the Quays are the quintessential animators; their films embody the enigma of cinematic cause and effect, of visual persistence, of filmic movement itself. If all animation creates these mysteries by its very nature, then only one tangential arm of the genre — light-years away from cartooning a la Disney, the deathless pope-king of popular animation — acknowledges it, a heritage of Soviet, Polish and Czech animators the Quays invoke as often as they're asked about "influences" by interviewers. Perhaps the most eccentric of all cinematic "secret histories," the lineage that leads up to *Street of Crocodiles* (and, more popularly, Tim Burton's *The Nightmare Before Christmas*) is firmly planted in traditions of puppeteering that run back to the Middle Ages (note the Punch and Judy motifs running through many of the films, including *This Unnameable Little Broom*), having crept alongside popular cinema, and animation, virtually since the first kinetoscope. For independent animators (as opposed to the studio assembly lines), making a film is akin to transcribing the Bible longhand — it's an intensely private, laborious, uncommercial act, and such films often reek of hermited obsession, going back to Ladislaw Starewicz, who as far back as 1912 began making stop-motion films using the rewired bodies of insects. The first of the trash-excavating puppet mavens, Starewicz was a true obsessive, his entomological mini-dramas — *The Revenge of the Kinematograph Cameraman*, *The Insect's Christmas*, *The Dragonfly and the Ant*, *Frogland*, *The Mascot*, *The Lily of Belgium* — often played out domestic comedy and Aesopian fables with dragonflies, grasshoppers, ants, stag beetles and frogs. (His first attempted film was of a live stag beetle fight; when they failed to provide enough action, he began moving them himself.) That his creatures were only barely anthropomorphized — insofar as they might wear hats and carry violins — is Starewicz's lingering legacy. They're still dead beetles (black jaws permanently opened to the sky), dead grasshoppers (folded wings passing as dinner jackets) and dead frogs (standing on their hind legs, their faces pointing forever upward). No matter how light-hearted the scenario, his films play like ghoulish pantomimes for entomophobes.

Perhaps we can count on Starewicz having been largely unaware of the gulf between his Mother Goose narrative sensibility and his bug corpses. Other animators, the variety seeking the sort of dark poetry the Quays have attained a Baudelairean fluency with, have proved just as important as influences often despite their use of entirely different mediums. Alexander Alexeieff (grandfather, incidentally, of indie director Alexander Rockwell) and his wife Claire Parker have explored the netherworld between 2-D and 3-D animation since the early 30s with their pinboard films — comprised of images formed of shadows cast within a surface made of thousands of movable pins. You may recall Alexeieff's pinboard work from the opening sequence of Welles' *The Trial*, but better he be defined in the annals of "experimental" animation by *Night on Bald Mountain*, a moody black mass that features pre-morphing transformations and 3-D models, and which preceded Disney's version of Mussorgsky by seven years; *Pictures at an Exhibition*, which utilizes two pinboards simultaneously; and *The Nose*, a Magritte-ish adaptation of Gogol that must've had an impact on the Quays, what with its shifting perspectives, hapless Everyman hero and perpetual East European night.

Of course, most animators have been trapped in the nursery ghetto, including Alexander Ptushko, a Ukrainian animator whose 1935 *The New Gulliver* is considered the world's first puppet feature. Notably, the Quays have never suggested that George Pal's Puppetoons were ever an influence; Pal's Hungarian roots and the films' stark landscapes and fluid, often startling movements could simply not surmount the Hollywood cartoon taint of the things. (Pal even assembled an evil army out of nuts and bolts in *Tulips Shall Grow*.) Jiri Trnka, on the other hand, is seen as a mentor, despite the fact that Pal's films were much more widely available to American audiences years earlier. Trnka was, after all, still a Czech and still trucking in Czech puppeteering traditions, even when satirizing American genres in wonders like *Song of the Prairie*. That film, with its hilarious Georgian figures and elaborate mise-en-scene, is a high-spirited lark compared to the epic A *Midsummer Night's Dream*, a massive and ravishing feature shot in Cinemascope. Trnka's puppet-operas, and the equally fanciful work of fellow Czechs Bretislav Pojar and Karel Zeman (whose everything-and-the-kitchen-sink version of *Baron Munchausen* is still the best), broke technical ground without providing the Quays, or us, with much thematic grist. (Even Starewicz's Walpurgisnacht sequence in *The Mascot* reveals a more modernist sensibility.)

Rather, the Polish animators Walerian Borowczyk and Jan Lenica have had, the Quays maintain, the most significant impact on their work, despite the fact that most of the Poles' films are not puppet animation — or even a hybrid a la Alexeieff, though pixilated live action is common. It's easy to see what was so galvanizing: films like *Labyrinth*, *Renaissance*, *Dom*, *A*, *Le Dictionnaire de Joachin*, *Le Theatre de Monsieur et Madame Kabal* and *Les Jeux des Anges* create self-consciously 2-D worlds ruled by dislocating strangeness, horrific savagery and Theatre of Cruelty surrealism. (In fact, Lenica went on to adapt Jarry in *Ubu and the Great Gidouille*.) In Lenica's *Labyrinth*, a Magritte-style Icarus descends to a city populated by all manner of self-cannibalizing mutant life: a dinosaur skeleton baying at the moon, trenchcoated lizardmen hunting down young girls, etc. Once the dapper witness's inappropriateness is recognized he's torn to pieces by a flock of vultures. In Borowczyk's *Les Jeux des Anges*, a metropolis of hapless angels spends most of its time butchering itself, rivers of blue blood flowing from the severed heads and wings.

Beautiful and appalling at the same time, the films of Lenica and Borowczyk were perhaps the first of their kind, the animated equivalent to *Maldoror*, Sade and Artaud. Seeing them through the scrim of Quayness, the Polish films represent a liberation of vision, of access to modernist despair otherwise alien to animated films. The means to the vision was new, too; in Borowczyk's *Renaissance*, decimated objects meticulously reenact their own destruction backwards, reassembling themselves, establishing a relational paradox between *things* the Quays have been exploring ever since. On top of that, Borowczyk moved from animations into live action features with no discernible textual or thematic compromise, a shift the Quays made as well (although, as they said in regards to mid-production funding difficulties on *Institute Benjamenta*, "we could probably animate the entire thing just as easily.").

In terms of the Quay's poetic syntax — their associative whorl of mystic relationships and lyrical disquiet — their closest kin (as the Quays themselves admit in a Norwegian interview) is Youri Norstein, a Russian animator whose *Tale of Tales* remains something of a Holy Grail for animation fans in America. (It can only be seen on a Japanese laserdisc unavailable here.) Graphically halfway between Gustav Doré and Maurice Sendak, *Tale of Tales* is a folkartish tapestry littered with elliptical connections and startling images. My favorite, amid the fog-blanketed forests and apples in the snow, is of a lonesome, rather Sendakian wolf huddled over a fire in a dark roadside ditch, the head-lights of passing cars falling over him and the surrounding trees like a lighthouse beam. What's felt in scenes like this is what's vital to the film, and what significance each sequence bears to another is difficult to discern with certainty; Norstein's children's book characters leave us unprepared for a degree of meditative mystery on a par with *Rehearsals for Extinct Anatomies*.

The Quays themselves are ironically pragmatic about the whole issue of ancestry: "Our own vision has been crucially marred by these masters who as it conveniently seems will never be known and so the dupery continues and no one will ever know." They're half-right: few will ever realize because most of the animators they extol as vital to the history of the art form are still largely unseen on these shores. (Starewicz, Alexeieff and Trnka have been made available on tape in limited quantities.) But as for the dupery, the Quays seem sui generis even to the most jaded viewers, and that may be their largest achievement. The smallest moment in their films can make us feel as if we've never known the true and quiet force of film before: the string twisting up on itself from just a touch of the protagonist's desiccated finger in *Street of Crocodiles*, the camera waiting for the bullet to pass through a particularly troublesome pine cone before continuing along its path in *Stille Nacht III*, the ladder, caressed by disembodied hands, suddenly sprouting leaves out of the focal plane in *The Comb*. As wholes, Quay films are carefully considered answers to the question of how many angels can dance on the head of a pin — and we realize the question is fruitless, it doesn't ever matter, what matters is the dance itself.

(*Film Comment*, September – October 1994)

CROSSING THE FRONTIERS: ROAD MOVIES

A breath away from the millennium and here we are on the road again, in a flamboyantly tinted early-model Caddy or T-Bird with a gas tank full of broken dreams and a warm gun on the seat beside us, either heading somewhere or leaving somewhere far behind, and either way we're lost somewhere in the middle. Something desperate and thirsty has been happening in film culture this last decade: the crush of road movies since the Reagan years is unparalleled, not even approached in sheer number by the post-WWII noirs and the late-60's-early-70's counter culture hotrods, the most famous of which, *Easy Rider*, is old enough to get a driver's license of its own. Of course, as Albert Brooks made clear in his *Easy Rider* riff *Lost in America* (1985), in which a frustrated '80s yuppie couple imitate their favorite movie — disastrously — by taking to the freeways in a mobile home, everything but the landscape itself has changed.

It's the Last Chance Gas Station on the movie map, reeking of the ruination and hope and restlessness our collective culture seems overcome by every quarter century or so, and if the signs are worth reading, we've cleaved into a new psychosocial gridlock, where the questions regarding mass identity and national meaning become too big for traditional answers and speeding toward the outskirts, preferably in a convertible, seems the wisest recourse. Indeed, the petrol already expended since the late '80s could fuel the clover leaves of America for an entire summer month: *Candy Mountain, Down By Law, Sherman's March, Raising Arizona, Near Dark, Midnight Run, Promised Land, Rain Man, Patti Rocks, Miles from Home, Miracle Mile, Drugstore Cowboy, Landscape in the Mist, Powwow Highway, Pink Cadillac, Homer & Eddie, Coupe de Ville, Alligator Eyes, Cold Feet, Wild at Heart, Thelma & Louise, Leaving Normal, Terminator 2, My Own Private Idaho, Until the End of the World, The Sheltering Sky, Delusion, Night on Earth, Roadside Prophets, Highway 61, Motorama, Guncrazy, The Living End, One False Move, Falling Down, True Romance, Dust Devil, Poetic Justice, Josh and S.A.M., Over the Hill, Road Scholar, Kalifornia, Highway Patrolman, A Perfect World, Even Cowgirls Get the Blues, Natural Born Killers, The Getaway, Boys on the Side, Across the Moon, Speed, The Chase, Dumb & Dumber, Kingpin, Cobb, Ulysses' Gaze, The Adventures of Priscilla, Queen of the Desert, To Wong Foo, Thanks for Everything, Julie Newmar, Love and a '45, Mad Love, The Doom Generation, Manny & Lo, Freeway, Flirting with Disaster, Fargo, Feeling Minnesota, The Trigger Effect, Dead Man, Bottle Rocket, Traveller, My Fellow Americans, Crash, Lost Highway* and so on. That this list is more or less split down the middle between indie idiosyncracy and Hollywood formula-mongering merely attests to the genre's infinite flexibility; no matter how many medium cool recyclings of *Badlands* the studios grind out, idiosyncrats like Gus Van Sant, Jim Jarmusch, Ross McElwee, the Coens and Greg Araki have still managed to find new reasons to light out for the frontier.

Of course, the recent deluge is a product of its generation, raised on TV and the open-ended, road-like form of the weekly serial. Two time-honored examples, *The Fugitive* and *Route 66*, have both been recycled as cash cows (summer blockbuster and short-lived TV retro-series, respectively), even though the Andrew Davis/Harrison Ford film, for all its box office pay dirt, couldn't approximate the three-year night of the David Janssen show. While too few shows capitalized on TV's potential for perpetuity, the media's very use of narrative space — the weekly scenery changes and transitional architecture of series like *Wagon Train, Star Trek, Have Gun — Will Travel, Movin' On, The Dukes of Hazzard,*

CHiPS and *B.J. and the Bear* — helped redefine our visual culture's sub-conscious predication on neatly concluded plotlines. At the same time, just as Spielberg (*Duel*), Coppola (*The Rain People*), Scorsese (*Boxcar Bertha*) and Bogdanovich (*Paper Moon*) all test-drove the genre's high-ways at least once, the second generation of post-baby boom movie brats have fallen for the autoAmerican allure and nihilistic cool of the genre in a big way, having been raised on Terence Malick, Dennis Hopper and Francis Coppola rather than Godard, Powell and Nicholas Ray. Every year, independent film festivals from Sundance on down to the New York Underground Film Festival regularly feature scores of beg-borrow-&-steal indies set in a car on the road to nowhere. Being cheap to finance helps, but even so, you get the sense that virtually no self-respecting film school tyro can resist the still-resonant topography of vanishing points, billboards and motels, the extrasocietal wilderness where the snug compression of urban culture peters out into one long empty stretch of entropic disorder.

There's something essentially American about it (regardless of how both Germans and Australians are also helplessly drawn to the para-digm), and something essentially transgressive. Indeed, why make a road movie at the end of the century if not to cut across the genre's timeworn iconography? Girlfriends, gays, transvestites, blacks, Native Americans, the elderly, children, the handicapped, vampires, pets — *everybody* has packed into the nearest stolen roadster, slapped an Elvis tape into the stereo and left their ruined lives behind. If they're not explicitly in search of *Easy Rider*'s "American Dream," their six-cylin-dered tail-chasings search for a freedom the frontier — cinematic and otherwise — haven't afforded since the Gold Rush (or, perhaps, *The Gold Rush*). Which makes the genre's exploding demographics seem more like poignant truth than a merely hyperextended formula. It's more than identity politics infiltrating a convenient and hip film tradition; in the road movie we have a matrix of human desire and the last-ditch search for self, and who is more plagued by hunger and lostness than the socially disenfranchised? Though not by any means the road movie's first genre-throttle, it was the fuck-em-all sisterhood of *Thelma & Louise* (1991) that established the frontier of modern nomadism as the domain of conflicting social — not necessarily economic — forces.

Ridley Scott's film imbued many of the form's outcast cliches with an unheralded radical chic, including the final seppuku over the Grand Canyon, which took Barry Newman's driving into a brick wall in the pretentious final moments of *Vanishing Point* (1971) and powerfully politicized it into zeitgeisthood. Suddenly road trips weren't solely the avenues of fate or tragedy or criminal whim; now, every tribe, fringe ideology and hue of Benetton Color could gas up for an escapist rip, flouting the law and flying their own everyday flags of discontent and exclusion. Thus, the very notion of the outlaw is redefined (the road movie being the modern anti-hero's original stomping ground); Fonda and Hopper, both young white men with gas tanks full of cash and a mind-expanding world of time on their hands, don't seem to have as much of a natural birthright to the backroads as the HIV-positive pair of randy misanthropes in *The Living End*, the narcoleptic lost boy of *My Own Private Idaho*, the amateur Cheyenne revolutionaries of *Powwow Highway*, the abused children of *Guncrazy*, *Motorama* or *Freeway*.

Even so, road movies are too cool to seriously address sociopolitical issues; instead, they express the fury and suffering at the extremities of civilized life, and give their restless protagonists the false hope of a one-way ticket to nowhere. As the Indian mystic M.N. Chatterjee put it, if you don't know where you're going, any road will get you there. The journey's the thing, and anyone who thinks differently is just wasting gas. Once Hopper and Peter Fonda declared "the American Dream" as their destination, it became obvious that where you were going hardly mattered, and that the Dream was the road itself, even if it runs in a circle and ends in hapless carnage.

And it always did; like noir and its living-dead neo-incarnations, road movies are cowled in spontaneous turmoil and dead-end fatalism, never more than a few roadstops away from abject lawlessness and haphazard bloodletting. The genre has always been inherently schizoid, offsetting our mad romance with the internal combustion engine, upholstery, tailfins and endless asphalt with a seemingly unpreventable collapse into failure and pain. From *Detour* (1945), with its shallow graves and deathful fits of bad luck, to the naive highway cop blasted off his motorcycle in a Darwinian display of random selection at the end of *Electra Glide in Blue* (1973), to the glossy shotgun weddings of *Wild at Heart*,

True Romance, Falling Down, Kalifornia and *Lost Highway*, road movies have always been songs of the doomed, warnings that once you enter the open hinterlands between cities, you're essentially on your own. I may be headed for the proverbial brick wall, sez the pariah heroes of *Gun Crazy, Pierrot le Fou, Scarecrow, Dirty Mary Crazy Larry, Stroszek* et al., but at least I'm doing the driving.

Simplicity itself structurally, the road movie has always been a virtually unique class of cinematic beast, built around narrative form rather than milieu; *The Wizard of Oz* is as much a genre number as *Wild at Heart*, its landscape no less grim, its journey no less circular and helpless. (Wizard or no wizard, Dorothy ended up back in the Depression-era Kansas badlands, still parentless and sulky and subject to the dog-destroying caprices of Mrs. Gulch.) The pattern, and mood, of the road trip haunts us like a Jungian archetype, from Ulysses to Kerouac, from the Diaspora and the settling of the American west to the real-life road movies starring Christ (who may as well have driven into a brick wall), Columbus, Jayne Mansfield, Neal Armstrong and O.J. Still, more to the point, road movies have become ineluctably tied to the cheap-and-nasty aesthetics of rock 'n roll (with Chuck Berry's "Route 66" as the first unofficial anthem), rebel youth culture and the no-future potential of crazed automobile use, and therefore to the hormone-shocked, Mustang-crazed libido of every modern teenager since James Dean picked the black marble on the road to Salinas. The geography of the car itself, and the accompanying postwar car culture, has traveled a contemporaneous vector, the vehicles themselves transforming from stately, tank-sized comfort zones to agents of speed, sex and sleek design, the uneven sprawl of the first roads giving way to the Gordian-knot engineering of cloverleaf freeways. Few cultural developments outside of the first atomic bomb test at Los Alamos have had as decisive an impact on movies as the postwar evolution of American car culture. The structure of the car, designed to both conform to our bodies' shortcomings and powerfully extend them into the world like the manifested projections of a collective ego, has become how we regard the world (through the screen-like, Panavision-shaped lens of the windshield and, like a miniature movie within a movie, the rearview mirror), how we measure the width of continents (which have all gotten significantly smaller), how we simultaneously close ourselves up within our self-made universes and gain access to every forgotten corner of the globe. Suitably, many road movies have found brilliant visual wisdom in exploring our complex relationship with the interior of the automobile: the quiet observation of a bank robbery from the getaway car's backseat in Joseph H. Lewis' *Gun Crazy* (1949), the chilling menace of the highway cop tapping on the driver-side window in *Psycho* (1960), the seedy sedan intimacy of the door-to-door Bible hawkers in *Salesman* (1969), Dennis Weaver's car's slow morph into an iron maiden of paranoid tension in *Duel* (1971). One of the most eloquent car scenes anywhere is in the otherwise non-road movie *Prime Cut* (1972), in which a life-or-death wheat field pursuit stops dead for all concerned when an empty Cadillac gets noisily eaten by a grain combine — even Lee Marvin is given pause.

Few road movies have ever been as in touch with the reality of cars, and with their own road-movie-ness, as Monte Hellman's long-unseen, long-martyred *Two-Lane Blacktop* (1971). Uncompromised, Rorschach-inconclusive, legendary yet as real as highway weeds, Hellman's stripped-down masterpiece is so expressive of basic existential identity and destination dilemmas that every frame has the poignant, needy ache of a child fruitlessly asking about God. It's simultaneously all-American and radically anti-Hollywood, authentic and effortlessly iconic. Echoes of Beckett and *Godot*, which Hellman staged in the 60s, abound; think of emptied-out motorheads James Taylor and Dennis Wilson as the lost ones stuck in a ritual dialogue, petulant hitchhiker Laurie Bird as Pozzo and Warren Oates's G.T.O.-driving jabbermouth as Lucky. Still, for all its metaphoric spin, witnessing *Blacktop* is being thrust into the dusty, dirt-poor midday of American road culture (most of it "found"), surrounded by overgrown barrens and the angry chortle of car engines. (*Blacktop* even lists its cars as cast members.) Taylor is the Driver, Wilson is the Mechanic, their life is a series of impromptu drag races against local drivers, almost always winning with their custom dragster in a primer-gray '55 Chevy shell. Oates (whose credit reads "G.T.O.") is a slumming dude with a hot car he knows nothing about; the cross-country race between the two vehicles that passes for the film's plot is arrived at so casually you could miss it. Along the way, a la

Antonioni, the wager is neglected (by the drivers *and* Hellman) and forgotten. Though scrupulously unfaddish, Hellman's acidic, calm but desperate vision is far from ignorant of its place and time: Wilson steals local Southern plates to slap on his Chevy because "I get nervous in this part of the country," while a quiet roadhouse confrontation with a redneck chills Oates into stymied silence.

Roadtripping may have been a drop-out, turn-on hot rod cliche even in 1971, but nobody told Hellman, whose frustrated odyssey feels like the first and last of the real road movies. The druggy rhythms, the down time, the meaningless forward motion — the movie itself is like a long drive to nowhere. And it never ends: like his characters, Hellman never admits the frontier is gone, that the road has an end, and simply lets the film grind down and burn in the projector gate instead. Hellman knew that implicit in the hermetic inner world of the car is its antagonistic association with the outside world (high speed car crashes being a mundane yet intensely cinematic cultural phenomena), and more importantly, the brute reality that the traveling itself, to the extent that it itself represents a question, may never be satisfactorily answered and finished. The annals of modern highway lore are filled with treks cut short by hard luck and cruelty, the travelers ground to a permanent halt in the loneliest, most degenerated backwater in the hemisphere. Your average road movie turns the too-real despair of transient losers into modern myth, outfitting it with moviehouse spectacles (psychosis, gunplay, mad chases, post-apocalyptic anarchy, you name it) and coloring it a laconic suede-shoe blue. "You ever been in a time machine?" arch-felon Kevin Costner asks his young, kidnapped passenger in *A Perfect World*. "That there's the past," he says in pure road movie patois, pointing to the ass-end of the highway they're on, "and up there, well, there's the future. This here is the present — enjoy it while you can."

Though a deathless movie species, road movies are rarely hits, and if mass audiences aren't exactly rabid for causeway action short of *T2*, perhaps that's because the genre epitomizes so much of what's uneasy and lost and temporal about the culture. Still, not all Industry band wagons are fueled by greed, and box office receipts alone do not a zeitgeist make. Just a moderate success like *Thelma & Louise* can reawaken our wanderlusty dreams of salvation, place roadside wreaths up and down the semi-paved hills of our consciousness, and signpost a hot corner of cinematic discourse for Hollywood to powerlunch over. Certainly the contemporary craze for hot asphalt, purple T-birds and allusions to the Eisenhower era constitutes a conscious effort by moviemakers to wire into the present-day thirst for the road movie topos by way of nostalgia for the Ghosts of Counter Culture Past. (Given a reasonable passage of years, every decade has its plunderable cliches; the Quentin Tarantino-scripted *True Romance* evokes the '50s with the ghost of Elvis, the '60s with its *Bonnie & Clyde* simulacrum, the '70s with Sonny Chiba movies, the '80s with Joel Silver and John Woo references.) The road movie is finally perceived as a means and end to itself, finally a franchised form, and suddenly the subject isn't the road so much as The Road, invoking the mode's legacy as the main text to a degree Monte Hellman and *Vanishing Point*'s Richard Sarafian wouldn't have dared. David Lynch's Cuisinarting of *The Wizard of Oz* in *Wild at Heart* was only the first step; the airless, obsessive journies of David Cronenberg's *Crash* may be close to the last. "And now we return to *Bullitt*, already in progress," Christian Slater chirps as he pulls his Caddy onto Sunset Boulevard in *True Romance*, and he speaks for a whole generation of movieheads.

Indeed, *Thelma & Louise* couldn't have existed without a tradition of macho-dominated interstate rambling to counteract. Tamra Davis' *Guncrazy*, far from being a remake of Lewis' *Gun Crazy*, rehashes *Badlands* for Judy Blume fans, revisiting the mobile homes, roadside churches and teenage ennui of '70s teen fiction. Dominic Sena's *Kalifornia* also reworks the Charlie Starkweather scenario, but with a particularly odious postmod twist: the film's serial killer and bimbo sweetheart are paired with a couple of urban art yuppies researching serial killers by visiting their homes. It's a predictable enough fate for a mainstream project longing to express outlaw impulses it cannot properly access. What you get are films so reflexive there's simply no there there, only a trunkload of undigested images from older movies. The titles themselves are dead giveaways to the scavenged, self-conscious tone of the movies: *Coupe de Ville*, *Pink Cadillac*, *Promised Land*, *Roadside Prophets*, *Road Trip to Heaven*, etc., and perhaps chintziest of all, *Road Scholar*, a documentary of the book by the same title by poet and radio commentator Andrei Codrescu. A Romanian naturalized to the

United States since the '60s, Codrescu took to the road in a '68 Caddy, armed with a book advance, a photographer and a film crew. Always a droll, sardonic essayist about the mad hilarities of the American quotidian, Codrescu acknowledges in both film and book how such an artificially conceived and prepared peregrination is a doubtful project at best. He's right, though his declamations to that effect hardly mitigate *Road Scholar*'s strained sense of self-importance. Codrescu's merely a member of an expanding demimonde, exploiting the road movie's seepage into other forms, including other highly publicized volumes of New Journalism with titles like *Road Fever*, *Highway 50*, *Storm Country* and *South of Haunted Dreams* (with portentous subtitles like "A Personal Journey Through the Mid-Atlantic" and "A Journey Through the Heart of America"), concept rock albums, performance art, photo essays (beginning with Michael Lesy's *Wisconsin Death Trip*) and a mounting slew of nonfiction cinema: Robert Kramer's 4 1/2-hour epic *Route 1*, Errol Morris' memory lane chase *The Thin Blue Line*, Ulrike Ottinger's 9-hour, real-time exploration of Outer Mongolia, *Taiga*, Robert Epstein and Jeffrey Friedman's *Where Are We?: Our Trip Through America*, the several chronicles of Oliver North's 1992 journey down the campaign trail for a North Carolina senatorship, MTV's quasi-doc teen-odyssey series *Road Rules*, etc. The dubious strain of such earnestly undertaken expeditions, searching as they do for Truth or, if you will, Hopper's American Dream, has been well understood in real road movies ever since Farley Granger is shot down in the rain in *They Live By Night*. Whatever might be found on the road, it won't resemble any universal truth, it will elude those explicitly searching for it, and it won't be easy to tie to the hood and bring home.

In an age where the American populace can create controversy over which image of Elvis — young or old-&-bloated — to put on a postage stamp, the road movie cannot help but turn in on itself, exploiting its own heritage. This may be a matter of socioeconomic friction; in the postwar years, the desperate flight to greener pastures seemed a viable recourse for many Americans sick of rummaging through the trash heap of their decimated lives. Come the '60s, the reckless joyride became the most authentic, expressive and rowdiest way for a new generation of self-exploring Americans to redefine their territory and at the same time thumb their noses at their parents' Levittown-style middle class of two-car garages and automated kitchens. Today, there's little frontier to speak of and little hope of national rediscovery, and the movies confirm the general sense of post-Gen-X defeatism by transforming the traveled landscape into a bricolage of cinematic tropes — especially the omnipresent stench of burnt gunpowder and smoking bodies — and by being, with or without a helpful dollop of irony, unabashed Road Movies. Characters hit the road less for any concrete, plot-driven reason than because they've seen a lot of movies — they're *in* a Road Movie, ferChrissake — and that's what you do. Objectively speaking, what could be more of a dead end than that?

How far can a genre self-reflex before, like a snake eating its tail, it simply disappears? More than likely, road movies will suffer the further humiliations of sanitization, learn-about-yourself melodramas a la *Rain Man*, and media saturation, setting up an inevitable tension. Predicated for the most part on heartbreak and post-noirish melancholia, on the precept that road trips never end as we hope and instead thrust us into an environment ruled by misfortune and dog-eat-dog brutality, road movies are bound to frustrate any effort to shoe-horn them into multiplex formulas. Instead, we may be nearing the age of the anti-road movie, or the revisionist road movie, when the genre will autonomously shuck off the blubber of the mainstream marketplace and once again return to the ragged outskirts of pop culture so beautifully traveled in the genre's best films — *Detour, Gun Crazy, Faster Pussycat, Kill! Kill!, Weekend, Salesmen, Two-Lane Blacktop, Duel, Kings of the Road, Going Places, Stroszek, Paris, Texas, Drugstore Cowboy*. Perhaps once again the image of a faded luxury model from yesteryear soaring through the heat ripples and fog and endless night of a flat turnpike or overgrown backstreet, dashed hopes trailing behind it like so much exhaust, will conjure not the tired postmod cliches of a hyperactive pop consciousness, but the mysterious, detrital lyricism of human hunger and loneliness we've all felt on the road ourselves, the engine humming beneath us, our future sprawling out across the earth like cruel desert sunlight, just a wheel turn from madness, and a just few miles from home.

(*Sight & Sound*, January 1994)

NOTES ON TWO *DETOURS*

A man and woman are driving down an empty desert highway; she's asleep, he's thinking to himself in voiceover, ruminating on where she might be from, who she is, that it won't matter in a few hours once he gets to Hollywood and ditches the car he's driving, property of a dead man, a man he didn't kill but whose pockets he rifled and whose identity he assumed after rolling the body into a roadside ditch. Just as he figures he can skirt the circumstantial rattrap he's found himself in, she sits up, eyes wide, her sour expression turned suddenly demonic, and — as if she had heard his thoughts on the soundtrack — demands in a voice that could turn milk, "*Where* did you leave his body?!"

Welcome to Endsville. The country is "noir," and this ferocious, unnerving moment of clairvoyance is from Edgar G. Ulmer's *Detour*, both noir's greatest, direst dirge and possibly the least likely film ever to attract a cult. Road movie ideogram, skid row bad dream and the answer to the decidedly unmusical question *how could things get any worse?*, *Detour* still bruises with each viewing; dashed off 47 years ago in four days and on a paper route budget, it feels like an exhumed artifact from a lawless, graceless time, a post-industrial Dark Age. To truly understand *Detour*, we must enter into a world where, according to the film's fated naif-hero Tom Neal, "whichever way you turn, Fate sticks out a foot to trip you." Today, the wellworn terrain of movie lowlife belongs to serial killers, cannibals and crack dealers; bad things never happen to good people. In 1945, we had the average schmoe sucked into a dark criminal nightmare for no better reason than wrong place, wrong time. For all its kitsch, shortcuts and uproarious vernacular, *Detour* remains a humbling lesson in the democracy of disaster.

Detour has remained one of the lucky classics to avoid the obligatory modernizing remake (not so lucky were *D.O.A.*, *The Big Clock*, *The Postman Always Rings Twice*, *Criss Cross*, *Kiss Me Deadly*, *Out of the Past*, *Cape Fear*, *A Kiss Before Dying*, *The Narrow Margin*, *The Desperate Hours*, etc.). That is, until now, and with a difference: Wade Williams's *Detour* (1991) is an ostensible remake that plays more like a reincarnation of the first film, brought back to life for the sheer retro love of it. No other film — indeed, no other genre — has ever spawned so worshipful a homage as this: in a straight-faced post-mod fit of iconicity, Williams convinced look-alike Tom Neal Jr. to play his Dad playing the original role. Williams shot along the same stretch of Arizona highway with the same camera model Ulmer used in 1945, constructed sets with the same constricting dimensions as the original, employed the same lighting and lenses (nothing as high-tech as a zoom lens was allowed), and used the same car — not the same model, the *same car*, a '41 Lincoln convertible the director tracked down in Boston. That Williams's *Detour redux* nevertheless has a berserk flavor all its own is no surprise: regarding the first film as a sacred text and attempting, in fact, to reconstruct it in a kind of timeless void as if nearly 50 years of intervening history and culture had never occurred, the new *Detour* is a head-shaking fusion of period gloom and movie-nut innocence. It's a work of fanatical nostalgia that doesn't acknowledge for a second that it's about the past.

Though doggedly hermetic, as though it was filmed within an unreformed cinephiliac's fusty skull, Williams's unreleased *Detour* is a touchstone that, sight unseen, heralded some kind of critical mass for the neo-noir fad. Think of it as a secret text that in a stroke marked the aesthetic dead-end of struggling to recapture the doomy heartache of the postwar era almost 50 years later, and expressed how peculiar and trapped-in-a-vacuum the resulting cinema can seem. Few films of the last 15 years, try as they might via sadomasochistic ritual, softcore sex and absurd violence, can capture the philosophical toughness of original noir; there are more base hits when the filmmakers go back to the source: *The Grifters, After Dark, My Sweet* and *Miami Blues* are all based on real blood-&-puddle fiction, the kind they used to sell in drugstore bookracks. Quentin Tarantino's *Pulp Fiction*, as its evocative title suggests, is merely a protracted textual pun on the real McCoy.

Still, ever since retro-noir gained sudden popular and academic cachet with *Chinatown* (1974), the first major hit to attempt reconstructing an old film era (and do it with no small dollop of irony and romantic nostalgia), the genre has remained deathlessly hip, inspiring an eager late-century glacier of copies, co-optations, tributes, academic musings and inanely dehistoricized retro attitude. Of the major film genres, it is easily America's favorite. Starting in earnest with *Body Heat* (1981), movies brimming with betrayals, smoke, femme fatales, Venetian blinds and outlaw roadtrips spawned like fruitflies. A woeful pastiche musical, *City of Angels*, won Tonys in 1990. Comic superheroes entered the mean streets for real in D.C.'s *Watchmen*, while music videos regularly hosed down the dark studio streets. Critic David Thomson actually wrote a novel, *Suspects*, constructed around the expanded biographies of more than 80 noir and quasi-noir film characters, centering on the imagined lost brotherhood between Jeff Bailey (Robert Mitchum in *Out of the Past*) and George Bailey (James Stewart in *It's a Wonderful Life*). Poets, notably Brooks Haxton with *Dead Reckoning*, published book-length poems of crime and misfortune told in noirish first person. Nearly every scuffed-knuckle word of Jim Thompson's fiction was sold to the movies (eventually even his seminal short story, *This World, Then the Fireworks*, was made into a retro-noir indie), as Black Lizard Books made a bundle reissuing his long-out-of-print novels along with those of Charles Willeford and David Goodis. Martin Goldsmith's original *Detour*, published in 1938, became one of the rarest and most sought-after paperbacks of all time.

There's no fooling ourselves: given to re-enacting a begone era's bone-deep desperation because it simply seems cool, we've gotten soft. Graphic bloodshed or not, movies have gotten less cynical, less willing to confront fear and loathing. All that has been successfully shanghaied is the attitude, all ruthless voguing with the real shadows and scary guts left behind. No movie of the post-New Morning in America era could possibly contain Neal and his relentless, blow-by-blow description of his descent into Hell anymore than it could end as *Detour* properly does, with its hero slumped over a late night diner stool mulling over the calamities that make up his ruined life. Neal is the human animal wrecked, spent and without a future — and it's no pose, no ironic joke, no expression of punkish rage. Fate is no laughing matter in the wasteland.

The films had the boatload of German Expressionists directing and shooting them to thank for their infamous visual patois, but the deeper mark was in the shocking nihilism of the stories, the majority of them penned by homegrown writers: A.I. Bezzerides, David Goodis, Sydney Boehm, Daniel Mainwaring, Charles Schnee, Jules Furthmman, etc., as well as the Henry James of noir, Jim Thompson. Wars being what they are, Americans came home from WWII believing in the Dark Side, no longer simply the evil Other-to-be-vanquished, and as a result 1945 America was a veritable primordial soup of societal disillusionment. (Embodying a backlash to relentlessly cheery wartime propaganda is yet another way to interpret noir's moment in history.) Vets came home to broken families, lost jobs, unreliant wives and — perhaps most of all — the inability to trust and embrace the innocence and calm of peacetime life. The most expressive take on this is the Chandler-written *The Blue Dahlia* (1946), which finds a numb Alan Ladd returning from the war to find his kid dead and his wife whoring. The American Dream, the sustaining thematic blueprint for our culture up to and during the war, was butchered and buried in these films. With Dresden, Okinawa and Dachau behind you, who'd be able to swallow *Stella Dallas*, *Babes in Arms* or even *The Maltese Falcon*, with its genteel patter and off-screen killings? (*Cahiers du cinema* auteurist critic Luc Moullet defined Ulmer's pervasive theme to be "the great loneliness of man without God.") Perhaps it was with *Double Indemnity* (1944) that the cold-blooded reality of it hit the world: two amoral bastards plot the death of an innocent jerk, and we watch them do it, hoping it works. The darkness has been with us ever since. This was culture-confessional cinema, our collective life: living day by dark day in a world ruled by jungle law, bad luck and the force of evil. If the ur-schmuck Tom Neal was us, then so was maniac cop Robert Ryan, hopeless puppet Farley Granger, whiskey-voiced mud-slinger Ida Lupino, mountain-of-trouble Lawrence Tierney.

"I think the man in the hat did something terrible," said sky-high William Hurt in *The Big Chill* whilst watching an anonymous noir on late night TV, and that one line could define the whole cycle. Men in hats began doing truly terrible things before WWII, but the gap between '30s movies and postwar fare is as broad as Lee Marvin's mean streak. During the Depression, movie crooks were amiable, charming, self-pow-ered rule-breakers who got the Hays Code bullet in the end — they would've, if they could've, gone straight. They'd been dealt a bad hand, you see, but it's nothing compared to what was dished out to most noir characters, who never get off the ground. Look at Jimmy Cagney: from nervy, anti-authoritarian rogue in the pre-war *Angels with Dirty Faces* (1938), to smalltime, self-immolating psychobeast in the postwar *White Heat* (1949). There weren't any Dead End Kids hanging around Cody Jarrett; this guy couldn't attract flies.

Politically, the genre is surprisingly resonant, even Marxist (or Social Darwinist, depending on the how you read the films' ethics) in its expression of class struggle. The lone noir man has no recourse to the law and knows it; if justice is to be served, he'll have to serve it, with no guarantees to neatness or the safety of bystanders. If you hold faith with the cops you'll probably end up under an inch of loose soil. It's American anarchism, textualized for the masses. What other set of films this side of Godard is so proudly proletariat? The little man is tom-mygun fodder for the corrupt, well-staffed corporate Mr. Bigs, who acquired their wealth while the less fortunate and duplicitous went to war — you can't tell the difference between, say, George Macready's officious smoothie in *Gilda* (1946) and a legitimate entrepreneur. Cops, if they're honest, are often the last holdouts of cynical virtue, guys with lousy jobs who've been screwed by the system. While a murder was for solving in the '30s, in noir it's only to be feared and avenged. Lawrence Tierney slaughters two people in the first five minutes of *Born to Kill* (1947), for no better reason than they upset him. The question from there on is not who will find him out, but who he'll kill next.

As exemplified in Ulmer's *Detour*, the genre usually kills even the hope for cleansing mayhem — violence is usually quick, unspectacular and unsatisfying. As Neal's noir Charlie Brown blurts to the audience near the beginning of his jeremiad: "I'll listen to it, but I know what you're gonna hand me even before you open your mouths... You're gonna tell me you don't believe my story about how Haskell died and give me that don't-make-me-laugh expression on your smug faces." By the looks of him, we might've. Who says he *is* telling the truth? This guy's always been a dark cloud: even a $10 tip for his pre-road nightclub piano-playing (at the Break 'O Dawn Club) is nothing more than "a piece of paper crawling with germs." Hitchhiking, filthy and penniless, his every grouse about the world is faithfully fulfilled. Later, driving the dead man's Lincoln — a man who staked him for a meal and whose body he never gave a thought to burying — Neal meets up with a true force of nature, a veritable Evil Spirit in the form of Ann Savage, indisputably the shrillest, most horrifying noir harpy of all. Conversationally, Neal says she looks like she's a Phoenix girl; "Are Phoenix girls that bad?" she wearily replies. You've got to see her to believe her; sex-starved, consumptive and drunk on sour viciousness, Savage, as Vera Whatever Her Name Was, soon engages Neal in a spare, motel-room *No Exit* nightmare from which he will never quite escape.

A masterpiece of on-shot set pieces and bad preservation — it's the Watts Towers to *Gun Crazy*'s stainless steel prefab diner — Ulmer's *Detour* gains another heartbreaking post-mod spin when paired with the off-screen life story of Neal himself, who began as an ex-Ivy League Tinseltown stud, servicing nearly every woman in the business — most famously, Joan Crawford, who got him fired from M-G-M when he grew tired of her. Relegated to B-movies, Neal made headlines by kicking the shit out of Franchot Tone over actress Barbara Payton (who eventually died a Sunset Strip hooker), and eventually shot his third wife dead in mid-coitus. Despite the fact that he went to an Idlewild diner (!) afterwards and bragged drunkenly about killing her, during the murder trial he claimed that they'd wrestled with the weapon — and that she had forced him to perform cunnilingus on her at gunpoint, all demonstrated in the courtroom to the delight of the press photographers.

He served seven years in prison for manslaughter anyway, and died 18 months after being released, when Tom Jr. was 15. Suddenly *Detour* seems imbued with a harrowingly realism, as Neal tells his story walking, forecasting (in the words of writer/noir-maven Barry Gifford) "his own hellish spiral from rich-kid Northwestern and Harvard University grad to Hollywood lout and wifeslayer. Even the daylight in this movie is cloudy." The tacked-on, the-law-catches-up ending, absent in Martin Goldsmith's novel and Williams's remake, comes off years later as less comeuppance than the final, fateful slap in the face: "Someday a car will pick me up I never thumbed." In the new *Detour*, Neal Jr. just walks into the fog alone, heading down the road and presumably into a hard life of no small payments.

Like a dog chasing his tail, the 80s-90s neo-neo-noir hall of mirrors comes around to the new *Detour*, a piece of kitschy trash culture voodoo with a true B attitude and not a trace of irony. It's a film Warhol would have loved, not least for it being seemingly oblivious to its own freakhood. Williams, a TV and indie film distributor whose previous credits include directing *Midnight Movie Massacre* and a shame-faced associate producer credit on Tobe Hooper's disastrous *Invaders from Mars* remake, freely admits to a hapless fanaticism when it comes to the first *Detour*, preferring writer Goldsmith over Ulmer as the film's true auteur and considering Ann Savage "possibly the finest actress to ever walk a soundstage." While sniffing out the original Lincoln used in Ulmer's film might be going a little far, other aspects of the remake's retro territory make good sense: the use of the archaic two-color Cinecolor process, which gives the film an old-plastic, spoiled pastel veneer, and the integration of subplots from the novel Ulmer didn't have time to shoot. The chief missing plot thread here is that of Sue, Neal's girlfriend who heads to L.A. in search of stardom and ends up waiting tables and attempting — none too successfully — to screw her way to the top. That Neal Jr. mourns ruefully in the diner that he can never link up with her now, not with a few murders hanging over his head, packs a new punch — she thinks he's dead, and good riddance to bad rubbish.

Though it lacks the original's grainy cheapness and authentic place in history, Williams's *Detour* has a bizarre ontological relationship with its ancestor — seeing it without a thorough foreknowledge of the original movie would be a bit like a New Guinea tribesman tripping through Madame Tussaud's. While other remakes endeavor to perfect or modernize what's flawed or dated, the new *Detour* glorifies *both* films' low-budget shortcuts and '40s ambience. Neal Jr. and Lea Lavish (her real name, in the Ann Savage role) act less than recast themselves as the old actors — which sounds lousy, but get a load of Lavish, who makes up for what she lacks in monstrousness with snotty, chin-stuck-way-out hubris, a sour cross between Savage and Pat Benatar. If the half-polished '40s-style acting isn't wholly deliberate, it's purposeful, as necessary to the film as the Lincoln's blood-red upholstery, seen for the first time in color.

Naturally, Neal Jr. is a walking boneyard haunted by the Ghosts of Hollywood Past. Providing Williams's film with a few extra layers of questionable hyperreality, resembling his father enough to impart chills on any noir-read audience, this guy is subtext in an old suit, proving once more that real life and movies can beget each other over and over again in a furious recycling whorl. Neal's line readings are just amateurish enough to hint at the restless, ex-orphan punk underneath the period trappings, a Hollywood fringe youth whose mother died when he was one and who had been shipped around between relatives while his movie-star Dad did time for killing the kid's shrewish stepmom. While remaining a stilted hologram of its progenitor, the remake of *Detour* nearly bursts its seams with real, if extra-cinematic, suffering. Back to back, who can resist characterizing the two Neals, and the two *Detours*, as consecutive generations of Americans plagued by the same post-WWII blight and socioeconomic dream-death.

But if you're talking zeitgeist (then or now), you can't get more noir than Neal and Savage in that '41 Lincoln, the original noir fool and the hitchhiking noir bitch. Her we first see closely in silhouette, gazing straight ahead, as the Everyguy driving observes to himself (and us, in Goldsmith's endlessly quotable dialogue), "She was young, not more than 24... Man, she looked like she'd just been thrown off the crummiest freight train in the world..." And, as he thinks she has a kind of beauty anyhow, "a beauty that's almost homely because it's so real," she quickly turns and faces him — and us — as if she could *hear* the film's narration. Her life-hating glare is the most unsettling in American film. Everything else is just Hollywood.

(*Bright Lights Film Journal*, #15, 1995)

GENUINE B NOIR: JAMES B. HARRIS

It has been fashionable of late to ring the death knell for B movies. Be it at the hands of escalating film costs, the blockbuster mentality or the skid row dumping ground of home video, the authentic B has become a cinematic dodo, as obsolete as the newsreel, the biblical epic or — let's face it — the musical. The Bs of yore — smaller budgeted cousins to As that the studios churned out to fill out bijou double bills — are famous for being unpoliced petri dishes of moviemaking brio. Studios paid as little regard to the making of Bs as to the making of cartoons (after years of Bugs and Daffy, Jack Warner was reportedly shocked to find that his studio was not responsible for Mickey Mouse), and thus filmmakers were allowed elbow room for idiosyncrasy, genre-bending, expressionistic visual styles and often harrowing nihilism. Formula could be futzed: in the cheaper noirs, for instance, happy endings and Mr. Clean heroics could be avoided altogether. The hard-luck Underman of Edgar G. Ulmer's *Detour* is lost on a highway to Hell you'll never find on any studio A-list map. (*Detour* was the product of the Poverty Row stalwart Producer's Releasing Corp.) We've come a long way. Nowadays mainstream movies rarely have the nerve to defy their designated demographics. All things being equal, the untamed nation of straight-to-video films, with their endless self-cloning sequels, is closer in spirit to old serials and exploitation indies. Once someone like Steven Seagal has become ensconced in the A lists, you know there's no room left in the movie culture food chain for Bs anymore.

Perhaps this is why the sullen, impulsive films of James B. Harris have been consistently overlooked and underseen. Genuine B noirs in the purest non-reflexive sense of the word, Harris's films are inglorious, pipe-dream-beleaguered gutterdives, with the cheap integrity of bygone pulp fiction. In a fitful career that has run from being Stanley Kubrick's producer on *The Killing* (1956), *Paths of Glory* (1957) and *Lolita* (1961) to the director of the idiosyncratic melodramas *Fast-Walking*, *Cop* and *Boiling Point*, Harris has kept faith with the basic principles of genre without succumbing to neo-anything, homage or pretension. The interface with Jim Thompson (co-writer of *The Killing* and *Paths of Glory*) is not incidental; Harris's later films come closer to Thompson's down-&-dirty sensibility than anyone has, because he doesn't strain to be retro. For Harris, the original dead-end alleyway of noir never faded into the Method decathlon of the 70s or the smirky cash cow farm of the 80s and 90s. It has always been there; you just need to look under the right rock.

Sporadic producing credits aside (including Don Siegel's forgettable 1977 Charles Bronson thriller *Telefon*), Harris's oeuvre is limited to five films, the first of which, *The Bedford Incident* (1965), is a taut if mundane atomic-sub thriller (co-produced by star Richard Widmark) that showed the strain of having to stand shivering in the shadow cast by Kubrick's *Dr. Strangelove*. Eight years later, Harris emitted *Some Call It Loving* (1973), a woozy, rarely seen post-hippie version of the Sleeping Beauty tale (adapted from a John Collier story) starring soft-porn-auteur-to-be Zalman King, a thoroughly druggy Richard Pryor and the implacable Tisa Farrow. It wasn't until *Fast-Walking* (1982) — nine years later — that Harris began to stake his own post-noir territory.

Like Harris's subsequent films, *Fast-Walking* is a character study masquerading as a genre film, a risky strategy that has usually garnered little more than critical antipathy and befuddlement. As with *Cop* (1988) and *Boiling Point* (1993), *Fast-Walking* was positioned as a formula thriller — a prison film — but what we got instead was a quirky melange of debauched characters back-stabbing each other in and around one of cinema's strangest, and most sparsely populated, correctional facilities. James Woods, apparently Harris's lowlife actor of choice, plays "Fast-Walking" Miniver, a happily corrupt, pot-smoking prison guard given to daydreamy money-making schemes and playing the SoCal prison's various socioeconomic forces against each other. He pimps for the local migrant workers, would certainly run drugs if he thought he could avoid getting set up, and generally occupies a rung on the moral ladder only a notch higher — and often several notches lower — than the inmates he guards. As played by Woods, Miniver is less hardened riffraff than a congenital worm, a weasely, grift-happy class clown to whom everyone is potentially both partner and mark. The perambulations of the rather dubious story (involving the attempted assassination of a newly arrived black activist inmate) are further fueled by Miniver's cousin Wasco (Tim McIntyre), an inmate with administrative duties who slowly reveals himself to be a megalomanic despot with delusions of grandeur and the outspoken intentions of taking over the big house's drug trade from Kubrick alumni Timothy Carey.

As befits Harris's oddball upending of genre conventions, McIntyre's powermad autocrat all but steals the movie — the first bitter taste of Harris's aesthetic, which emphasizes the fallout from outlaw culture over the culture itself. Re-entering the noir sensibility freshly, and without any reference to its cliches as a cinematic style, Harris reveals his concern to be how the genre forms, affects and poisons its people. The characters in *Fast-Walking* wander through the movie nursing their own twisted agendas, and the movie can barely keep track. Wasco is a freakish, unpredictable creation designed to warp the formula, not fulfill it.

Not surprisingly, like all of Harris's movies, *Fast-Walking* flopped, a square peg that never fit into the audiences' round-hole notion of pop moviemaking. Its source material is telling — Ernest Brawley's crime novel *The Rap* is exactly the kind of cheap, forgotten fiction whose unaffected aura neo-noir strives so cluelessly to capture. Harris's next film, *Cop*, may be his best and nastiest, and although novelist James Ellroy, upon whose early *Blood on the Moon* it was based, has said he doesn't like the film, he should. Its grimy, pugnacious, hypercynical vision of the urban universe is truer to the tenets of fiction like Ellroy's than any number of more fashionable and self-conscious 80s shots in the dark. Woods stars as Lloyd Hopkins, a rabid LA detective obsessed with the savage murder of a young woman. What puts Hopkins in a whole separate phylum than the usual burnt-out movie cops is his boiling mad-dog spite — faced every day with the squalor and filth of human potential, Hopkins sees himself as an angel of justice on a sick planet, with as little regard for the law as for the criminals he hunts. Woods's persona at this point in his career was defined by sleazy opportunism; whereas the Woods characters in *Salvador* and *Fast-Walking* would wheedle, writhe and rationalize in the name of greed, in *Cop* he does the same in the name of uncorkable fury. A single shot early on illustrates the Hopkins worldview: roaches struggling helplessly in a thickened puddle of blood. The ultimate moral pragmatist, he routinely tells his young daughter violent case histories at bedtime. "Innocence kills," he spits back when his wife objects, "I see it every fucking day."

Indeed, *Cop* concerns itself with oft-ignored police-story questions — how *do* you come home and tell your daughter fairy tales after seeing a teenage girl eviscerated and hung from her toes? Other genre pieces would take sides — is Hopkins correct in his compulsive dredging of the scumbanks, or is he, as his soon-to-be-ex-wife says, "deeply disturbed"? — whereas *Cop* concludes that not only are both true, but that both *must* be true, one logically born of the other. Harris's film is a moody skulk of de-evolved motivations and chum-drunk cruelty, with its few untainted characters (including fidgety rape victim-turned-radical feminist Lesley Ann Warren) merely representing the betrayed martyrs of modern innocence.

With his own gore-worn code of righteousness (contrasted with his superiors, who are all born-again Christians), Hopkins is the ultimate Harris hero, a crash-and-burn idealist so well acquainted with the soft white underbelly that it has eroded his reason down to its black-or-white, live-or-die extremities. In the film's climactic moment, as Hopkins corners the nutcase killer (Steven Lambert), justice is both served and perverted. "You're a cop," the psycho says, "you gotta take me in." "Well, there's some good news and some bad news," Hopkins replies, at the tail end of a series of bloody murders, departmental scandal and the trainwreck of his homelife. "The good news is you're right, I'm a cop and

I gotta take you in. The bad news is I've been suspended, and I don't give a fuck." He shotguns the killer's head off. Cut to black.

Just as the original noirs did, *Cop* dares us to accept an honest fatalism, and yet we seem markedly less capable of digesting the bitter pill than the post-WWII audiences of *They Live By Night*, *The Big Heat* or *Born to Kill*. Harris's next film, the ersatz Wesley Snipes policier *Boiling Point*, is nearly an object lesson in how to betray audience expectations. Promoted as a rippling, guncrazy action epic in the spirit of *Passenger 57*, *Boiling Point* is actually a modern B-type study in loneliness and failed relationships.

Based on yet another not-unjustly neglected pulp fiction (Gerald Patievich's *Money Men*), the film volleys between the doomed efforts of three characters — Snipes's embittered, divorced federal agent, Dennis Hopper's menopausal ex-con with a headful of balderdash, Viggo Mortenson's gullible copslayer — to reassemble their decimated lives. Intent on proving themselves worthy of the film's women (including Valerie Perrine as Hopper's ex-wife and Lolita Davidovich as the only heart-o'-gold hooker in town), all three speed towards a brick wall of self-delusion, natural-born violence and their own crushing limitations. Snipes can barely concentrate on his job for fear of losing his son and wife forever; when he forces himself into their home in the middle of the night, he is confronted with his wife's lover, who is bigger, saner and more responsible than he is. Like *Cop*'s hydrophobic hero, Snipes has driven his family away with his bullet-headed pursuit of vice, not his love of or respect for the law. Once he realizes he's been replaced as his son's father, he simply decides to turn in his badge — with his private life a smoking ruin, he couldn't otherwise give two shits about justice.

Hopper's Red, like Fast-Walking and Wasco, suffers from a gambler's addiction to easy money, and of course his attempts at a last heist go terribly awry. As the cleancut, disaffected triggerman, Mortenson is pure sociopath, matter-of-factly shotgunning grifter after grifter at Hopper's behest. Taking place almost entirely at night, *Boiling Point* is a closed circle — Harris clearly demarcates a thematic sump for his born losers to live and die in. The peripheral characters, especially Snipes's wife, appear to be leading perfectly normal lives. *Boiling Point*'s central terrain is the hopeless shadow zone of smalltime law and crooks, each sucked deeper and deeper into their own hard-luck tragedies.

Inevitably, *Boiling Point* was drubbed by critics, discontented with its lack of thrills and its aura of sour melancholy. That Harris has been permitted (albeit infrequently) by the system to make his resolutely unprofitable movies at all is a Hollywood miracle. Hitting 65 when *Boiling Point* was released, Harris remains something of an anachronism, occupying the barren no-man's-land between budget-bloated movie "events" and video quickies — two modes of the same late-capitalism sensibility. Unfettered by the principles of commerce, or even of art (why did Snipes, a legitimate above-the-board star at that point, do Harris's film?), Harris's movies are small, wild, sad and nasty in ways we've forgotten films can be. Like true Bs, they're more interesting for their wayward narratives and ragged grit — a movie world where anything dark and cruel can happen.

(*Sight & Sound*, November 1993)

SINISTER URGES:
THE LEGACY OF EDWARD D. WOOD JR.

It might very well say something dark and degenerate about our culture that we've turned Edward D. Wood Jr. into a kind of disturbed cottage industry. The neverending tsunami of film fests, video documentaries, the Bad Movie books effortlessly collapsing into testaments of Woodmania, reams of Woodian reminiscence (including the sublime 1992 oral biography by Rudolph Grey entitled, oddly, *The Nightmare of Ecstasy*) and, ultimately, the sweet and stylized 1994 Hollywood biopic directed by Tim Burton — spawning all this and more, Wood has become, despite himself, a permanent fixture in the pop culture pantheon, an icon of desperate misfithood. In a postmod world of faux sleaze, neo-noir and true crime TV, he's the real McCoy: the patron saint of the lunatic fringe, a skidrow wildcard and gargantuan substance abuser whose bizarre life and deranged films are as seductive as cheap carny trash whispered into the ear of a trailer-park whore.

Whereas most inept filmmakers working on the border of mainstream culture have been by definition ignored, forgotten and certainly not released on video (albeit infrequently distributed by public domain companies like Something Weird Video and Bogus Video), Wood's popularity has continued to snowball. The more we know about him, the more fascinating he becomes. Still, as a filmmaker and scriptwriter Wood is too often dismissed as merely inept — though staggeringly funny, now-classic movies like *Glen or Glenda* (1953), *Jailbait* (1954), *Bride of the Monster* (1955), *The Violent Years* (1956, dir. Fritz Eichorn), *The Bride and the Beast* (1958), *Night of the Ghouls* (1959), *Plan 9 from Outer Space* (1959), *The Sinister Urge* (1961), *Orgy of the Dead* (1965, dir. A.C. Stephens, a.k.a. Stephen Apostoloff) and *Fugitive Girls* (1971, dir. Apostoloff) manage to revivify our notions of cinematic "badness." Whereas movies like Phil Tucker's immortal *Robot Monster* seethe with inimitable clumsiness, Wood's films are a mutant breed all their own, as distinct from normal films as Thalidomide babies are from healthy off-spring. They're the most hermetic films of all time, genre films from a parallel dimension. Take another look at *Plan 9* — with its Bressonian disregard for realistic acting, Wood's knotted Catch-22 dialogue, jaw-slackening discontinuity (day/night, Lugosi/6-foot chiropractor, tiny/huge tombstones), dazzling fusion of back-alley kitsch and Caligarian expressionism (wrinkled night backdrop, cardboard mausoleum, grave-yard grass carpet), Wood's magnum opus smacks less of ineptitude than of outright disturbance. There isn't a whiff of self-consciousness or affectation within a mile of these films — Wood meant every frame, and every frame implies a consciousness ill at ease with reality. The rheumy phases of the man's life — teenage weirdo, carnival geek, Tinseltown outskirter, transvestite (he boasted of storming the beaches at Nor-mandy wearing silk panties under his Marine issue), suicidal tosspot, pornographer, world-class lowlife — are both more compelling than his films and the inevitable source of their sorrow. (And his films *are* lone-some, in the same way very good films feel inhabited and full of life.) Grey's biography is easily the most tragic biography to hit the shelves in years, and watching Wood's films is in a very real sense like entering the dead-end dreams of an authentic American nut. That they're uproarious as well, and have single-handedly fostered an entire subgenre of film appreciation, simply adds to their legend.

But in the annals of Woodography, like most quasi-cult phenomena based nostalgically on trash culture initially intended for children (both *Star Trek* and *Star Wars* spring to mind), indexing the lunacy is preferred to analyzing it. And Wood left a legacy of uncredited writings, half-made movies and stag-loop appearances behind him, all the better for enthusiasts to explore with a figurative pick and flashlight like intrepid journeymen hunting down forgotten tombs in a Lovecraft story. Grey's bibliography/filmography runs 45 pages, and every year a new addition to the Wood corpus is discovered. (Using up to five pseudonyms, Wood spent the last years of his life churning out paperback smut, most of which is still lost to time.) *Night of the Ghouls* sat in storage for 23 years because Wood never paid the lab bill. In 1993, New York's Film Forum ran a Wood retro featuring the newly discovered *Married Too Young*, a 1962 melodrama partially scripted by Wood, probably during a weekend gin binge. Only the careers of giants like Hitchcock and Welles (who, in the form of Vincent D'Onofrio, puts in an appearance in *Ed Wood* as Wood's personal archangel) have been as obsessively anatomized. The quintessential anti-auteur, Wood was as significant in his way as anyone working in the medium — there could not have been a *Rocky Horror Picture Show*, nor its subsequent camp culture (or Burton's entire career; think about the use of Vincent Price in *Edward Scissorhands*) without Wood's influence. *Plan 9* et al. are not artistic constructs, they are vivid windows onto the nightmarish, senseless country pop culture can be when scored by despair and lostness.

At the New York press junket for Tim Burton's *Ed Wood*, I remember Patricia Arquette, who plays Wood's angelicized booze widow Kathy, letting loose with this humdinger of a Wood anecdote: "A beautiful story Kathy told me that's not in [Grey's] book was how one day she was wearing this kind of ochre, yellowish skirt suit, and came by to visit Eddie on the set, and he said 'O'Hara, I saw the most beautiful gardenia today and it's exactly the color of your suit and I'm going to go get it for you.' She said he ran off and came back with this gardenia which was exactly the color of her suit, but Eddie didn't realize it was rotting and that's why it was that color. He didn't realize it, he didn't see the ugliness of it, he saw only the beauty of it..."

Few other stories I've ever heard — and as Burton's film demonstrates, our cultural crawlspaces are loaded with them — have so beautifully captured the sad, decaying strangeness of the Wood paradigm. As winning and witty as Burton's film is, it and its attendant publicity is contingent on another untruth: that Wood was a dreamer who never got his chance, an unstoppable movie buff who kept making movies despite the handicaps of poverty, talentlessness and a cruel, unappreciative industry. This is utter nonsense: Wood was hardly just "talentless," and could not have made even a merely bad film if he had had the budget of *Cleopatra* to piss away. Anyone who has paid any attention to *Glenda, Plan 9, Bride of the Monster, The Sinister Urge, Orgy of the Dead,* etc. (even Wood-written nudies directed by other fools bore the man's unmistakable mark), could see there was something else at work there, something more than ineptitude, cheapness, alcoholism and fetishistic obsession. The collective regard of Wood as a Hollywood martyr defies the evidence; it's as if no one knows a rotten gardenia when they see one.

Even so, Burton is the closest thing to a genuine pop-cult auteur Hollywood's got, and his film remains the only American movie ever made about the true life of a moviemaker. In many ways, it's the movie Burton has been building up to, and simultaneously (like the subsequent *Mars Attacks!*) a swoony valentine sent with all love and rockets to every thirtysomething boomer who misspent his 70s childhood seeking out alternative universes by watching monster movies on local TV station "Creature Features" showcases, reading *Famous Monsters of Filmland*, eating Quisp cereal and generally floating free in the black-&-white broadcast ether where bad special effects, dying horror actors and laboratories filled with unscientific bric-a-brac were the norm. Anyone not dizzy with nostalgia for the first time they saw *White Zombie* on a rainy Saturday afternoon may not be as overcome, and inescapably the hermetic quality of Burton's lovesong invokes a suspect film culture that makes masterpieces out of the grade-Z effluvia we watched as introverted children too spastic to play football on the lawn with the rest of the kids. Indeed, with what good faith can we take Burton's film when it lionizes Wood (more or less in his own style) and still emerges as so immeasurably superior to Wood's own work? "Can you imagine how Wood himself would've reacted?" was a common press-junket musing, and, sure, that's easy: he would've loved Burton's film, he would've wanted to make a movie just like it, or any movie at all, immediately. He had a unquenchable jones for cinema, but he would have failed in the same inevitable way Burton succeeded. It was his nature.

Burton's movie may be funnier than Wood's films but for the same reasons: the fragility of the cardboard gravestones in *Plan 9*'s cemetery, for instance, is laugh-out-loud in both movies, but Burton's contextualizes it as comedy. Wood, of course, never did, and it's his dull-eyed escape from reason that has both inspired Burton and escaped him. Despite being one of the most successful film directors ever, Burton still characterizes himself as a Woodian misfit; he may have been an unpopular, unpromising kid, but Burton's proved that although many are called, few are chosen. His titanic popularity places him, like it or not, helplessly removed from Wood and Wood's genuine intimacy with the sour torments of the American century and its socioeconomic remorselessness, and with the corrupting moonshine sold everyday by the Movies as a utopian dimension we must view from a distance. In reality, Wood represents more than just the Worst; he is the sobbing ghost within the carpenter's-gothic bungalow of Hollywood's concept of itself. It's a case of the American Dream passing a lost loser on a desert highway like a convertible full of naked women. Wood is the reality of show business culture; Burton is the fantasy.

This is a large part of why *Ed Wood* tells only a sliver of the real story, the part leavened with ardor and heartfeltness: Wood's bonding with the dying, drug-addled Bela Lugosi (seamlessly reincarnated by Martin Landau), his guileless transvestism, his blind optimism and dreamy ambition. The real, nasty, more deranged story is ignored, the one in which Wood couldn't for the life of him film a single effective scene despite a lifetime of absorbing cinema, in which Wood wrestled pathetically (and publicly) with an utterly confused and obsessive sexual persona, in which Wood spent the actors' pay at the liquor store, in which everyone surrounding him was bitter with failure and booze and dope, in which he and his hootch-mate Kathy would get evicted from one hovel to the next in between pelting each other with lamps and occupying friends' living rooms like an infestation no spraying could kill.

For all his uniqueness, Wood is paradigmatic. Like nothing else on earth, movies like *Glenda* and *Plan 9* formulate the most evocative portrait we have of the 50s, an aesthetically barren polyester landscape where postwar optimism and class conformity failed to bury alive the culture's darker furies. The films' soft, defiant unrealness and mysterious torment seems to have sprung fully imagined like weeds from our own Eisenhower-era victory garden. They wear the aura of ruined lives, missed chances, twisted sensibilities scraping out their lives in the back alleys of society. Nowhere in the modern mythology is there a more eloquent postmortem on movie-bred postwar idealism: how a movie-crazed lad from Poughkeepsie goes to Hollywood, makes the worst movies in the world, pays his liquor bill writing cheap porn and dies boozy and homeless with nothing to his name besides a bottle of Old Crow and an angora sweater. Think of Tor Johnson's lumbering struggle to rise from a jerrybuilt grave in *Plan 9*, Wood's assembly of a chintzy, cross-dressing self-portrait from exploitation dross in *Glen or Glenda*, the hootch-swollen psychic Criswell nodding dumbly at the graveyard strippers in the Wood-scripted *Orgy of the Dead*; compare them all to, say, *Marty*, a contemporaneous, Oscar-winning rendering of postwar average-guyness, and somehow Wood's work seems the more honest, the more penetrating, a dead-real document of the outlying territories, the epic autobiography of a borderline personality. Seen this way, the Wood oeuvre makes him an unconscious parallel text to Artaud, Sade, Robert Walser and even Mark Rothko (who could be defined easily as a "bad" painter). Wood's achievement, which this late in the game is what we can safely call it, might even qualify him for sanctification as a Surrealist axiom, if only there were real Surrealists left to make that claim.

That Wood is a found absurdity, a plastic Jesus without a head on the crucifix factory assembly line of public culture, is a point proven by any film or book he produced; how could any writer feature this solemnly intoned line in no less than two movies?: "Friends, we are all interested in the future because that's where we'll spend the rest of our lives." Imagine the psyche that belched out this smidgen of wisdom, from the recently discovered manuscript *The Hollywood Rat Race* (for which plans of publication by St. Martin's Press have been scuttled): "Aim for the STARS [his caps], and if at the end of your life you've only reached MARS, remember one thing. STARS flicker in and flash out — MARS is a planet." The most treasured moments from the Wood corpus tend to be just as cryptic and painful: there's Criswell's opening speech for *Plan 9*, proclaiming that "future events like these will effect you in the future;" Wood himself crippled by his lovesick coveting of angora in *Glenda* (not only an astonishingly progressive movie about transvestism for 1953 but also a groundbreaking paean to fetishism); the ailing Bela Lugosi, his system so addled by alcohol that he sipped paraldehyde on the set of *Bride of the Monster*, trying to appear the victim of a rubber octopus when it was obviously the other way around. In what can only be described as *Plan 9*'s dramatic climax, silk-PJ-wearing alien Dudley Manlove pontificates to the idiot earthlings about the cosmic reverb of "the solaranite," a deadly weapon we will soon uncover which will "explode the actual particles of sunlight" and therein cause the demise of "the universe." Manlove likens the Earth to a gasoline-soaked ball, the sun to a can of gasoline, the sunlight to spilt gas. "Then we put a flame to the ball. The flame will speedily travel around the earth, along the line of gasoline to the can, or the sun itself. It will explode that source, and spread to every place that gasoline — our sunlight — touches. Explode the sunlight here, gentlemen, and you explode the universe."

There were hundreds of other exploitation filmmakers of Wood's era just as inept and moronic (Phil Tucker, William Grefe, Doris Wishman, Larry Buchanan, etc., all of whose films have the numb, ghastly affect of seeming to have been made by dead people), but none then or since have had the distinctive strangeness and naked innocence of Wood. It is not going too far to say he was a visionary — albeit a visionary whose special vision suggests debilitating delirium rather than genius, and whose work scans like a clubfooted parody of dementia praecox. As Criswell ranted in his Dadaist *Plan 9* prologue, "You are interested in the unknown. The mysterious. The unexplainable. That is why you are here." Amen.

(*City Paper*, October 5, 1994)

THE EIGHTH SEA: *PETER IBBETSON*

If a true symptom of far-gone cinephilia can be the willful transformation of film viewing itself into a craft, then no one has ever been as rapturously sick with movies as the Surrealists. In between the two world wars, Andre Breton and his motley assortment of itinerant, chess-playing, Parisian cafè-loitering cronies — opium eater/epistolary poet Jacques Vache, automatic writer Robert Desnos, partisan upstart Louis Aragon — famously restructured cinema-going in the Surrealist mode by entering a film in the middle and abandoning it for another once its storyline became clear. The resulting hodgepodge of decontextualized imagery was as personalized and ephemeral as genuine dreams, the highest order of aesthetic attainment for the Bretonistes. If this particularly feckless manner of filmgoing resembled the boudoir-hopping antics of restless Don Juans, that might as well have been the point: these guys were, after all, the first to acknowledge the libidinally unruly, pansexual aspects of sitting in the dark with complete strangers transfixed before a near-magical succession of looming images. In 1923 Aragon wrote that "I would like to see films made such that suddenly in the dark a woman would get up and say as she threw off her clothes, 'To the first of these gentlemen!'", and as feverishly adolescent as that randy free-love fantasy is, it's Surrealist through and through. Desnos, in his *Paris-Journal* reviews, went so far as to encourage audience members to seek out sexual partners in the dark during intermission. So, in retrospect, it makes perfect sense — or nonsense — that Surrealist partisan and poet Paul Eluard should discover Henry Hathaway's *Peter Ibbetson* (1935) by following a beautiful Parisian woman into a movie theater, oblivious to what was showing. Thus, the aleatory, lust-driven manner of discovering Hathaway's flamboyant *l'amour fou* delirium became a part of the film's nimbus — for Eluard, naturally, but for us as well. Hailed by Breton as "stupendous," "a triumph of Surrealist thought," and by Luis Bunuel as "one of the world's ten best films," the white light of *Ibbetson's* headlong, cosmic romanticism is as eerie and ravishing as a gravestone photograph of a beautiful girl. While Eluard's is one of art history's most notorious cinema trips, the film he stumbled on has in turn been all but forgotten; ignored at the time by nearly everyone except the avant garde, *Peter Ibbetson* is as rarely seen and rarely examined today as it is unique among early Hollywood genre pictures in its postauthorial determination to be seen through the scrim of Surrealist fervor. Of course, neither studio journeyman Hathaway, source novelist George Du Maurier (father of Daphne), intermediary playwright John Nathaniel Raphael, nor any of the five scriptwriters (including actress Constance Collier, who had acted in it on stage) had even the remotest connection with Breton's dream aesthetics or his pack of multimedia lost boys. (That Du Maurier's story had been filmed once before, forgettably, in 1921 as *Forever*, seems of little import to anyone involved.) Call it fortuity or fate, but Hathaway's *Peter Ibbetson* is, outside the few films the Surrealists managed to make themselves, perhaps the most distinctly surreal film of its era.

This perspective may well be afforded to us by hindsight. Who knows what nostalgic resonance we would glean instead from *Steamboat 'Round the Bend* or *Thanks a Million* (to name a few, substantially more popular 1935 Industry products) had Eluard's heedless, dressed-to-kill quarry led the lusty poet into a different theater? Even so, surely no other movie fit as snugly into the mid-30s Parisian zeitgeist as *Peter Ibbetson*. There's no denying Hathaway's foggy, romantic runaway train, a lush, straight-faced Hollywood weeper that beats down all comers in the mad love department — except perhaps Dali and Bunuel's *L'Age d'Or*, to which it was inevitably compared.

In classic Victorian secret-garden style, *Ibbetson*'s star-crossed lovers are introduced to us as children (Virginia Weidler and Dickie Moore), living in extraordinary luxury during "the middle of the last century," as an opening titlecard declares, "in a suburb of Paris where many English families had made their homes." The film is strong in the Maxfield Parrish-ish faith in cherry blossoms, open verandas and vine-draped marble, photographed with a silvery magic-hour sheen by vet Charles Lang, whose resume includes the like-realized sand castles *Death Takes a Holiday* and *The Ghost and Mrs. Muir.* Moore and Weidler, as Peter (nicknamed Gogo) and Mimsey, respectively, are first seen feuding in their adjoining gardens over the relative values of wagons and dollhouses; the sunlit squabble in Eden climaxes with Peter making a bratty point in the air with his thumb instead of index finger, a gesture Mimsey finds so misfitishly adorable she begs him to do it again and again. Naturally, a fantastical, prepubertal love-bond of the kind that only happened in fiction from "the last century" has formed between the two, a bond we know, because we've read Bronte, will haunt them their whole lives. Their springtime idyll is permanently disrupted when Peter's mother suddenly dies and leaves him in the custody of his rather Dickensian uncle, played with loathsome rigidity by Douglass Dumbrille. The scene where Dumbrille informs the orphaned Peter that he's taking the boy home with him to London, away from Mimsey, is murder on the tear-ducts: standing one step behind Moore, Weidler is all moonish cheeks, banana curls and frightened eyes. As Moore cries in frustration at the prospect of leaving his home and life-mate forever, she soberly steps up beside him and, in a close-up, gently places her thumb into his semi-clenched fist.

Hathaway's camera last glimpses the six-year-old Mimsey sitting high in the leaves of a giant oak, sobbing quietly, followed by another title matter-of-factly turning the page on "the first chapter in the strange foreshadowed life of Peter Ibbetson." Next we're in London years later, where Peter has matured into a strapping and beautiful Gary Cooper (Mimsey wouldn't be so lucky, growing into the colorless, snake-eyed Ann Harding). A brilliant young architect plagued by terminal restlessness (we know why, even if he can't quite remember), Peter takes an impromptu sentimental journey to Paris, where he and Cockney flirt Ida Lupino visit Peter and Mimsey's decaying estates. The memories hit Peter hard; upon returning home, employer Donald Meek asks about the bachelor's vacation-time liaisons. "There was a lady," Peter says. "She was very beautiful. She was eight years old, still wore a white dress, and I shall never forget her."

Weidler *was* beautiful, as only pouty little girls can be, and so the appearance of ice queen Harding, as the Duchess who commissions Peter to build new stables on her husband's land, is the film's only disappointment. Hardly a woman I'd choose to have a fated, incorporeal love affair with, Harding made a short career during the 30s as a patrician tragedienne, and if one barely notices her stiff-lipped paleness in the midst of *Ibbetson*'s high-flown soap, credit Hathaway, who managed to make her usual pallor shine with a warm dreaminess.

We know straight away that the Duchess is Mimsey (as I said, we've read Bronte), and though the coquetry between them is intense, Peter and Mimsey remain oblivious after months of close quarters as the stables are being built, despite several instances of suggested clairvoyance. Even the fact that they both apparently shared a dream doesn't clue them in, though it certainly portends to us the crazily melodramatic path the story begins to take. The pivotal moment occurs once the Duke, a prototypical pompous ass played by John Halliday, accuses the two of having an affair. Peter declares his love, that up until he met the Duchess all other women have faded before the memory of "a little girl in a little garden," a curse he has now been freed of. In a glazed state of shock, realizing who he is, Harding reverts to their childhood patois, choking out "crick!", to which Cooper replies, slowly and with a big grin, "crack."

Then true melodrama sets in like a state of euphoric dementia. Once the Duke pulls a gun on the two kismet-beset lovers, Peter fends him off by breaking a chair over his head and killing the old sod. "Death ends the second chapter...," the title card tells us, with Peter sent for life to a subterranean jail, and Harding back to the Duke's huge mansion alone, where she passes the days too depressed to get out of bed. On his filthy straw matte, Peter's continually taunted by the other prisoners ("He's got a date with the Duchess tonight!"), forever kicking their teeth in and then getting beaten by the semi-lycanthropic guards. One beating breaks his back, and that's when the tale turns a faery corner: paralyzed, Peter is indeed greeted in his dreams by the Duchess, who painstakingly tries to teach him to release the physical world and live exclusively in dreams. Peter can't buy all this at once; "Who's to say what is real and what is not real," insists Harding, a line, like many, that could have very well fallen from the manifesto-ready lips of Desnos or Breton. To prove to him he's not just dreaming on his own, the Duchess promises in their shared dream to send him her ring during the waking day; as she fades like an apparition, the hand bearing the ring floats disembodied outside of Peter's cell. "Remember it!" she implores from the shadows.

When the ring comes, Peter becomes positively imbued with the soul of a Surrealist poet: "It looks like a ring, but it isn't. It's the walls of a world. Inside it is the magic of all desire, inside it is where she lives, and everything inside leads to her, every street, every path, and the eighth sea. It's our world." Eluard must've felt as if he'd stumbled onto the Holy Grail of romantic, co-optable junk cinema with this one, a mainstream Hollywood movie that quite without realizing it began to speak Surrealist lingo, both thematically and textually ("the eighth sea"?). *Peter Ibbetson* does in fact make all other love stories seem half-hearted and hopelessly earthbound by comparison; you can't get much more *fou* than its astral manifestation of emotive power. Peter and Mimsey conduct their romance within their shared dreams, otherwise rarely moving from their respective beds, hoping to sleep and perchance dream again. In dreams they are eternally young, and can presumably go anywhere; the landscape of their bonded subconscious is as utterly malleable as it is fraught with the occasional hazards of doubt and fear. First they visit the old garden and finish building that wagon, and then move into pure Rousseauvian fantasy, transversing open valleys and lofty mountaintops. This is contrapuntal to their bizarre, Oblomovian waking existences (naturally given short shrift by Hathaway), resigned as they are to complete inactivity and apathy toward all things concrete. Every moment awake is spent waiting for sleep and another ethereal rendezvous. "As long as we live!" Harding exclaims, "Years and years and years!"

"And so, many years went by...", we're told in perhaps the film's most alarming card, and we see it's so: Harding's an elderly duchess and Cooper's still a bed-ridden convict, now sporting a white beard. Meeting in the sun-dappled garden of their dreams (for, we presume, the umpteenth time), the lovers begin to worry about their old bodies dying out from under them like thirsty horses crossing Death Valley. "We're too close to Heaven," Harding says, but the transition from dreams to Paradise turns out to be a painless one. And with his loved one calling for him at the other end of a beatific beam of sunlight, Peter-as-old-man extends a withered hand up from the dungeon shadows and completely surrenders the physical world at last.

It's easy to see why of all the American films Breton & Co. saw in the 30s, *Peter Ibbetson* alone could be compared to the favorite Surrealist house movie *L'Age d'Or*, the two of them cited by Breton in his novel *L'amour fou* (1937) as the only two true expressions "of the exaltation of total love as I envision it." Truly, they are two sides — pre-Freudian phantasmorgia and anarchic art crime — of the same brassy love-vs.-society coin. (Presumably the boys hadn't caught Hathaway's more obscure fantasy *The Witching Hour* (1934), based on an Augustus Thomas play about thought transference and mystical obsession, or a Hathaway-as-mystic cult would most certainly have formed.) All but shrugged off by American critics in 1935 as an absurd trifle and neglected on these shores since, *Ibbetson* has enjoyed a lofty reputation among French cinephiles. For critic and film historian Georges Sadoul, writing in his 1965 *Dictionnaire du films*, *Ibbetson* is "one of the most beautiful films about love ever made... Its brilliance is even more remarkable since the George Du Maurier novel does not match the film and since Henry Hathaway is not a director of consequence. But perhaps he had known that rare thing, true love."

A large degree of pragmatism being what has separated French and American audiences since Méliès, a movie as larky and nakedly emotional as *Ibbetson* could perhaps only be fully appreciated on the other side of the Atlantic. Still, even in Paris, it's far from famous or widely screened; Sadoul himself had to work from an age-old memory of the movie's first run, admitting "it is difficult to discuss this film without tending to invent certain details more than 25 years after being burnt by its flame." Indeed, Hathaway's will-o'-the-wisp has all the intensity of a fever dream, from its devastatingly teary childhood elegy to the crushing melancholy of a lifelong love requited only in dreams, which is rationally to say not at all. While Eluard and Breton may well have adored *Peter Ibbetson* for its irrational regard for love over all else, even reality, there's no overlooking the angelic (but not explicitly Christian) sweetness Hathaway has saturated the film with, an uncloying effervescence so tangible and affecting it could slide any preposterousness down the lump-stuck throat of the most hard-hearted of viewers. A overlooked freak masterpiece of the sort most often found in the corpora of Rouben Mamoulian or James Whale, and easily Hathaway's most remarkable film, *Peter Ibbetson* is still relatively inaccessible today. Even with the rare late-night cable appearance, TV showings have been less regular than solar eclipses; it also remains perpetually unavailable on video. If only an ambitious revival house programmer somewhere would screen a print of it — you could follow a beautiful stranger inside, and let it change your life.

(*Film Comment*, July – August 1993)

ON STANLEY KWAN

If moviegoing is the communal, chrome-plated clone of sleep, and movies of dreams (and indeed, isn't a matinee a luxurious midday nap running with the ripest of semiconscious imagery?), are the subconscious lives of this century denser, juicier, more voracious for the experience of consuming all that lanternlight? Or is our sense of interiority merely driven quicker into pure cyberwhatever by the tide of visual matter, archetypal narratives and boiled-down physical beauty? Perhaps both, perhaps neither, but certainly cinema-as-unconscious remains a potent metaphor by which we can attempt to understand our submissive, hypnotic relationship with movies. Perhaps this is why dreams in movies always seem silly and redundant, and why surrealism as an aesthetic strategy has had little success on film beyond the particular mordancy of Bunuel. The currency of movies is already so soaked in subconscious spirits that most willful irrationality has the sourness of dead wine.

Like dreams, movies can be analyzed but also relished, autopsied but also surrendered to, and perhaps what matters more is *what* about them is dreamlike: the structuring of desire, the idealization of love and fear, the entrance into unknown space, the blithe acceptance of

sensory disjunctions, the sudden totemic meanings invested into incidental objects or gestures, etc. This is movies at their moviest. Even so,
like good Freudians reading a dream for its codes, most filmmakers dis-
avow or fail to recognize this more lyrical, emotionally mysterious
aspect of their craft; only a few dare to take this inherent dreaminess as
their films' formal sense of self; and perhaps only one can do so without
affectation or strain or even explicit overtures to subconscious syntax:
Stanley Kwan.

For Kwan (or Kwan Kam Pang) is a romantic, not an ironist, and his
films are songs of crushed love. Subconsciousness is not a subtext so
much as it is a suggestion for structure; Kwan's films are all tiered by
levels of consciousness, and heartbroken over the tension between
them. In *Rouge* the supernatural pass into the natural urban world (and,
eventually, into the world of *other* Hong Kong films) as if it's a crushing-
ly sad dream; in *Actress* the braiding of film history, fictional film present and documentary self-regard creates a fugue of mourning and awe
for the short life of a real silent-screen star; in *Red Rose, White Rose*, a
life divided by two tragic romances is itself divided into two separate
narratives, continuously punctuated by conflicting points of view and
deux ex machina strokes of poetic hypertext.

Kwan's primary instinct is indeed dialectic, but to a purely elegiac
end. Few films feel so *woven*. It's a cinema of quiet mortality, where
beauty signifies its own evanescence, and where love is too strong for
time to break or for us to bear in peace. Because his films are marked
with the signposts of the "women's picture" melodrama, Kwan is often
characterized as a grad student of the Sirk school. But the most famous
of movie melodramatists like Sirk, Stahl, Minnelli and Fassbinder are
luridly intense, gilded with irony, and flaming with primary colors and
emotions. In short, they (or their hindsighted positions in the canon)
are yet another mutant born of the postmod high/low art coupling, and
very often the acclaim these artists receive is tinged with defensive-
ness, rationalization and the clubby, self-congratulating ooze of camp.
Closer in temperament to the serene, heartfelt tones of Borzage, Kwan's
praxeological-yet-pop vision is more diaphanous and singsong, more
concerned with the blooming reserve of inner life than the stylized emotional explosions of melodrama per se. Hardly ever sensational, Kwan's

tales are trancey, reflexive and unerringly modest — like most of us (excluding, perhaps, actors), Kwan's characters are not novas of unrestrained passion (think the maenadic Dorothy Malone), but decent, fragile people realizing they're standing in the center of a tragedy, and that life will always flow on around them.

I can't differentiate between common melodrama and Kwan's achievements enough; by the same token, Kwan's films are almost radically meditative within the volcanic dreamscape of Hong Kong moviemaking. They are, however, as equally infused with movie-movieness. While the best Woo and Hark films are *about* the pulp cinema their makers have consumed, digested and regurgitated at twice the speed, Kwan's films take the very acts of moviemaking and movieviewing as their methodology. It's a popular trope for smart filmmakers (Godard, Welles, Rivette, Makavejev, Ackermann, Tarantino, etc.), but rarely does it overcome its own Zeno-like cleverness. Kwan's use of the movie apparatus is genuinely felt, grounded in a sense of cinema as our clearest and most reflective culture, our most powerful communal rite, and our most poignant view of ourselves; life, after all, never measures up to our dreams, be they conscious, subconscious or cinematic. *Rouge* and *Actress*, Kwan's masterpieces, are both as beautiful and sad as their own view of movies and the irretrievable past they represent.

Appropriately, given his themes, Kwan's visual style is ferociously gorgeous — limpid, shadowy, roseate. At their most Bertoluccian (and he does have an Italian eye for composition, if an Oriental sense of space and scale, a synergy Bertolucci failed to achieve with *The Last Emperor*), Kwan's images are deep, precise and warm, jampacked with mirrors, scrims, doorways and burnished tchotckes. (His most-used cinematographer is Christopher Doyle.) But he's the least decadent of filmmakers. Rare is the indulgent malingering over a lovely composition or symbol-laden image — Kwan's cuts follow the desires of his characters, and therefore rarely rest on even the most breathtaking incidentals.

What's more interesting is how flexible his luscious mise-en-scene is, coolly rupturing narrative flow with metafictive asides and ellipses, constructing an entire movie, *Actress*, like a cube of interrelating but separate film forms — romantic fiction, documentary, archival footage, film history re-creation. Yet Kwan doesn't showboat style-wise; his interpolations and textual cross-stitches seem all of a piece, converging on the same sense of loss and farewell. Kwan's cosmos is deeply lovelorn, and so his films come fragmented with yearning. If his films, even in their ostensible realism, succumb to an ardent, pearly dreaminess, it is simply the formal and emotional manner by which Kwan addresses cinema.

Kwan is in his 40s, and still not one of his six films has seen a legitimate U.S. release. Stateside distributors don't seem to understand Hong Kong films of any stripe; only John Woo's Americanized shotgun wingdings have seemed suitably and wholly of a genre, and therefore releasable. For all of their success and worldwide notoriety, HK films still don't get seen except in mini-festival retro groupings and on home video. If they're not quite *maudit*, then they're victims of their own irrepressible energies. They're hardly saleable as somber, mainland Chinese-style art films are; even contemplative romances like Kwan's are still too saturated in their own pop culture milieu, which is one of the most intense and fantastic in the world. This, it seems to me, calls the cards on this nation's art film audience, which generally imbibes at the pipe of foreign culture as long as it's not *too* foreign, too berserk, too characteristically itself. Even Kwan's easily translatable daydreams are apparently too heady for America's upscale filmgoers, whose secure notion of Asian cinema remains tethered to the flawlessly color-coordinated political angst of Gong Li.

Kwan began as an assistant director in television and for Ann Hui on *Boat People*. His first two films, *Women* ('85) and *Love Unto Waste* ('86), narrowly predated the international discovery of Hong Kong film, and are therefore relatively difficult to see here. They do not seem, in any case, to herald the revelation of *Rouge*; at the same time, *Love Unto Waste* is a strange, elliptical film in which overtraditional plot elements recede behind a frustrated aura of ruefulness. Ostensibly a murder mystery (with Chow Yun-Fat as the rakish detective on the case), Kwan's second film is actually a disquieted portrait of a group of 30-ish, Lost Generation-type Hong Kong yuppies (including a jaded Taiwanese model) as they dissolutely drink, eat, mingle romances and try to come to grips with the death of their friend. It's well-titled — all of the characters wander through the film stunned and uncomprehending of their wasted youths and empty futures. Chow's clownish cop becomes one of them, gamely picking over the wasteland of his life and hoping for better things. (The survivors' confused lives overshadow the murder, which is never solved — shades of *L'Avventura*.) At times clumsy and unfocused, *Love Unto Waste* is nevertheless imprinted with Kwan's woebegone sensibility; whereas another filmmaker might caricaturize or romanticize the subject's ennui and heartlessness, Kwan sees it as a miniature, workaday tragedy.

Rouge ('88), his third film, was just as significant a find for English-speaking cinephiles as *A Better Tomorrow* and *Peking Opera Blues*. Stylistically at odds with the frenetic, acrobatic elan of other HK ghost movies, and seemingly languid enough to get indeed lost in the furor, *Rouge* nevertheless established the presence of a unique vision, half self-regarding pop, half Proustian meditation on time, love and destiny. Essentially an upending of the Orpheus-Eurydice myth, *Rouge* begins with a restrained version of a Makavejevian tableau: the doe-eyed Anita Mui silently observed against a floral-printed wall, looking into the camera as if it's a mirror and applying make-up. The titular make-up is in fact the film's effortlessly eloquent ruling metaphor, embodied by the rouge locket Mui carries with her from world to world: just as Mui's regal Depression-era prostitute could be more or less demarcated from the women outside the brothel by her make-up, so her wandering ghost passes for mortal by applying same. Similarly, her desperate existence beyond the Veil begins with the disreputable traditional Peking opera, and ends within the chintzy, set-bound universe of HK ghost movies — rouge represents the sheer scrim between reality and myth, social appearance, spectacle, movies.

All the more moving, then, that this desolate Eurydice must return from the underworld to find her wayward Orpheus. In lengthy flashback sequences to early-century Hong Kong with its opium dens, local dynasties and courtesans, Mui's Fleur is wooed by Chan (HK staple Leslie Cheung), a slumming son of a wealthy family. She is the elusive Cleopatra of demimondaines, forever keeping him waiting and spurning his most extraordinary advances (having an enormous bed installed in the whorehouse for their use alone, etc.). Of course they fall in love, languishing about, singing to each other in an opium daze, and only once they tender the notion of marriage does his family intervene and forbid an alliance. A Taoism-styled Romantic suicide pact is their only recourse; this way, they can meet in the netherworld and be together.

Much of their saga is gradually gathered as *Rouge*'s weave rolls on, but we know very early that only Fleur died: Kwan cuts abruptly from the first brothel scene to 1987 Hong Kong, where Fleur, unaged, appears unceremoniously and approaches a yuppie newspaperman (Leung Man Chi), looking to take out a personal ad for her lost lover. Fleur essentially haunts the bespectacled urbanite until he agrees to help her find Chan, who must still be alive. Fleur's journey to the end of night is a hushed, confounding nightmare: lonesome and drained of the assurance she once possessed as queen of the courtesans, her ghostliness is implicit in her timeless beauty, her sadness, her ambiguous relationship to materiality (in one quick moment, she looks out the window and the streetlights go dark). There are no F/X, merely circumstantial mysteries. "Sounds like dialog in an obsolete Cantonese movie," the reporter says to Fleur at one point, slyly linking again Fleur's orphic tragedy with the losses we all incur with the passage of time and, implicitly, the passage of popular culture.

Kwan is clearly fascinated by the whiplash of culture as it speeds by us, and in *Rouge* we're witness to reconstitutions of the past as restless ghost, as opera, as old Chinese movies, as new yet myth-mired moviemaking. *Rouge*'s beauty lies in its seeming to be so simple a film, and in fact being so manifold, so variegated in its sorrow. Even the modern reporter gets his moment in the soft shadows: walking alone at night, he and his cynical fiancee ask each other if like Fleur they'd die for each other, and ruefully admit they would not. They're not quite sure if this is a lack of emotional conviction (Fleur's ghost being a victim of societal norms as well as her own romanticism) or merely sound judgment, and Kwan lets this heartsick question dangle like a last apple, rotting on the branch.

Kwan's next film, *Full Moon in New York* ('90) was little seen even in festivals, but no such dismal fate befell *Actress* (*Ruan Ling Yu*, also known as *Center Stage*; '92), simultaneously Kwan's most audacious and most tender film. As silent-screen star Ruan ("the Chinese Garbo," and if there's a living director who'd love to get his hands on Garbo, it's Kwan), Maggie Cheung won at Berlin, and the film was roundly heralded and showcased in retros, though again not deemed by American distributors suitable for release per se. Among a great many things, *Actress* is the Hong Kong film industry's most impassioned lovesong to itself and its own legacy, which dates back to the teens. You need no more evidence of cinema's native melancholy — its elegiac sense of passing time and fading beauty — than to survey the manner in which various national film industries have memorialized themselves over the years. Like the Italian, French and American cinemas, Hong Kong loves to wax nostalgic, and *Actress* is nothing if not a eulogistic swoon.

Movies are like time capsules no one can bear to keep buried for very long; they are the record of a boundless mythic past that we continually, woefully, ache to reexamine, relive and remourn. No one is as profoundly aware of this as Kwan, and his quadripartite strategy for *Actress*, though more instinctive than syllogistic, acknowledges the questions we suspend between dreams, fantasies, reality and film. It's pure elegy, a pantoum about cinema as the capture, and therefore the dissolution, of time and beauty, and though the film operates on four narrative levels interactively, never is its emotional web disturbed. We and Kwan are meditating on Ruan and her life just as Cheung is in discussing her own role with her off-camera director, and just as Ruan is, implicitly, in real footage from her own movies. The films scans like emotional notes for a biography rather than the polished, historical product, and for that it may be the most entrancing and inspired biopic ever made. The passage from level to level never sinks into post-Godardian hijinks constructed solely to display the director's postmod wiseassness. *Actress* is, rather, serious about its subject and its empathy for that subject; it is poem, not deconstruction.

Inevitably, physical beauty becomes another central issue, one which Kwan embraces (unlike, say, Zhang Yimou, whose insistent use of world-famous knockout Gong Li has been relatively suspect). In this film at least, Cheung is as ravishing as any woman ever captured on film, and for Kwan she's the whole issue of screen beauty made flesh. Characteristically, Kwan seeps the movie in the pleasure principle of female loveliness because he knows it matters, and because that's the fuel Ruan's career ran on. (Beauty is crucial to Kwan, whereas to Zhang it seems incidental and opportunistically used.) Ruan herself died in a mysteriously motivated suicide at 25, so the long-lost time and radiance represented by her films and by *Actress* itself has a tragic and poignantly archetypal cast. The weft of *Actress* rarely investigates the matter of beauty so much as honors it, considering its tragedies and gifts.

If I sound dwalmy, blame Kwan, whose narratives often seem drunk on love, roping us into their woozy passions. Cheung's Ruan is a true heartbreaker: radiant, demure, sweet and compassionate, a larger-than-life goddess of impossible poise, tenderness and confident modesty. The bulk of the film follows Ruan's last few years, including the making of her most famous films, a painful divorce, a sensibly maintained yet unruly lovelife, and copious scandal, all relegated by Kwan to the thematic backseat behind the in-between moments that really make up any life. Ruan is seen more often than not watching other people with undisguised joy, her untroubled depth of character obviating any cliched notion of destructive celebrity or egomania. In fact, the Chinese film industry, though perfectly capable then of producing true movie stars and stirring public obsessions, is depicted as a humbly casual, and decidedly small, business, with few hierarchies or power-plays. It's not, at any rate, a system that overwhelms or underaccomodates Ruan, whose kindness seems to rub off on everyone around her like static. (Kwan doesn't believe in villains.) Photographing his actress with Von Sternbergian fervor, Kwan was apparently hypnotized, as is easy to be, by Cheung's quiet smiles and luxurious movements. It's for her grace and lambency as much as for her acting that Cheung won at Berlin, and though that may seem questionable in the abstract, *being* is at least as vital to cinema as *acting*, and always has been. In one simply framed scene where she delicately crouches beside a director thoughtfully squatting on the studio lot, Cheung and Kwan effortlessly transform a simple gesture into the raw stuff of dreammaking.

Kwan's newest film, *Red Rose, White Rose*, is no less a ballad, nor any less a dialectic. Close in spirit and arc to *The Conformist*, *Red Rose* is, like Kwan's other films, a bruised love story, a luxuriant portrait of romantic disaster. As in the Bertolucci classic, *Red Rose* is an opalescently visualized study in reverse *bovarysme*; in defying their hearts and striving to be what they inherently are not, both films' heroes lay waste to their lives and the lives around them (though in Kwan, the fallout hardly has a political chill). Just as similarly, Kwan's film harbors a Flaubertian sense of satire, a gentle, reluctant mocking that lurks underneath the surface of the film like an undertow. The interface between Bertolucci and Kwan is not incidental, though a significant difference lies in Kwan focusing on the women and the consequences of his hero's neurotic behavior — as if Bertolucci's sympathies had wrested with the victimized Stefania Sandrelli and Dominique Sanda rather than the tragically spineless Jean-Louis Trintignant.

As its title suggests, Kwan's film illustrates its crisis by dividing itself neatly in half; even the frequent intertitles — rephrased dialogue, stream of consciousness, poetic digression, omniscient exposition — are halved, one side English, one side Cantonese, like an open, bilingual book of the movie's latent emotional text. (Of course, the titles also invoke silent film, with which Kwan is intimately involved aesthetically; here, perhaps, he's using titles as they always should have been used and never truly were.) The film chronicles the life of Zhen-bao (Winston Chao), a young engineer, as it is split and then rendered impotent by two painful liaisons. The elliptical titles and calm narration have a ruminative, philosophical tone, but Kwan's visuals are as lanternlit and multilayered as ever; there's never a romantic moment that Kwan doesn't make sure we can't feel under our skin, and he knows that milieu and context matter as much as the object of desire itself.

Zhen-bao's first "rose" is Jiao-rui, the coquettish wife of a college friend Zhen-bao comes to live with in Shanghai. Played with astonishing warmth and feline elegance by Joan Chen, Jiao-rui is a spoiled, flirtatious, decadent, bulimic philanderer, as beguiling as she is amoral. She's unsafe at any speed, and though he knows it, Zhen-bao eventually — Kwan is a master at evocative foreplay — initiates an affair while his friend is away on business. What begins as a dallying snowballs into a full-blown l'amour fou, surprising no one so much as Jiao-rui, whose affairs have been, up to now, disposable. It's when she cables her husband, asking for a divorce so she and Zhen-bao can marry, that Zhen-bao is first confronted with his own ruin — he righteously abandons her, knowing full well that marriage to Jiao-rui would never allow him the social acceptance and professional opportunity he seeks.

Another of Kwan's urban hollow men, Zhen-bao trades passion for status and pays the obligatory price, something he never seems quite aware of until the end, when he and Jiao-rui meet on a trolley years later and he begins sobbing. Up until that chilly moment, Kwan is more interested in the wages of ambition paid out by Jiao-rui as well as Zhen-bao's "white rose," Yan-li (Veronica Yip). Zhen-bao's carefully chosen wife, Yan-li is a selfless, wilted, dim girl railroaded into the role of obedient Chinese wife. For Zhen-bao, it is a union built for success, but for the ineffectual Yan-li it's death on the installment plan — she slowly goes mad in tiny ways, sitting on the toilet for hours, fondling a special swatch of cloth dazedly as her husband pumps away on top of her at night. When she has a daughter, she and the baby are surrounded in the hospital by clucking family members assuring themselves that the next child will be a boy, and then the family will celebrate. Kwan's unsettling inspection of traditional Chinese gender roles is right there in that bed; you know as Yan-li inevitably must that her little girl is due for the same fate as she.

For Kwan, the dynamic of *Red Rose, White Rose* lay between the two women, who dictate the film's look as well. Each has her own attendant tonal scheme: Jiao-rui's is shadowy, rich and umbered, while Yan-li's is washed-out and pale (a dead-on parody of her own wedding cake). Kwan's laconic narration tells Zhen-bao's story, but the film itself is the tale of two women — another dialectic. The tenor of the later film is less easy to nail down than earlier Kwans; it's more ruminative, objective, detached, and the disenchantment with patriarchal systems that's under the velvet cloak of every Kwan film is for once thrust into the daylight. It's an anti-romance that considers its own passage and significance at every step, like *Actress* but more philosophical; you could characterize it as a dramatic essay that ponders itself and its methodologies just as it ponders love, beauty and life's capricious twistings.

What will become of Kwan in the new, Chinese-owned Hong Kong? He's the least provincial of HK filmmakers, and having shot films both in New York and mainland China as well as in Hong Kong, perhaps he's already moved beyond the need for national roots. Simultaneously lyrical without being pretty or grand, and postmodern without being calculating, the ego-superego fusion of Kwan's filmmaking remains unique. The balance of guileless sophistication and genuine feeling would be a perilous tightrope walk for another director, but for Kwan it is an intuitional response to, a personal definition of, cinema. "Personal" in a purely interpretive sense; far from inaccessible or even extravagantly formal, Kwan's films are purehearted, modest and wise — of how many other living filmmakers could that be said? How many dead? Vigo, Renoir, Mizoguchi and Ray are Kwan's grandfathers, and he may very well be their sole heir.

(*Film Comment*, May – June 1996)

LONG BLACK LIMOUSINE: POP BIOPICS

"Is everybody in? Is *everybody* in? Is everybody *in*? The ceremony is about to begin," intones Val Kilmer at the opening of Oliver Stone's rose-bespectacled mastodon *The Doors*, and even though the words were Jim Morrison's, it was quite obviously the film itself that was pure ceremony. Like any film genre worth its rock salt, the pop music biopic is a self-fulfilling ritual, contrived of tropes and significations propagated in the hothouse of cinematic hyperbole, and thriving jauntily at a respectable remove from the reality on which it is based. Unlike most based-on-a-true-story movies, it traffics in a culture myth that is not only not dead, a lie or buried in history, it's our most ferociously beloved bedtime story — the grandstanding, fire-breathing music genius/god courting Untimely Death by way of his or her essential extraordinariness. Ever since *The Pride of the Yankees* converted the ordinary biopic — as in *Disraeli, Wilson, The Story of Alexander Graham Bell*, any number of Paul Muni vehicles, et al. — into love-and-death pop idolatry, our modern pop heroes, who do little more than sing, play guitar and exude raw, churlish magnetism, must die at their stories' ends like ailing kings. Room must be made, time and time again, for new and younger dynasts.

It's a ceremony of the innocent, certainly, and as such movies from

The Glenn Miller Story to *La Bamba*, no matter how fanciful and hagio-graphic, express a truth about pop culture: that the life-affirming 3 1/2-minute jukebox ditty does in fact often end with a plane crash (or at least an overdose), that the Mach 1 rise to glory so often endured by pop stars has tragedy and early death written all over it, and yet no one ever seems to heed the heritage. (Per capita, the life expectancy of pop stars must be shorter than, say, nuclear power workers.) It's the American Dream distilled down to its grain-alcohol essence, instant splendor and celebrity twinned inexorably to disaster. At the same time, there's nothing more Romantic, and if it was good enough for Keats, it's good enough for Buddy Holly. Pop music, or more specifically rock 'n roll, is both an essentially cinematic beast and the frankest manifestation of life force modern culture has ever produced — which may amount to the same thing. Thus, its biopics create and then lament the frustrated dreamtime of our collective fantasies, which, with the creation of youth culture after WWII, have never before been more powerful or seductive. The 90s guitar group Radiohead was right: everybody wants to be Jim Morrison. Few of us wants to die at 28, however, and therein lies the par-adox no true cultural obsession can live without.

Perhaps the question isn't whether we all want to be rock 'n roll stars so much as that we all can be; pop biopics have always adored the deathless tale of a guileless rube stumbling into success and attaining godhood by virtue of unschooled talent and good will, and eventually falling victim to Fame, the System, or just plain Fate. On a very real level, this is pure Americana, the arena of cheap Armageddons; wherever a pop idol crashes and burns, it's always an American phenomena, thanks to one man — Elvis, who cut his first Sun record less than a year before generational archetype James Dean smacked up his Porsche on Highway 41. If Dean cut the mold, Elvis sold it to the world. The hayseed Christ of pop music, the Greatest Story Ever Told, the King of kings, Elvis served as the prototype for every pop form imaginable, biopics includ-ed. Perhaps mysteriously, even if it took more than 20 years for the crush of iconolatry, wealth and drug abuse to boomerang back at him, the classic trajectory of Elvis' life is still clung to popularly as a modern tragedy — as if he was *meant* to die sometime before getting fat, mid-dle-aged and campy, didn't, and we'll just pretend he did. Perhaps even more mysteriously, no major Elvis biopic has ever been produced, outside of a handful of American TV movies and spirit-of-Elvis guest appearances in postmod-ish Industry offspring like *Heartbreak Hotel*, *True Romance*, *The Dark Half* and *Death Becomes Her* (which also gave us an ageless Morrison). Though undeniably pivotal and totemic, Elvis' story may be too archetypal: modest country schmuck to instant sensation worshiped by millions to lonely despot slumped dead over his gold-plated, diamond-encrusted toilet, successful but empty and wasted by fame. It's the same story, one way or another, at the core of *The Buddy Holly Story*, *The Doors*, *La Bamba*, *Lady Sings the Blues*, *Sweet Dreams*, *Sid & Nancy*, *BackBeat*, *The Rose*, *Selena*, etc.; it's the true story of pop culture, true because it's ours, we made it and we live by it. (Its prevalence shows no signs of waning; a Kurt Cobain biopic is inevitable — call it *Nevermind* — starring either Brad Pitt or Ethan Hawke.) Still, it's possible to overtell the story, and Elvis as an icon may be too familiar, a face, name, voice and swagger so ubiquitous in the universal consciousness we don't need a major movie of his life anymore than we need one of our own. The paradigm survives, of course, and in essence we watch Elvis live and die over and over again in other peoples' tales, like the wax Gary Gilmore being executed, and revived, every minute or so at Madame Tussaud's. The King is dead, long live the King.

To the naked eye, the Elvis legend seems simultaneously chintzy and debauched, and it's somehow fitting that TV movies, the kitschiest and least self-important in America, have felt most comfortable exploring Elvis — you can imagine the man watching them himself, a gun in his lap. *Elvis*, *Elvis and Me* and *Elvis and the Beauty Queen* (starring Kurt Russell, Dale Midkiff and Don Johnson, respectively) all regard the premier pop saga with the misty, maternal sentiment of supermarket tabloids, the sort that report live Elvis sightings — and publish photographs of them — even to this day. The most thorough, John Carpenter's *Elvis*, lavishes more angst upon Elvis' relationship with his dependent mother (Shelley Winters) than upon the King's various jailbait romances (as the other two movies do) or the frighteningly hollow nature of absolute fame, which TV could never have the wisdom to examine. All three movies are tinged with rue, without ever being explicit as to why. It's assumed we know the rest of the story, and we do, all too well.

The pop music biopic didn't begin with Elvis; it just suddenly had more at stake, just as rock always seemed to be more immediate, more dangerous, more a matter of life or death, than jazz. The pop biopics dealing with pre-Elvis phenomena — *The Glenn Miller Story*, *With a Song in My Heart*, *The Benny Goodman Story*, *The Gene Krupa Story*, *St. Louis Blues*, *Young Man with a Horn*, *The Fabulous Dorseys* (in which Tommy and Jimmy play themselves, badly), *The Jolson Story*, *I'll Cry Tomorrow*, *The Five Pennies*, etc. — center on either hit songs or tearful comeback chronicles, and we're never asked to understand their protagonists as charismatic pop idols. What they did — how they played — mattered most; who they were, and why they were popular, mattered least. With Elvis, the dimensions of pop expanded nova-like to nearly every neglected corner of the media quotidian, and consumers weren't merely record buyers anymore, they were *fans*, hungry, crazy and dizzy with sexual awe. Suddenly the nature of pop music changed, from simple entertainment to something that could control your life. The stories, and lives, of its artists took on a Rimbaldian intensity. Glenn Miller was never seen as musically compensating for a tortured off-stage existence, and although Gene Krupa and Lillian Roth battled dope and booze behind the scenes in *The Gene Krupa Story* and *I'll Cry Tomorrow*, it was just a lost weekend or two, and there was light at the ends of their respective tunnels. After Elvis, one could not have fame without paying for it with flesh and blood. (You'd have to pay for salvation that way, too — take a big step backward and you're looking at Christ himself, the first foredoomed pop idol.) It was a phenomena Ken Russell has tried to comment on in his particularly semi-toxic manner with *Lisztomania*, which immolates itself trying to demonstrate that musical fame has stayed more or less the same over the centuries, when in fact the kind Roger Daltrey knows about is no older than the 45 rpm single — or perhaps just as old.

Russell's *Tommy* could qualify as a genre piece as well, insofar as the album from which it sprang, at its roots, is a freshmanically metaphoric transcription of Pete Townshend's ascension into the public eye. Certainly its denouement, wherein Tommy is ravaged by his disciples, displays the post-adolescent angst of a real pop star; no one else would have the audacity to blame the fans for his projected fall from power. Like a true last temptation, the onus of responsibility for a pop star's doom must lie with him or her — if only subtextually — or it's pointless. Even climbing aboard an airplane is a choice made at the end of one's rainbow, as in the various versions of that infamous plane trip in *The Buddy Holly Story* and *La Bamba* (though *Buddy Holly's* fatal journey is summed up in an ominous title card). Both Holly and Richie Valens could've bussed it, but such was the nature of their role in popular history that if they had, another plane would've crashed, somewhere, sometime. (Valens even had portentous dreams about plane crashes for years before.) One wonders when a Big Bopper biopic will be produced, providing us with a fully triangulated vision of that same air passage, the same damnation, that same ill-fated day when, as Don McLean said, the music died.

All modern pop biopics are by nature hagiographic, but, haunted by the ghost of Elvis, they're also inevitably tempted by the forces of darkness. The bitter destiny balances the music's natural elan. And without the buoyancy of youthful privilege, the crashes and ODs and asphyxiations would have no resonance. So, pop biopics are often pilgrims' progresses, for the most part brimming with hope, and the more mundane the pre-stardom lives seem, the more remarkable the rise and fall. This pattern fit the agrarian tincture of country/folk music best, exemplified by George Hamilton as Hank Williams in *Your Cheatin' Heart*, David Carradine as Woody Guthrie in *Bound for Glory*, Sissy Spacek as Loretta Lynn in *Coal Miner's Daughter* and Jessica Lange as Patsy Cline in *Sweet Dreams*. Here, the Elvis mountain-boy cliche has its purest expression: dirt-poor Ozark hillbilly sings like a mockingbird, gets noticed, becomes simultaneously sanctified and cursed by his or her Nashville ascendancy. What's fascinating in these films' use of the Elvis myth is the tension between the idolized stage persona, which in its attainment of musical sublimity is beyond reproach, and the violent yet mundane chaos of their real lives. This conjures a sense of classical tragedy as well as the inevitable creep of nasty housewife gossip; the dialectic between larger-than-life demigod and next-door victim of spousal abuse is irresistible, especially to Middle America. If fame is created by the consumer, then here it's fueled by hate as much as love. Alternating scenes of domestic savagery and performance epiphany, *Coal Miner's Daughter* and *Sweet Dreams* are two sides of the same buffalo nickel — Cline's death in yet another plane crash pays for Lynn's survival, so to speak, a point *Coal Miner's Daughter* makes explicitly by featuring Cline (Beverly D'Angelo) as Lynn's surrogate big sister, the one damned by fortune and men. After that, *Sweet Dreams* scans like a eulogy; in every throb of Cline's voice, and Lange's muscular body, we can see the end. All we see in *Coal Miner's Daughter* is placid decades of headlining at the Grand Ole Opry.

Each brand of music has its own narrative zone, however Elvis-ized. If country is the land of misused homemakers-turned-songbirds, then jazz, in the contemporary biopic, is a frontier of racial spite and wholesale self-destruction. Compare *St. Louis Blues* to *Leadbelly*, *Lady Sings the Blues* and *Bird*, and you'll see hagiography slowly turn sour in the gut. As these are the only notable examples of black pop biopics (with *What's Love Got to Do With It?*, the subgenre's sole tale of triumph), it's safe to say that Hollywood remains racial light-years from the well-paved inroads of Motown. (Perhaps that's a secret reason for the dearth of Elvis biopics; "You said that if you ever found a white boy who could sing colored," someone says to Colonel Tom Parker in Carpenter's *Elvis*, "you'd make a fortune.") Gordon Parks' *Leadbelly* is fraught with post-Confederacy rage, just as it deepens the stakes paid for iconhood. Huddie Ledbetter's particular ring of Movie Hell — years spent on the chain gangs of Depression-era Texas and Louisiana — gave his music, and his biography, instant cache of a caliber unseen anywhere else, while simultaneously sanctifying the man as a free-range Johnny Appleseed a la *Bound for Glory*. A spoonful of bitter honesty helps the hero worship go down, and so *Lady Sings the Blues* and *Bird* each travel the dark byroad of junkiedom, implying that like a poet's madness, smack-fueled dissolution is the price you pay for jazz glory. Gracelessly directed by Sidney J. Furie, *Lady Sings the Blues* makes all the stops on the way down to the gutter, with a few racist detours along the way: Billie Holliday as preteen whorehouse slave, rape victim, whore, freak nightclub sensation, junkie, Carnegie Hall star, corpse. She's a black cross between Anne Sexton and Patsy Cline — it's implied, mostly by Diana Ross' performance, that Holliday's terminal combat with heroin *deepened* her singing, gave it resonance. Still, like most of its brethren,

Furie's film mutates the facts of Holliday's life into a three-act soaper; better is Ross, who establishes a precedent (see *Bound for Glory, Coal Miner's Daughter, The Buddy Holly Story, The Doors,* etc.) by singing Holliday's vocals herself. (Ironic, then, that the appalling Michel Legrand score swells and croons as if in a jazz-less void.) In pop terms, the honorable and brave practice of recreating an artist's vocal achievements anew musters an aesthetic catch-22 — if Holliday paid such high stakes for her art, what did Ross pay? If Holliday is worthy of a sentimental, teary movie of her life because of her singing, why isn't Ross? (Perhaps Ross will be, someday; the scenes of Ross' impersonator doing Ross doing Holliday will be fascinating.) On one hand, it's as if an actor played Van Gogh by painting "Sunflowers" himself, his own way. On the other, of course, it's a moot point — Holliday's voice isn't duplicated so much as approximated, and her biopic is a dream version of her life, just as the movies are dream versions of everything. While we're there the real Billie Holliday doesn't even exist. This is a principle violated years later in *What's Love Got To Do with It?*, which closes with footage of the real Tina Turner strutting her stuff; whatever substantial empathy we had with Angela Bassett throughout the film is summarily obliterated in the presence of the real McCoy. Shaken from the trance of the movie's dreamtime, we're left with a foot in each world, at home in neither.

Clint Eastwood's *Bird*, on the other hand, creates a indelible nightclub shadowland around its Charlie Parker, a dark troposphere of failure and obsession hovering over a chillingly believable enterprise of self-demolition. Seen as a sort of persecuted Galileo of the saxophone with Baudelairean tendencies, Forest Whitaker's Parker makes as much of a project of his life as he does his music, one aiming into the grave as the other targets out toward immortality — hell and heaven. One cannot exist without the other — it's a tale Western civilization likes to tell itself above all others. Bird is just another troubled saint tempting the devil and death to do God's work, which is to say, his own, and if he martyrs himself in the process, that simply validates the effort.

Perhaps rock 'n roll was ricocheting too freshly and frenetically around the popular consciousness for full-scale biopics to be made before *The Buddy Holly Story* (1978), which stands as the first true rock biography. An unassuming pie-plate of latent 50s nostalgia, *Buddy*

Holly's drama came with the shrugging breakup of The Crickets; it wasn't much, and that was okay. All that was necessary was our knowledge of Holly's premature death to charge even the most mundane recording-studio squabble with poignancy. Gary Busey's Holly seemed to have just come off an iron-pumping jag, but the film's modesty fit Holly's own, and the real story did the real work. *La Bamba*, coming nine years later, matched this formula meticulously, draining Richie Valens (Lou Diamond Phillips) of any serious dramatic fire — his delinquent brother has more problems, and more reason to escape the barrio. Richie has the plane crash, after all; who needs more than that? When the good die young, the whole world mourns.

Death is to rock what lightning strikes are to summertime, and the only sure reason why Dennis Wilson, Brian Jones, Keith Moon, John Bonham, Ricky Nelson, Bob Marley and Peter Tosh are not already the subjects of movies is the sometimes formidable pricetag of music rights. (As of this writing, big-budget Joplin and Hendrix bios are in the works.) Todd Haynes's infamous *Superstar*, in which he biographies the top-40 life and bulimic death of Karen Carpenter via animated Barbie Dolls, remains a hostage to lawsuits held by both Richard Carpenter and Mattel. Fictionalizing the descent is a popular alternative: in *The Rose*, a thinly disguised tour of duty through Joplin territory, Bette Midler's rock mama careens toward the boneyard on a river of original songs and belted covers of Motown faves, mixing her own brand of stage attitude generously into the Janis legend. *Eddie & the Cruisers* remakes the his-death-was-a-sham-he-just-*disappeared* Morrison yarn (complete with copious references to the Lizard King's poet-of-choice, Rimbaud) with Springsteen-ish songs by John Cafferty and the Beaver Brown Band. Most interesting of all when considered as a biopic, *Pink Floyd The Wall* finally tackles Roger Waters' Syd Barrett question once and for all, even casting the otherwise somnambulistic Bob Geldof because of his resemblance to Barrett. Like the album, Alan Parker's film attempts to literalize the imagery of a mind deranged by fame and alienation, heading inexorably toward the nuthouse; love it or not, it could pass for a film the quite mad Barrett might have made about himself, which may have been the point. If only someone would do the same for Elvis, Morrison or Cobain.

Or Sid Vicious. Alex Cox's *Sid & Nancy* has the raw strength to become a biopic prototype — as if anyone else's life might ever resemble Sid's. Perhaps the best that could be objectively said about Vicious is that he was in the right place at the right time — once; otherwise, he was an impenetrably dim working-class sod whose lack of talent or ambition left him completely unprepared for the demands and indulgences of fame. No one was as vulnerable, or succumbed as easily. Vicious and Nancy Spungen were hardly candles that burn twice as bright but half as long — they were merely innocents plowed over by the steamroller of pop history. Arguably the greatest of all pop music biopics, *Sid & Nancy* hits the gutter early on and loiters there for the duration, splitting the burden of ruin between punk fame and the most harrowing of dysfunctional relationships. In his way, Vicious constitutes the nether edge of the Elvis paradigm: by virtue of his worthlessness, he's the Greatest Punk, the ultimate negation of pop values. His death, and Nancy's (that is, suicide *and* murder), represent not a Faustian pact with the devil but with the culture's own anger. If anyone has been sacrificed for rock 'n roll, it's Sid and Nancy.

Though still sporadically produced, rock biopics have reached a state of happy self-fascination, maturing alongside the baby boomer generation, who finally want their own childhood myths reenacted for them in 35mm. Jim McBride's *Great Balls of Fire* was a conspicuous failure not because of Dennis Quaid's Daffy Duck-like performance but because the time for a Jerry Lee Lewis bio had long since passed. No one cared by 1989, and one couldn't be sure audiences would have ever cared — Lewis' only claim to notoriety was marrying his 13-year-old cousin. There was no premature death, no tragedy, no Calvary for Jerry Lee. *What's Love Got To Do with It?* was another story, fraught with crucifixions, and was therefore a minor hit (and gratuitous Oscar nominee). While Angela Bassett's Turner, like Busey's Buddy, looked as if she spent six hours a day in the gym, she still suffered through her career arc weathering Ike, rock's most renowned wifebeater, in the classic Susan Hayward manner. What's interesting about *What's Love* is its built-in triumphant ending, for which Turner herself has been amply celebrated. She seemed destined for a Holliday-esque finale, but walked across the street in bare feet instead. It's truly a tale for the '90s.

Perhaps the most lavish, and blindly worshipful, pop biopic of all is *The Doors*, a misty-eyed counter-culture valentine in which the tragedy of Morrison's over-indulged life is seen as some sort of homage to the Old Gods. Stone stages concerts as if they were gargantuan pagan orgies, literally superimposes dancing shamans over Morrison's drugged-up stage shenanigans, and likens the man more than once to the earthly avatar of Dionysus. *The Doors* manages to be more pretentious about Morrison than he was about himself, and sometimes, at least, Stone seemed to know it. ("Did you have a good world when you died?" Kilmer reads from Morrison's poems, "Enough to base a movie on?") All the same, perhaps moderation is not what the Jim Morrison story required, either; he was the closest thing rock has yet had to a Poe, and if Stone overdid the Gothic New Age mythopoeia, it was in the service of expressing what Morrison meant to his many, and most enraptured, fans. (Stone's dreaminess is not uncommon — see Dan Sugarman's bio *No One Here Gets Out Alive*, in which the author unequivocally admits to believing Morrison to be "a god.") *The Doors*, and Kilmer's scarily accurate portrayal, make one point crystal clear: that Morrison, whatever else he may or may not have been, was Elvis with the backwoods bashfulness removed, leaving only the raw sexuality. More than anyone, even Mick Jagger, Morrison represented the ideal of hedonism in the hearts of teenagers everywhere. The will to fuck that had been in the music all along was, finally, standing right there on the stage, in black leather pants.

While sex motivated rock, death became its proudly displayed battle scar. The two needed each other, which may be why John Lennon had to die before any of the Beatles got straight biopics of their own. If the Beatles seem to have fallen out of the loop in regards to biographies, it may be because each survived youth and fame to lead successful subsequent careers. (We're not counting the curious and eerie simulacra *Beatlemania*, which took the Ross-Holliday principle way too far, and the post-Python parody *All You Need Is Cash*, which still may say more about "The Beatles" than any other cultural document.) An odious American TV movie, *John & Yoko — A Love Story*, was the first, coming five years after Lennon's murder. This Sandor Stern-directed skulduggery served only as a forum for dozens of actual Beatles recordings, an opportunity afforded a low-budget TV quickie by the good offices of Michael Jackson (who got his comeuppance, whether he knows it or not, with the wretched mini-series *The Jacksons*). Lennon's legacy was approached with great wisdom and savvy in both Christopher Munch's *The Hours and Times* and Iain Softley's *BackBeat*, both using the same actor, Ian Hart (who could well make a career of it as he ages, ending up a few movies down the line sprawled across the sidewalk outside the Dakota). For doubtlessly deplorable reasons, neither film was allowed to use the Lennon-McCartney songs, and both circumvented the handicap breezily by featuring early cover tunes or no music at all. Munch's film may be the cleverest and most thought-provoking movie take on a pop legend yet, exploring a single weekend early in the Beatles' career and using it to speculate upon the sexual tensions between Lennon and Brian Epstein, as well as explore Lennon's tentative relationship with worldwide fame. Shot for next to nothing and in black-and-white, *The Hours and Times* seeks to attain a truth about its resident pop idol, not glorify him. Lennon is on the cusp of the best years of his life; Munch lets the audience conjure the tragedy themselves.

There's no such subtext in *BackBeat*, in which Hart's Lennon is the young proto-punk art student of the Hamburg days. Instead, the tragic arc is Stu Suttcliffe's, who went from being a piece of unnecessary Beatle furniture and latent Lennon lover to art martyr, dead in his 20s of an aneurism. It hardly seems like much of a loss compared to Lennon's death decades later, and appropriately *BackBeat* only comes alive when Hart's onscreen. Curiously, both films ponder on the viability of Lennon being at least semi-gay, using the biopic strategy for varying subtle what-if scenarios. Hardly scandal-mongering, both films do this with genuine sensitivity, and if the proposition has little basis in fact, the films still make up a text unique to the genre — mourning the loss of a rock star, and the universal youth he signified, by wondering aloud if at the beginning he was drastically different than we remembered him, or very much the same.

But Lennon had already starred in his own biopic, hadn't he? What is *A Hard Day's Night* if not a semi-fictionalized version of the Beatles' lives? Few viewers then or now have bothered to recognize what an odd, metatextual creature Richard Lester's movie is, what with the Fab Four playing themselves — internationally worshiped pop idols named John, Paul, George and Ringo constantly besieged by fans and fame — ambling through their lives as if it were a Mack Sennett comedy. Sure, Babe Ruth played himself in *The Pride of the Yankees*, but that whole film wasn't structured around the bristling contradictions between biography, documentary and outright fiction. *A Hard Day's Night* could be, and is, all three, and may be the best biopic any rock star will ever get, insofar as it captures its protagonists at the height of their powers, gives them all the best lines and cancels any question of likeness or musical impersonation. If so, what about *Abba: The Movie*? What about Arlo Guthrie playing himself in his self-created folktale *Alice's Restaurant*? Sonny and Cher in *Good Times*, The Monkees in *Head*, Bob Dylan in *Renaldo & Clara*, Prince in *Purple Rain*? What about Paul Simon, as himself in a screenplay he wrote, in *One-Trick Pony*? What about the bizarre transformation from glitter rockers to superheroes in *KISS Meets the Phantom of the Park*? Or star-manipulated "documentaries" like *Bring On the Night* and *Truth or Dare*? If not kosher biopics per se, then surely films like these participate in the same current of cultural dreaming. In the mass consciousness, reality matters less than spectacle, and even the shrewdest of pop stars can get lost between the two. If they didn't, it wouldn't be rock 'n roll.

(*Celluloid Jukebox*, BFI, 1995)

A UNIVERSAL MOVIE:
FOUND FOOTAGE FILMS

Of all the countless varieties of filmic expression, none is as clearly a
product of evolution as found footage films, rising naturally and
inevitably from the visual culture like saplings from a landfill. Though an
established precinct of experimental filmmaking since *Rose Hobart*
(1936-39), Joseph Cornell's seminal reconfiguration of the 1931 programmer *East of Borneo*, found footage films have suddenly, in the last
15 years, reached full-fledged zeitgeisthood. We are, after all, poised at
the cusp of the cinematic centennial, chin-deep as a society in a full
century's worth of film bites, media icons and archetypal effluvia. Film
culture is much more, after all, than the few hundred movies that get
released every year, or the few dozen TV shows that get broadcast:
though largely forgotten and reportedly accounting for the larger bulk of
film production, the wide and wonderful world of incidental cinema is
where footage is most often "found": educational films, industrial pro-
mos, training shorts, military films, commercials, videos, travelogues,
porn loops, home movies, archival footage, forgotten TV productions,
documentaries both short and long about every subject under the sun
produced by both solitary filmmakers and omnipotent corporations,

news film, propaganda, "personal" cinema, stock shots, outtakes, public service instruction, ad infinitum.

Trash it all may be, strictly speaking, but many of found footage's leading proponents — Bruce Conner, Craig Baldwin, Abigail Child, Ken Jacobs, Oleg Kovalov — will be quick to point out found footage's modern-art lineage of Picasso, Duchamp, ready-mades, Dada and assemblage, often with strong ties to more contemporary pop art, punk and Burroughsian collage. Additionally, as per revered found footage vet Ken Jacobs, if we have come to think, dream and daydream in the syntax and iconography of movies, then excavating "lost" footage can be considered akin to psychoanalysis — culture studies at its most therapeutic. Which is all to say it's postmodernism incarnate; found footage cannot help but inherently address the manner and relevance of visual representation, and its own scavenged nature.

It's also hopelessly cool. With a mile-high scrap heap of ephemeral culture at our disposal, it's no surprise in a world of neo-genres and post-MTV reflexivity that found footage has crawled out from the underground into the light of mainstream pop consciousness. Most conspicuously, videos from all manner of musical beast — from Public Enemy to David Bowie and far beyond — have been formed from recuperated images. (Indeed, *Rose Hobart*, scored and cut to pop songs of the early 30s, may have been the first music video). Following suit, cable TV conjured up *Dream On*, the cable TV sitcom that regularly incorporated snippets of old movies and TV shows to punctuate its hero's hapless relationship with the world, and *Mystery Science Theater 3000*, in which an on-screen three-man Greek chorus adds an additional, sardonic scrim of text — referencing everything from Shemp Howard to Wilhelm Reich — to old, rotten B-movies and thereby recreating them as new viewing experiences. Similarly, and with all irony presumably intended, *Beavis & Butt-head* treats actual MTV videos as "found" and subject to the de-evolved comments and channel surfing of its primitively drawn and characterized protagonists. (The animated duo's 1997 movie was, unfortunately, found-footage-free.) Popularly, the radical reuse of electronic footage can run from brainless mock-voyeurism (*America's Funniest Home Videos*) to the cynical frisson of 1992's election-time documentary *Feed*, in which hilarious co-opted glimpses of Bush,

Tsongas, Clinton et al. were pulled straight from the airwaves and thus represent the most immediate variety of found footage yet — found before it was even lost. Even Hollywood has consciously played hit-and-run with the found footage aesthetic, from Woody Allen's *What's Up, Tiger Lily?*, and the Steve Martin hash *Dead Men Don't Wear Plaid* to the computerized graftings of *Last Action Hero, In the Line of Fire, Forrest Gump* and the Paula Abdul-meets-Louis Armstrong Coke commercials. Oliver Stone fashioned his epic day-in-court thesis *JFK* around the most notorious piece of found footage of all: the Zapruder film, which a few daring critics put on their ten-best lists for '91. Mark Rappaport's popular video *Rock Hudson's Home Movies* (1992) reimagines Hollywood imagery as a sardonic, postmod episode of *This Is Your Life* from beyond the grave, taking us on a dry-eyed psychosexual tour of Hudson's homophobic screen career and transforming *Pillow Talk* into a Chinese box of sexual conundrums. Video stores are stuffed with smirky compilations of public-domain trailers, industrials, old nudies, TV ads and general ephemera. Alternative cinema pro Barbara Hammer's delightful 1992 feature *Nitrate Kisses* used, in turn, discarded outtakes from the classic 1933 avant-garde short *Lot in Sodom* — you know the snake has truly swallowed its tail when yesterday's experimental movie is today's recyclable image-bank.

Found footage has been an inexhaustible resource for the underground since Bunuel began *L'Age d'Or* (1930) with scrap science footage of scorpions. Cornell's ersatz love poem to 30s starlet Rose Hobart notwithstanding, it wasn't until 1958, and Bruce Conner's *A Movie*, that the subgenre was authentically born — a form of film made without cameras, culling images instead from the junk drawer of movie past and present. In the catalog that accompanied New York's Anthology Film Archives 1993 retro *Recycled Images*, Conner waxes dialectic about his formative cinematic experiences: "I would see third-rate, cheap movies that came out of Poverty Row in Hollywood. They had a stock footage library and would use the same images again and again. When there was a scene in New York introduced, you would see the same shot of the Brooklyn Bridge... Also, it was cheaper to shoot in front of a rear projection screen in the studio instead of going out. People were walking in front of *a movie!* Cowboys would pick up their guns and point them, and up would pop shots taken from previous and larger productions: Indians attacking and things like that. So I became aware that there was a "universal movie" that was being made all the time! It's classic images. It's the *Mona Lisa*, it's the Sistine Chapel, it's the Statue of Liberty... It seemed natural that I would make this movie called *A Movie*."

Indeed, one of the philosophical linchpins of found footage films is the arresting disparity between the filmmakers' formal/political purposes and the intent of the original footage (it's the only brand of movie in which every frame has two, often conflicting authorial intentions), as well as the fact that the very borrowing of the images forces them to be non-definitive — *A Movie*'s many pieces of dislocated imagery no longer belong exclusively to their sources, nor do they belong exclusively to *A Movie*. By decontextualizing cinematic fragments, filmmakers like Conner send them into a free-associative abyss, where they can signify nearly anything in nearly any context. In addition, the process explodes the notion of free-standing "works," implicitly insisting that all films everywhere are part of Conner's "universal movie."

Tossed together from stock footage, stag loops, travelogue excerpts and other now-standard sources of meaningless imagery, *A Movie* is a tour-de-force of Kuleshovian editing jokes (cutting between a submarine commander looking through a periscope, a semi-nude girl and a mushroom cloud), juxtapositional metaphors and outright nonsense, all set to a lush Respighi piece. Relatively apolitical and free of dogma, Conner's films make exquisitely poetic sense of yesteryear's earnest incidentals. No other found-footage filmmaker manages to locate such mysterious lyrical moments within such banal material — witness the grade school science-film glimpse of a girl watching a tissue rise in the air in *Valse Triste* (1979), or the sad, leering Marilyn Monroe stag film repeated five times to the tune of "I'm Through with Love" sung by America's favorite suicide blonde in *Marilyn X 5* (1968-73).

Given the monstrous heap and many species of visual culture available, it's no surprise there are more found-footage films than stars in the sky; since the 60s, Ernie Gehr, Chick Strand, Stan Brakhage, Caroline Avery, Scott Bartlett, Donna Cameron, Emily Breer, Heather MacAdams, Keith Sanborn, Jack Chambers, Nina Fonoroff, Joyce Wieland, Greta Snider, Al Razutis, Saul Levine, Mary Filippo, David Rimmer, Stan

Vanderbeek, Laurie Dunphy, Jerry Tartaglia and Leslie Thornton have all contributed significant works to the landscape. Since the creation of images — normally the first leg of the filmmaking journey — is beside the point, the ersatz archaeological glories of discovery, and control, dominate the tactics of the genre: How will I contextually alter this imagery, and why? The degree of autonomy exercised over the footage can vary wildly, from the untouched Dada of George Landow's self-explanatory *Film In Which There Appear Sprocket Holes, Edge Lettering, Dirt Particles, Etc.* (1966) and Conner's *Ten Second Film* (1965), which is literally ten seconds of countdown leader, to the Uzi-fire films of Abigail Child, collected under the umbrella title *Is This What You Were Born For?* (1981-88). Mixing refuse footage with sequences she'd shot herself and then mercilessly spliced up as if they were found, Child's cacophonous films interrogate all manner of cultural ills with the energy of a jackhammer, and make MTV look sodden by comparison. With individual titles like *Mercy, Mayhem* and *Covert Action*, Child's ferocious torrents of pure collage come off like sweaty delirium-tremen accelerations of media-saturated modern life — sitting through her full oeuvre can have the effect of being slammed in the stomach and the head at the same time.

All films collaged from refuse footage struggle between the interrogation of mass media image-use and the examination of the fragility of cinematic meaning itself, usually meeting somewhere in the middle. Emphasizing the latter, on the far horizons of recreated imagery, lies the manipulation of cinematic sequentiality as enacted by deus ex machina Ken Jacobs in his "nervous system" performances like 1992's *XCXHX-EXRXRXIXEXSX*, employing two modified, asynchronous projectors (controlled by Jacobs) and a few minutes of a 1920 French stag movie (*Cherries*) that the artist mutates into an epic, frame-by-frame reordering of film time. Phil Solomon's *The Secret Garden* (1988) represents another degree of separation, consisting of clips from *The Wizard of Oz*, the obscure French version of *The Secret Garden* and a Polish rendition of *The Garden of Eden*, edited into a single image-myth about dysfunctional families and distorted into near abstraction through optical printing. With its mottled glimpses of familiar nursery-time cliches, cryptic subtitles and eventual descent into pure lightshow, Solomon's film degenerates the essence of its found images — which struggle to retain their faerie contexts — until they nearly disappear altogether in a dreamy mock-tribute to nitrate decay. Cut-and-crash filmmaker Lewis Klahr's *Her Fragrant Emulsion* (1987) reorders footage in yet another way: vertically, with shots of unclad motorcycle-movie-queen Mimsy Farmer apparently cut lengthwise and glued onto blank emulsion. As the film unspools, the images overlap, appear and disappear in thick strands, only intermittently allowing the projector to lock in on a solid image of palm trees or Farmer's sun-soaked blondness. Alongside Cornell's decades-old paean to *his* favorite never-was movie idol, it's the wisest, swooniest film elegy we have for the phenomena of the Hollywood heroine.

The methodological fulcrum for artists like Jacobs, Child, Klahr and Solomon has been the transmutability of the film stuff, altering it on such a fundamental level that its native identity is almost wholly obscured and thus rescued from its proper ephemeral destiny. Cinematic context being what it is, however, any notion of transmutability must be left open-ended. Whatever's "found" is sometimes left untouched, better to ponder its essential "foundness": avant-garde elder statesman Hollis Frampton took an old documentary about the planting of a garden and merely retitled it — *Works and Days* (1969). Though otherwise identical to the original film, Frampton's is, like Borges' *Don Quixote* by Pierre Menard, undeniably a separate work. Jacobs' *Perfect Film* (1986) is news footage taken at the scene of Malcolm X's assassination found by Jacobs in a Canal Street bin and simply spliced end to end. Left "perfectly" itself, without the filmmaker's editorial intervention, the film fragments become both objective history and the filmmaker's sliest statement about authorial power, a tack he takes as well in *Urban Peasants* (1975), comprised of his wife's aunt's home movies, with little or no sign of a controlling hand. Primitivist in spirit, *Urban Peasants* acquires a moving significance generated solely and organically by the natural passage of time and evolving social forces outside the film, in high contrast to Alan Berliner's enervating *The Family Album* (1986) which, perhaps because the home movies are edited into a nostalgic form and dressed-up with a cue-heavy soundtrack, more acutely resembles... well, watching someone else's home movies.

Long the private stomping ground of secluded avant-gardists of all tactical strategies, found footage films acquired arthouse cachet with the wide release and video sales of *The Atomic Cafè* (1982). A didactic feature-length survey of the Cold War era's nuclear fever cobbled together out of all manner of educational baloney by archivists Jayne Loader and Kevin and Pierce Rafferty, *The Atomic Cafè* is less filmic experiment than an early audiovisual attempt at culture studies, casting a cold eye on the methods by which our culture lied to itself about the grim realities of atomic warfare. Viewing *Cafè* again, I was overwhelmed by both the sheer idiocy of the Eisenhower-era media mindset and by how the same time-stuck, bedlamite visuals of atomic foolishness could have become so much more than merely political in the hands of an artist.

Still, if the materials at hand are the detritus of an unavoidably politicized mass media, political creatures are bound to emerge. The collapse of the Soviet Union opened a veritable Pandora's Box of previously unseen (in the West) governmental cinema, which in turn begat scathing found footage assemblages ripping the former USSR's ideological patterns of force to shreds. Oleg Kovalov's *Garden of Scorpions* (1991) and Andrei Zagdansky's *Interpretation of Dreams* (1990) are bastard offspring crawling from the wreckage of nearly 70 years of righteous propagandizing. The glasnost rediscovery of Freud inspired Zagdansky's dialectical essay, in which most of 20th century's political aberrations are reevaluated through the tongue-in-cheek application of psychoanalytic theory, whereas *Garden of Scorpions* wryly turns the legacy of fist-pounding Soviet agitprop in on itself, ending up atop a debris heap of socialist camp. A chop-shop of melodrama, half-baked educational films, cartoons, musicals, news footage, snippets from the films of Eisenstein, Vertov and Pudovkin, *Garden* explicitly acknowledges its debt to the Kuleshov method: interpolating the impassive face of an actor with shots of food, a child and a corpse, and garnering praise for the eloquent expressions of hunger, love and grief. By subverting the intended meaning of celluloid by experimenting with its context, Kuleshov laid the foundation for the montage/collage aesthetic; from then on, it's been an avenue of visual experience whose principles of expression are founded in subversion — formal, emotional, historical, political or otherwise. The bulk of Kovalov's irreverent blitz is ripped from an uproariously earnest 1955 drama *The Case of Corporal Kotschetkov*, wherein a fresh-faced Soviet soldier stationed on the homefront of the Cold War falls in love with a young girl, only to be informed by officials that she and her pie-cooking grandmother are both capitalist spies. Material from the Khrushchev era is worked in in ingenious ways: at one point, Cpl. Kotschetkov passes into a foggy delirium from some of Grandma's presumably poisoned food and hallucinates Khrushchev's trip to Paris and New York, with garish capitalism radiating from every neon light, Peking Opera dancers leaping about to "Blue Suede Shoes," and guest appearances by Yves Montand, Marilyn Monroe and Frank Sinatra.

It's something of a testament to the expressive, "discoverable" nature of found footage that it can simultaneously hum with satire and lyrical beauty, and yet both *The Atomic Café* and *Garden of Scorpions* fail to engage the sense of surreal poignance that lurks beneath their absurd, government-produced components. Sometimes the footage sings its own song: hearkening back (and, unavoidably, forward) to the deliberate dissolution of *The Secret Garden*, Dutch filmmaker Peter Delpeut's *Lyrical Nitrate* (1991) is nothing more than scrap celluloid from several nitrate-stock early-century films found by Delpeut in an Amsterdam attic and rescued halfway through the process of dissolving into goo. Presented with little authorial interference (and in their original tinted color), the random fragments — travelogues of Stockholm and the Alps, disconnected bits of stagy drama and passion play, simple film portraits — are both ravishingly beautiful and teetering on the edge of entropy, an edge they topple over in the final sequence, where a kitschy Adam & Eve tableau is completely overcome with nightmarish nitrate breakdown. *Lyrical Nitrate* is possibly the most reflexive of all found footage films, taking as its solitary subject the fragile impermanence of cinematic imagery and its subjects. Looking into the nitrate-lit eyes of the film's many portraited children, it's immediately palpable that both they and movies could never be as innocent again. Delpeut's next, *The Forbidden Quest* (1993), uses reams of early documentary footage to fabricate a 1905 ocean voyage to Antarctica that climaxes in shipwreck, bloodshed and an encounter with the valley of Heaven. "Inspired" by Eliot, Jules Verne and Poe's *Narrative of Arthur Gordon*

Pym, as well as by many actual accounts of the day, *The Forbidden Quest* is an old-fashioned Boys' Own adventure saga whose antiquated imagery — much of it employed because of its timeworn grittiness — tell its own, very real stories despite its new pulpy context.

On a hermetic narrative island all its own, David Blair's *Wax, or the Discovery of Television Among the Bees* (1991) is a nuclear-powered bughouse rave that incorporates found footage into a cyperspatial stew that belongs to the post-atomic tradition of cultural discourse that runs from Thomas Pynchon to Epcot Center to the Weekly World News. Blair's furious current of electronic imagery, computer animation, found archival footage, and fresh tape shot on-location at Trinity Site resembles the paranoid cosmologies of longtime amphetamine junkies. Blair not only edits historical imagery to his own deranged ends, but electronically warps them as well, dropping them like knotted helixes into a mad plot about beekeepers, alien telecommunications and the Gulf War. In the various alternative decipherings of *Wax*'s post-atomic dustbin, the most frequently cited interfaces are J.G. Ballard and William S. Burroughs, whose narrative function/form experiments and field trips through the post-industrial junkyard are obvious ancestors to Blair's televisual hyperbole and to found footage films at large.

The cut-&-paste Ghost of Postmodernism Past, Burroughs also lingers over perhaps the most infamous, and proudly "derriere-garde," of found footage purveyors, Craig Baldwin, a polemical San Francisco-based "media savage" whose films naturally spring from his work as a programmer of alternative media and collector of industrials, typically characterized as offering "a delightful rear entry into a pop cultural limbo of transcendent banality." His notorious bricolage narrative, *Tribulation 99: Alien Anomalies Under America* (1991), is an unparalleled achievement in wicked social satire and reformulation of hopelessly disparate pieces of ephemera (everything from Japanese sci-fi to Caribbean travelogues) into a hellzapoppin secret history of modern politics that itself executes media credibility and exposes our crazed thirst as a society for half-meaningful imagery. In a hilariously far-reaching conspiracy theory "rant" that entwines aliens, Atlantis, inner earth theory, Armageddon theology, killer bees and shrapnel from nearly every major political fallout of the last 50 years, Baldwin breathlessly flambes every notion of political purpose this country's ever held dear. (Found footage tends to begat conspirational symbol systems — "The illusion-shattering truth about the coming apocalypse and the official cover-up!" Baldwin's *Trib 99* paperback screams — possibly because, taken out of its original propagandistic context, the footage of mass control often appears terrifying, shockingly lamebrained and hilarious.) According to Baldwin's conspirational narrator, Eisenhower met with the alien "Quetzals," the CIA was invented for the sole reason of monitoring their activities, and a veritable laundry list of western hemisphere hotbeds — Guatemala, El Salvador, Nicaragua, Panama, etc. — are pinpointed as Quetzal ground zeroes. Early on, the 1949 suicide of Secretary of Defense James Forrestal is illustrated by an obvious dummy tossed from a high window and the title "UNDER TELEPATHIC ORDERS?" An activist at heart, Baldwin is also a post-punk "cargo culturist" whose garage-band politique sees no reason to tread lightly; representing Noriega with Lon Chaney's Wolfman and Castro with a flea-bitten Moses are characteristic tropes.

Before *Tribulation 99* came *Wild Gunman* (1978), an otherwise trad found footage exercise employing sequences culled from a gunfight video game whose course of visuals are predicated on the player's participation, and *RocketKitKongoKit* (1985), an incisive historical firecracker that set the mold for Baldwin's politically incendiary subsequent work: bizarre found images are coupled with authentic, disturbing news footage of Zaire under Mobutu's reign, supported by a just-the-facts narration of Mobutu's step-by-step exploitation of his country and ties to foreign governments, including ours. His first post-*Trib 99* exercise in "cinema povera," *¡O No Coronado!* (1992), continues Baldwin's interrogative course, this time reconstructing the historiography surrounding the Spanish conquest of the New World as personified, in all his disaster-prone, loot-and-kill buffoonery, by Francisco Vasquez de Coronado, who journeyed across Mexico and the Southwest searching haplessly for the Seven Cities of Gold, a trek marked by tragedy, cannibalism, wholesale slaughter and madness. Simultaneously a risible, factually accurate chronicle of Coronado's mishaps (one every schoolkid should see) and an outright parody of cinematic historicization (Baldwin pillages countless costume dramas and swashbucklers, as well as picture books, serials, *Gulliver's Travels* and kitschy re-enactments Baldwin shot himself), *Coronado!* is an object lesson in how to revivify the most moribund cinematic avenues. If only Baldwin had been commissioned to make *A Brief History of Time, Wild Palms, The Civil War* or *Hoffa.* Instead, Baldwin took on the personally vital subject of copyright out-lawry and freedom of expression with *Sonic Outlaws* (1995), a ballsy, half-straight documentary/half found-footage probe into the Negativland-U2 scandal, encompassing an astonishing breadth of covert media protest (including a group of shopping guerillas who steal Barbie and G.I. Joe dolls, switch their voice discs, and then return them to store shelves). As political movies go, Baldwin's are wrecking balls in perpetual swing.

At the core of the found footage aesthetic lies a malcontented urge to uncover the dark submovie — a true "secret cinema" — underneath the skin of generic mainstream media, like a pentimento seething with taboo truths and subversive impulses. Demarginalization isn't viable, or necessarily desired. In this age of recycling, no irony could possibly be lost on Baldwin and his contemporaries as the movies they amalgamate out of forgotten filmic offscourings prove more resonant and complex by far than the original product. For a creative culture otherwise ruled by the naked force of commodity, it's the ultimate justice.

(*Film Comment*, November – December 1993)

OUSMANE SEMBENE

The poet Robert Lowell changed the face of American poetry with the admonishment "why not say what really happened"; no filmmaker anywhere in the world has taken as strong a stock in that ruling principle as Senegal's Ousmane Sembene, called too often (but not unjustly) "the father of African cinema." His films make nearly all other modes of cinematic discourse seem decadent by comparison — cluttered with decorous images, imperialist indulgences, frivolous material and a reliance on technical gimmickry to move audiences. Rather, films like *Borom Sarret* (1963), *Emitai* (1971), *Xala* (1974), *Ceddo* (1976), and Sembene's recent masterwork *Guelwaar* (1992) all possess a natural-born faith in the naked austerity of events, expressed via amateurish (yet relaxed) performances, a seemingly artless mise-en-scene, and a sense of Shaker-like utilitarianism. Camera movement is rare, close-ups even rarer, and many of the images have the fading, over-exposed tint of aging home movies. Whether it be famine, political upheaval, religious squabbling or racial exploitation, things are as they are in Sembene's world, presented with all the demi-Catholic severity of Bresson, but with a distinctly African grit and appreciation of folly. And whereas Satyajit Ray or other regional filmmakers steeped in different traditions might locate lyricism within similar precincts, Sembene eschews even the most elemental cinematic flourishes. Dead-serious just-so-stories perpetually teetering on the fulcra of the basest human factors — greed, pride, fear, intolerance, etc., Sembene's modern folk art has all the power and glory of Old Testament mythos, while casting an ice-cold contemporary eye at the socioeconomic tarpit of African nations wrangling with their newfound independence and the crippling reverb of colonial control.

Like a flower's tropistic bowing to the sun, most political cinematic aesthetics are often predetermined in a virtually Darwinian sense by their culture's particular legacy of oppression, colonialism, fundamentalism, protracted warfare or will to power. Political movies can't help but bring their social landscape to bear on their own form, just as European cathedrals are really "about" the Crusades if you look closely enough. Filmwise, the silent Soviets served the principles of Socialist control by way of propaganda calibrated with an almost trigonometric sense of manipulative purpose, while Allied wartime cinema used the tropes of dime-novel entertainment to stir the masses. Italian neo-realism reclaimed its peasantry with the movies' first willful *cinema povera* riff, encouraging the form of their films to reflect their subject, while in the roiling 60s, more restless South European filmmakers like Gillo Pontecorvo and Costa-Gavras began using the raw nerviness of in-your-face suspense thrillers for their post-mortems on local political wounds everyone else had hoped were long scabbed over. Agitprop documentaries, from *Triumph of the Will* to *Shoah*, all purport to *be* truth within their various subjective strategies, and can have, of course, notoriously mercurial and mysterious relationships to reality. *JFK* and *Malcolm X*, the last decade's most aggressive juggernauts of American political intent, do their frenzied dances to the tune of MTV editing rhythms and glowing Spielbergian power-shots. Less powerful, and less wealthy, cultures have a habit of consequently paring down their films' scope to the most basic of political realities: poverty, the vestiges of colonialism, the tangible meat-&-potatoes of class struggle. Third World cinematic traditions are therefore often and almost by definition politically structured, and guided like none other by the limited resources of filmmaker and subject alike.

Few oeuvres exemplify this hand-to-mouth politique as well as Ousmane Sembene's. Unlike Ray, who began like Sembene by making his first Indian groundbreaker *Pather Panchali* without any visible means of support but who then went on to become the revered grand master in one of the world's most rapacious film cultures, Sembene still makes his dirt-cheap movies on the fly 30 years later (with found locations and actors), and for a poor, troubled culture whose regional cinema was, until recently, virtually nonexistent outside of Sembene and a handful of contemporaries. From the beginning, his films are as stripped of nonessentials as the scrub desert in which they're most often set. Initially a renowned novelist in France, but with limited distribution in the Francophone West African areas where the vast majority of people are illiterate and speak only native tongues like Senegal's Wolof, Sembene switched to film in 1963 so he could ostensibly engage in a direct dialogue with his countrymen, and indeed his films leave the arid wastes of Senegal as rarely as Pagnol's leave Provence. Sembene has claimed to have realized the power of cinema upon seeing the defiant athletic prowess of Jesse Owens at the 1936 Berlin Olympics in Leni Riefenstahl's *Olympiad*; typically, the images of the black Owens outracing Hitler's ubermensch, not Riefenstahl's fabulously fascistic visuals, are what caught his imagination. What's most readily apparent in Sembene's own films is his spare, ascetic approach to narrative, formulating tales with the same simplicity and straightforward moral identity as the fables related by village *griots*. That the rest of the world might be watching as well, and that Senegalese citizens often opt as we do for glossy Hollywood product over technically crude yet relevant local cinema, couldn't come as much of a surprise to Sembene, who studied in Moscow under Mark Donskoi and whose adventurous life (as WWII infantryman, longshoreman, labor leader, celebrated author) and work eventually circle back to the dusty, pragmatic verities of life in a Senegalese village, where the tribulations of clashing cultures are both universal and distinctively post-colonialist.

A disarmingly simple, unmitigated day-in-the-miserable-life of an iconic Dakar cart driver, *Borom Sarret* singlehandedly staked Sembene's turf as a new and reckonable filmmaking presence, and at the same time claimed a place for sub-Saharan African cinema in the international gallery, where it has since snowballed in breadth and significance. Though hardly the first film to emerge from the region (*Mouramani*, a film from Guinea, appeared in 1953), *Borom Sarret* was the first sub-Saharan movie to be widely screened outside of Africa, and its seminal success at film festivals essentially force-fed the notion of an African cinematic topos to an early-60s movie world otherwise infatuated with the stylized hyperart of Antonioni, Fellini, Resnais, Bergman, et al. Though only 20 minutes long, *Borom Sarret* sent epic-sized shockwaves through the European film culture that might say more about lingering post-colonialist culpability than the film itself. It's difficult today to see what was so surprising; Sembene's stripped-down style, tragic fatalism and brutal take on class collision are such natural expressions of his nation's mindscape that nothing short of recolonialization could've prevented it. For all its formal modesty, *Borom Sarret* is a harrowing, primitivist capsule of complex themes Sembene will readdress and explore in many later films. Neo-neo-realism and realpolitik soc-crit both, Sembene's mini-tragedy — wherein his naive and God-trusting Everyman loses everything at the hands of societal barriers, the advance of modern life and plain rotten luck — is built on dichotomies, a common Sembene strategy. Our hero-for-hire carts pregnant women and corpses both, and plies his trade in the edge sections of the city, the narrow avenue between undeveloped villages and Dakar's gentrified center, where peasants, and donkey carts, cannot go. Making hash of the traditional male warrior role around which African life was once centered, Sembene's urban outskirts are littered with shellshocked vets of the culture war. In the end, the cart-driver's wife sets out bitterly to buy via prostitution the food he has failed to supply. "All I can do now is die," Sembene's dehumanized protagonist says finally in his unemotional voiceover; the film's Job-like ordeal cuts right to the core of perhaps Sembene's most crucial j'accuse — the role of the new, black African elite in the decimation of their own nations.

The first sub-Saharan film to debut at Cannes, *Le noire de...* (*Black Girl*, 1965), is no less scathing, if not simply more explicit, in its encapsulated portrait of the colonialist instinct at work, focusing on its inherent racism. The scenario couldn't be simpler: Diouana, a beautiful young Senegalese woman with no French (she narrates in Wolof), takes a job with a white bourgeois family in Dakar caring for their children; when they move back to France, she accompanies them and soon finds herself reduced to virtual slavery with no days off and no contact with the outside world. (Explaining to a friend about Diouana's silence, the wife asserts that "she understands instinctively, like an animal.") If Diouana represents her people — *Black Girl* is nothing if not overtly metaphorical — she also represents their unconscious urge to follow the withdrawn colonialism home rather than have to reinvent themselves as free citizens. When the mounting tensions and suffocating anomie end in shocking, silent tragedy, *Black Girl* takes on the aura of minimalist manifesto — a salient, albeit pitiful, precursor to the spirit of *Thelma & Louise* as much as *Do the Right Thing*.

As Sembene has pointed out himself, his cinematic statements owe less to romantic notions of "negritude" — which by definition subtracts degrees of responsibility for the state of West African disarray from colonialists — than to the hard, gimme-food-and-shelter truths of quotidian living in Senegal, where blame falls squarely and without ambiguity upon the oppressive powers that be, black or white. Few filmmakers attest so eloquently to the integrity of native experience — as scholar Jay Leyda has said, no mere visitor to Senegal could have come to Sembene's seemingly de-aestheticized formal conclusions. Sembene's first genuine feature, *Mandabi* (1970), is a virtual comic flowchart of the traditional tribal world lost in modern-day red tape that, while still maintaining its quasi-biblical candor, evokes the spiraling nightmare of Steinbeck's *The Pearl*. Here, literacy, self-perpetuating bureaucracy and western systems of control are the new, black, French-speaking petty bourgeois's methods of sustaining power over the illiterate majority, and Sembene paints it all in broad, symbolic strokes — the anonymity of Dakar and its various institutions signify bureaucratic entropy on a continental scale. The hero, Ibrahima, is a vain, blustery Muslim living with two wives in the semi-developed Senegalese 'burbs, and who receives a money order (*mandabi* in Wolof) from his Parisian nephew. The mere news of the order drowns him in false friends, harrowing debts and much woeful interfacing with the city's indifferent corruption as he attempts to cash the cursed thing and repeatedly plays the sucker to modernity's more usurious elements. Sembene's films rarely end in any manner but disaster, and so Ibrahima's saga has an inexorable, Aesopian logic in which misfortune is the true wage of fools. Ibrahima, like other Sembene characters, has little depth and doesn't need it — he's a near-sighted, puffed-up Fred Flintstone in a world where water must be bought and a bag of rice makes for a luxurious feast. The nuances of his character are less important to Sembene's scheme than the character of the system that strips him of worth and dignity; Ibrahima is the representational peasant-pilgrim in the New World of the post-colonialist bourgeoisie, and as such need be nothing more than recognizably human, with ordinary human failings.

Mandabi was perhaps Sembene's first wholehearted interrogation of the self-governing Senegalese social system, complemented soon after by *Tauw* (1970), a short post-revolution, pre-Generation-X statement focusing on the dehumanizing relentlessness of dumb low-wage labor and a literal no-futurism for the West African youth culture that makes punk politics look like one long, spoiled whine. With *Emitai* (1971), he began exploring other manifestations of historical injustice — here, the exploitation and abduction-draft of non-nationalized tribesmen by the French during WWII. As in the dour pageantries of Miklos Jancsó and the Leninist firecrackers of Eisenstein et al., *Emitai* has no primary characters, just masses of social force. Instead, Sembene's deceptively casual sense of spatial anxiety, dividing our attention between the besieged village's ground zero and the "hidden" circle where the village's men endlessly debate about their situation, controls the action. Opening with a thrilling guns-vs.-spears battle scene (in which white officers lead black soldiers against their own countrymen) that stands as Sembene's *All Quiet on the Western Front*, *Emitai* is a classically clearcut, de-exoticized vision of African culture routed out and mauled by European needs. A lone desert tribe among many with its own language spoken throughout the film, the Diola are besieged by French wartime forces set on first kidnapping the tribe's young men at gunpoint for infantry service ("You have volunteered," the officer tells them, "You will have great war stories to tell your grandchildren."), and then looting the weary village of its supply of rice. Still, Sembene fastidiously resists a Manichean view of the matter; the elder Diola men hide themselves from the invaders and bicker endlessly about what to do — eventually deciding several times to sacrifice chickens to the god Emitai — while the women more pragmatically hide the rice and confront the troops as a veritable wall of passive resistance. Neither are the French authority figures ever evil or all-powerful; rather, on the exhausted edges of the eastern front, they're tired and half-witted, their positions transitory and makeshift. This powder-keg situation is only complicated by the appearance, and influence, of Emitai himself — plunging Sembene's usually pragmatic social universe into the sky-high mythos of Indian *masala* movies — and inevitably ends in an appalling assault on all things *afrique* that recalls several martyred waves of post-Stalinist Eastern Bloc cinema. A perpetual motion machine of ethical ambiguity and confrontational tension, *Emitai* may be the first Sembene film to explore and redress recent history from a Senegalese perspective, a strategy that Sembene continued in *Camp de Thiaroye* (1987).

A raw, subtle epic excavating yet another forgotten episode of downhome horror from WWII, *Thiaroye* is the first Pan-African feature produced completely without European technical aid or co-financing — it took nearly 30 years, but with this Algerian-Tunisian-Senegalese coproduction West Africa can truly be said to have its own film industry. Co-directed and written with Paris-trained filmmaker Theirno Faty Sow, *Thiaroye*'s historical imperative revolves not only around its protagonists' tragic fate at the hand of the French, but their very existence as history — for years the massacre of Senegalese infantrymen at the camp was purposefully repressed in all quarters.

What actually happened at Camp de Thiaroye in 1944 could be read as an abstract of colonialist friction; it conforms so expressively to Sembene's themes one could be tempted to suspect he fashioned it from whole cloth. But, as always, the film's sober relationship to how things were (are) remains Sembene's polemical crux. *Camp de Thiaroye* centers on the Senegalese infantrymen that returned from the war expecting to be repatriated to their individual villages, and were instead sequestered in the eponymous transit camp, where they are made to feel more like POWs (several are Buchenwald alumni) than victorious soldiers. As the voltage between the dispirited men and their French guards rises, culminating in the seizure of the camp by its prisoners, Sembene's reconstructed history lesson takes on the bitter menace of the familiar *Great Escape* prison-camp genre feeding upon itself like a cancer. Of course it climaxes in a massacre — dated in a title, Nov. 30, 1944, 10 Hours — which Sembene portrays with a hellish brio that's as close as he's ever come to hyperbole. Like *Emitai, Camp de Thiaroye* is an ensemble piece in which each character occupies his own point along the sociopolitical scale stretching between conformism with the oppressive powers and unbridled revolution. (The cultured Diola sergeant, who at first enjoys the privileges of his rank and later represents the rebellion at its most ferocious, tells *Emitai*'s village-slaughter story as his own, indelibly connecting the two films as the first thirds of a WWII trilogy begging to be completed.) Whereas the outrage of *Camp de Thiaroye*, though powerful, may preclude the gray-shaded, subtle dualities that make Sembene's other films so rich, *Ceddo, Xala* and *Guelwaar* are all more eloquently shaped as colloquies.

Ceddo is Sembene's only attempt to visualize and thereby reinvent pre-Christian, and pre-Muslim, African myth (a subgenre of African filmmaking that has since exploded), and also his only film to center on a strong woman, a textual aspect to his work that in the end reflects more about the post-colonialist culture than the artist. Set in the 17th century, on the cusp of the slave trade, *Ceddo* focuses on the religious patterns of power that threaten to tear a village apart: traditionally matriarchal, the villagers are torn for the most part between ceddos — adherents to the ancient myth systems — and Muslims, who along with the relatively peripheral influence of a Christian missionary, engage in a now-familiar brand of fundamental intolerance for the paganish ways of yore. A frustrated ceddo kidnaps the village's proud princess and holds her hostage in order to inspire an ideological critical mass among the village's leaders: the king, his opposing sons, his daughter's suitors, and the Iman himself, who is positively Ayatollah-ish in his bloodthirsty fervor for fatwas and forced conversions. As in *Emitai*, Sembene adeptly demarcates the mounting tensions between the two spaces: the village's central meeting ground where the king holds court, and the wild patch of scrubland where the ceddo holds the indignant princess, who refuses to be bound up and instead acknowledges a single length of rope stretched in the sand as the border of her imprisonment. Sembene takes great pains to construct his story by way of the formal injunctions of ceddo society — the role of griot and royal spokesman as middlemen in tribal exchanges, the manner by which champions are chosen to rescue the princess — and *Ceddo* has the ceremonial air of a Greek tragedy, complete with bloody finale (in a bracing fit of prairie justice, the princess takes the Iman out) and timeless aphorisms ("If a lizard teases a turkey, it's because there's a tree nearby"). *Ceddo* also harbors a handful of Sembene's most arresting images: a goat running horrorstruck through the flames of the burning village, the semi-nude Princess lounging in the desert dust, a dead man frozen in a crouch position and buried by his villagers in a giant mound of dirt with the tip of his bow jutting from the top as a marker.

Xala, at the other end of the aeon, is an uproarious comeuppance comedy set in contemporary Dakar and lampooning, once and for all, the new Senegalese ruling class's adoption of Eurogreed — El Hadj, the film's affluent demimonde joke-butt, even insists his chauffeur-driven Mercedes be washed with Evian. Sembene opens with a revolutionary mock-allegory preamble wherein Senegalese blacks storm (dancing) the Chamber of Commerce, eject the white officials and various symbolic objects of their regime out onto the building's front steps, and install a "pure" Socialist government while simultaneously receiving briefcases packed with cash; the biting irony of *Xala* is Sembene's broadest, and all the more arresting for his starkly lit, mock-doc visual style (it's a world without shadows), which often leaves you second-guessing what was a joke and what wasn't. As with nearly all of Sembene's films, the division between classes is limned by language — when the new leaders address their Wolof-speaking public, it's in French: "We have chosen socialism, the only true socialism, the African path to socialism, socialism with a human dimension," happily indulging in the blithe, straight-faced corruption practiced for so long by colonialists just before climbing into their limos and taking off.

Xala is Wolof for the curse of impotency, which is inflicted upon El Hadj by mistreated beggars on the eve of his third marriage. Taking on three wives is in itself both a pathetic display of masculine vanity and a Senegalese extravagance on par with getting a second beach home in Malibu, and El Hadj's impotence is perhaps Sembene's most incisive metaphor for his nation's economic vice and class-conflicted inertia.

"You're not a white man," one of El Hadj's mother-in-laws tells him, "You're neither fish nor fowl." As he tries to rid himself of the *xala* by visiting rural village marabouts (medicine men), one of whom he angers into reinstalling the *xala* by paying with a rubber check, El Hadj is revealed as a distillation of capitalistic tendencies who made much of his fortune by diverting supplies meant for famine-struck areas. Fittingly, the news of his impotence helps bring about his bankruptcy. Easily the most comical of Sembene's films — in the wedding-night shenanigans, it becomes refreshingly ribald — *Xala* has several separate currents of thematic action that collide in its final, chillingly unfunny moments: the disenfranchised, Hogarthian beggars return to El Hadj's home, ransack it, molest his first wife and offer El Hadj the only permanent cure for the *xala* — to strip naked and be spat upon, to which he eventually consents. This rite of humiliation, appalling in its visceral impact and predating Todd Haynes' *Poison* by some 16 years, is presumably Sembene's symbolic answer to the plague of greed and exploitation independent West African nations have inflicted on their own; the ritualistic destruction of dignity as a process by which to tear down divisions of class. *Xala*'s satire turns on a dime in this last scene and lays bare the naked suffering of Sembene's people in a way the film hadn't prepared us for — it's a sociocultural venus fly trap, luring us into the maw of honest sociopolitical pain.

Sembene's newest film, the lean and eloquent *Guelwaar*, takes the religious battlements of *Ceddo* into the 20th century, where the isolationist mania of both Christian and Muslim coalitions reaches a nadir in drought-stricken Senegal. Guelwaar himself is a radical, anti-interventionist activist assassinated before the film begins; we seem him intermittently in flashback, amid stirring *Malcolm X*-ish speech scenes. On the morning of his funeral, the mourners discover that his body's missing from the morgue, and all hell breaks loose. There's ghastly talk of the body being stolen by fetishists, among a great many other wild theories, while sharp comic points are scored off Guelwaar's eldest son, who's become a superior-minded French citizen, and Guelwaar's long-suffering wife, who has her own personal wake kneeling before her troublesome husband's empty suit: "Our next meeting will be tense," she says dryly. Soon it is discovered that the remains of Guelwaar, who's a baptized Catholic, have been mistakenly buried in the local Muslim cemetery, a bureaucratic gaffe that leads to a direct confrontation of faiths. While Guelwaar's family naturally wants to relocate the body in consecrated ground, the Muslims maintain no mistake was made and even the mere presence of infidels on their holy turf would be blasphemy punishable by death. This imbroglio's every intolerant wart is backlit by Sembene in his most perfectly realized scenario, as the two eventually face off in a riot-to-be stemmed only by a helpless constable negotiating the literal, and ideological, middle ground of the graveyard overlooked by looming high-tension towers. Sembene again conceives his dozen or so main characters (only two of which are experienced actors; the rest simply live in the village) as embodiments of social energy, and structures his drama spatially, as the two camps bicker over a patch of arid desert of no inherent value beyond what meaning is arbitrarily imposed upon it. And if any character of Sembene's could be said to wholly represent the filmmaker's political viewpoint, it's Guelwaar, the *agent provocateur* himself, whose only dogma was the ideal of a unified Africa unsundered by petty religious squabbling, bureaucratic chaos and class combat, and who went so far, as Guelwaar itself does, to condemn the African nations' reliance on "emergency aid" from other countries, Sir Bob Geldof or no Sir Bob Geldof. In *Guelwaar's* radical climax, after the successful reburial of the eponymous corpse, a truckload of food is overrun and destroyed by villagers as per Guelwaar's last public entreaty, seen in flashback.

Guelwaar draws the graph of Senegal's currently-raging Christian-Muslim civil war in miniature much as Jan Nemec's *A Report on the Party and the Guests* (1966) dissected the clockwork of Soviet totalitarianism through the invasion of a small outdoor party by oppressive, and wholly symbolic, forces. "We are no longer in the era of prophets," Sembene has said at a recent Lincoln Center screening in honor of his 70th birthday, regarding the anti-fundamentalist thrust of *Guelwaar*, and though the film's wrangling occurs mostly on sacred ground of one type or another, the terminal decimation of the supply truck brings us right back to the scorched-earth issue of economic independence and equality, Sembene's thematic sine qua non and indeed the basic brick of all political cinema. If a film won't *matter* on a fundamental level to his countrymen, as films rarely *matter* here, Sembene won't make it. Questioned about the shiftings of his politics through the years — the barrel of his interrogatory camera leveled at colonialists, fundamentalists, bourgeois and aspiring peasants in varying proportions — Sembene answered, "It's not me, it's my people that evolve. I live among them; I'm like the thermometer." Quite possibly the only filmmaker left in the world who cannot be bought and sold, Sembene represents the dying heritage of political films still possessed of a virginal faith in social change, a faith not in films for profit's sake, or even film's sake, but for ours.

(*Film Comment*, July – August 1993)

DESPLESCHIN'S *LA SENTINELLE*

Like a midnight stalk through the no man's land between the East and West portions of the old Berlin Wall, Arnaud Desplechin's *La Sentinelle* unfurls in a state of frustrated mystery and static menace, brimming with mirror-split images, portentous tremors and post-Cold War meta-crises. An unpopular entry in 1992's New York Film Festival finally finding stateside release in 1997, *La Sentinelle*'s landscape is cool and lunar, a personal sphere haphazardly scorched by the chaotic sunspots of political backdrafts. Emmanuel Salinger, as Desplechin's mystified forensics student Mathias, wanders privately through the film's world in a state of bug-eyed disquiet, striking a blind-and-silent bargain with history (his father was a respected Germany-based military attache) in between run-ins with freelancing spies, a defector smuggling ring posing as an operatic company, medical school weirdness, yuppie Defense Ministry diplos on the warpath, and the chilly appearance of a mummified head.

As Desplechin himself has acknowledged in a *Cahiers du cinema* article, *La Sentinelle* is a brooding, intuitive study in split consciousness; the far-ranging and sometimes dreamily abstruse perambulations of the plot are secondary to the film's dislocating textures and collision-course subtexts. Inevitably, this suggests that for all its realism and cold-blooded, Hitchcockian psychopathology, Desplechin's moody piece was organically grown from mood, fluke and happenstance. He explicitly celebrates the role of on-set serendipity above all else — allowing the story to grow its own tentacles by incorporating a random image or an actor's mid-scene stumble — and admits to "writing" much of the script in the editing room. Indeed, *La Sentinelle* is a spontaneously combustible experience as resistant to schematic readings as it is entranced with shadow-selves, human mysteries and roomfuls of sweaty suspicion.

On this un-thriller's strangely permafrosted surface, we're dealing with the fine, often surreal line between personal and political priorities, a line that, like much else in the film, roils from a druggy absurdism to Grand Guignol and back again. We open in the French Embassy in Bonn, late 1991, as an autumnal ambassador-type regales a gathering of comrades with the story of how Churchill and Stalin divided Europe between them, sans Roosevelt, conclusively ruing the passage of such epochal political climes. The past, political and otherwise, constantly informs and haunts the present, often as fond memories of the espionage bonanza that was the Cold War, sometimes as tangible residue — history leaving a trail behind it like a snail. In the background we first glimpse Mathias wandering the embassy grounds dispassionately; the geography of the scene positions Mathias where he remains throughout the film, in the frustrating position of being an unwitting insider who wants nothing more than to get out.

Nearly everyone he meets wants this un-spy to come in from the cold. Leaving Bonn, and the privileged circles of ambassadorship he's known his whole life, for an internship in Paris (where his sister lives), the introverted Mathias first crosses vectors with the Great Out There on the train, where a disheveled and ambagious bully of a border officer (Jean-Louis Richard) grills him regardless of his diplomatic semi-immunity — or possibly because of it — and never reveals what he's really looking for. "I've looked through your things, that bother you?" he prods Mathias. "So why are you here? Why do I have your trunks? You must have some idea..." Throwing his heaving bulk intimidatingly around the train compartment, hovering over the small-framed Mathias like a thunderhead, the grand inquisitor doesn't ask questions so much as pose koans. "Mathias Barillet... Student of forensic medicine, right? You take care of the dead. Good, someone has to." When Mathias asks flat out what the man wants, he bellows "To know who you are!"

This bureaucratic Bluto's brand of interrogative theater has a distinctly violative cast about it; Desplechin has referred to it as a figurative raping, leaving Mathias humiliated and bruised nearly from the outset. He finds shrugging the incident off even more difficult once he unpacks and discovers an addition to his baggage: a cured, shriveled human head that becomes, quite literally, the movie's guilt-ridden subconscious, bearing the burden for Mathias' many repressed anxieties, including fallen Catholicism, Oedipal angst, political apathy and latent homosexuality — or at least latent Otherness.

This *Night Must Fall*ish nogginful of guilt drives Mathias crazy — should he bury it? throw it away? — until he accepts responsibility for it and does what pathologists do best: dissect and analyze it, in grueling, meticulously flourescent-lit detail. We helplessly begin to wonder if Desplechin used a real mummified head. (He says he didn't.) *La Sentinelle* (the title refers firstly to Mathias' father, as a German-border agent, secondly to nearly every figure in the film) proceeds to then split time between Mathias' cloistered lab work — scraping skin samples, opening the scalp and skull, breaking off the jaw for dental examination — and his reluctant socialization into his vampy sister's stratosphere, which, to his dismay, is stacked high with Secret Service agents and diplo go-getters.

The cold eye that Desplechin casts on the severed head — its dark, shaggy rot often set cooly against the chromic sterility of the forensics lab — is again offset by the warm, sometimes disorienting messiness of Mathias' relationships with his somewhat neurotic sister (Marianne Denicourt), her winsome good-time-girlfriend Nathalie (Valerie Dreville), his powermad, *Richard III*-quoting Secret Service roommate William (Bruno Todeschini), and a touchy, ambivalent forensics colleague named Asher, to whom Mathias' off-hand question re: Jewishness becomes a joking sore spot between them. Desplechin makes no bones about obviating narrative logic for textural moments, and *La Sentinelle* is rife with non sequiturs, behavioral spasms and red

herrings, all the while floating on a nightened river of subtextual portent, photographed with crepuscular richness by Caroline Champetier.
"When I'm in the dissection lab, it's like I'm at the center," Mathias
explains to his sister, "it's calm, you know what to do. When I leave, I'm
out of synch." Like everyone in Desplechin's film, Mathias seems
plagued by secrets. He negotiates life with a severed head in his shoul-
der-bag, and most of us know how he feels.

Like the body in the trunk in Hitchcock's *Rope*, and Poe's heart under
the floorboard, Mathias' head puts a mordant spin on everything that
happens in the film merely by being in the room; we're always hyper-
aware of where Mathias had last sequestered it, whether in a trashcan
or station locker or toy globe. Eventually William and his blacksuited
cronies uncover the identity of Mathias' masquerading border buffoon
— he's a renegade French spy possibly working for the Soviets — and
become convinced Mathias is complicitous in some variety of covert
activity, the suspicion quite naturally centering on whatever it is he's
spiriting around under his coat. Desplechin's laconic, burnished daydream has a natural entropic arc, forcing Mathias' privatized relationship with the semi-dissected skull (and its former owner, a Russian
engineer sold into indentured labor in exchange for asylum) into a head-
on smash-up with the political reality of the world outside the forensics
lab: the sardonic cat-and-mouse games William plays culminate in a
shotgun-brandishing face-off over a piece of jawbone. Murder, betrayal,
treason — in Desplechin's universe, nothing is as it seems, or happens
for readily apparent reasons. It's the nature of the unanswered questions, the film's mysterioso, double-agent take on the post-WWII world
as a *Lady from Shanghai* funhouse, complete with mirrors, guns and
lurking motives, that is the film's lingering voice. Directed and performed with a pathologist's patience — *there's no hurry,* it says, *here's
death right here on the table* — *La Sentinelle*'s occulted ambience may
be best embodied in one sequence: Mathias' dismantling of the head's
leathery, thin-haired scalp and weather-worn skull with shears.
Desplechin closes off each shot with a quick fade-to-black, lending
some formal apprehension to the process; once Mathias' tweezers go
inside the darkness of the opened skull, we know he'll find more in there

than simple decayed tissue. As Mathias, as well as we, begin to realize, what that is will always remain a secret.

(*Film Comment*, May – June 1993)

THE GREAT AMERICAN BLONDE

Blondeness. That transcendent, preternatural, golden-apples-of-the-sun singularity of self; the blaze of cool, clean noonlight flowing like slow water from within a woman; mermaid-ness, Helen-ness, Godiva-ness. Natural or manufactured, human blondeness has no real equivalent in the natural world; nowhere else can you find a beast who can grow foot upon foot of soft spun gold quite like Debra Jo Fondren, that Playboy Playmate with hair down to the Cape of Good Hope, can. And it goes without saying that blondeness is a state of mind — several states, in fact, for the women (self-)blessed with it, the men who gaze slackjawed at it like rummies in a discount liquor store, and for the culture at large. Cultural blondeness is many things to as many people, but it is simultaneously one thing to us all: the empty-eyed, conscience-less, depraved, libertine, post-Aryan dream of sex heaven, of brain-dead pleasure.

To think blonde is to ponder our own unconquerable hungers, but make no mistake, Blondeness per se is an authentically 20th century construct. In past eras, there were blondes, but no Blondeness. To create it, you needed a universal form of visual experience, and indeed Blondeness — as personified in the prototypical blonde bimbo, the

Great American Peroxide Dish — is a peculiar invention of the movies and of the culture movies have spawned. Without movies or TV, there may be blondes, but there could not be Blondeness as we know it. There might be Joni Mitchell, but no Pamela Anderson.

The history of the blonde bimbo is one of the century's many secret histories; it began, strangely enough, with the coming of sound in movies. Why this is, precisely, is anyone's guess, but if you doubt me, try to find a Blonde movie star before 1929. Greta Garbo and Lillian Gish hardly qualify — both are far from bimbos, and dirty blondes to boot. Prior to the stock market crash, blonde hair was simply not fetishized as it is today; we preferred our movie women, whether vamps or madonnas, as brunettes. In fact, ordinary bimbos lingered as mere movie stereotypes until redhead Clara Bow emerged in the mid-20s and made the dumb-as-wood floozie an American classic. She was hot, horny, flirty and utterly empty, and audiences loved her. She was publicized as having It, but what we liked better was what she didn't have much of: clothes, brains or morals. An important precedent to blonde bimbohood, Bow established the paradigm: the primacy of raw, unpunished sexual allure as the modus operandi for popular entertainment. Movies-as-eye-sex was out in the open.

When conjoined with this principle, blondeness was like lightning over water; suddenly, our fantasies were arc-welded to the movies for all time. The first true blonde bimbo, Jean Harlow, hit big in Howard Hughes' *Hell's Angels* (1930), and spent the 30s etching out a unique and deathless screen persona: slatternly, smart-mouthed, worn-out and dumb. As far as you can tell from her movies, she never wore underwear. She's often credited for shifting men's sexual gaze from legs to breasts, but that was only because she didn't seem to care if you saw them or not. And Harlow was blonde the way the ocean is big; *platinum* was the term used, and they weren't kidding. Her blondeness would light up a room like an over-amped fluorescent light. Good thing she had a sharp tongue, because her looks demanded it — you could smell the barroom floors, sour cologne and bad luck all over her.

No one had ever seen blondeness like Harlow's before — perhaps the inherent properties of peroxide were still relatively unknown in 1930, making Harlow something of a pioneer. Her blondeness was integral to her character; if she had had normal hair, there would have been less depth, if you will, to her shallowness. In her movies, often Clark Gable or somebody would fall for a sophisticated brunette while Harlow yapped at his heels; by the end, he'd realize that he was in over his head and that he and the nova-haired trollop are made of the same low clay. He couldn't have romantic dreams about Harlow, but he sure could have a lot of fun fucking her.

Which is what Blondeness boils down to, of course, but then, so do movies. The first wave of blondies were cut in the Harlow mold, all aluminum sheen, deadly wisecracks and hands-on-hips. There was voluptuous trenchmouth/Marx Brothers cohort Thelma Todd (who, like Harlow, died tragically young), and Warner Bros. mainstay Joan Blondell, who always seemed utterly foolish and bubbleheaded, and strangely beautiful and smart, all at the same time. Fay Wray and Mae Clarke served as white-hot screaming machines in *King Kong* and *Frankenstein*. Like Todd and Blondell, Ginger Rogers lurked around as a proto-Harlow for years, snapping gum under a crystalline hairdo, before graduating to the Astaire partnership and more respectable climes. Her sassy harlots in *42nd Street* and *The Goldiggers of 1933* were showgirl leftovers, more prepared to sleep with the producer and get screwed than become a real star. That Rogers would become a star was, therefore, inevitable. Once we glimpsed true blinding bimboness, there was no turning back.

In no time the goofy Blonde was ripe for riffing — Carole Lombard, perhaps the sharpest and least Blonde (though rapturously blonde) of Golden Age actresses, spent several of her best performances sending the bimbo persona a mail bomb. In *My Man Godfrey*, *Nothing Sacred* and *Mr. & Mrs. Smith*, Lombard was the bimbo as Tasmanian Devil; only the simplest of fools would take her for a sex kitten. Her eyes burned with brilliance, and you were never tempted to regard her with mere sloppy, hormonal hankering. You were even less tempted by Mae West, the Queen Victoria of movie Blondes, with snow-white hair and a figure like the prow of a ship. Notorious, all-powerful and far from stupid, West is nevertheless a certified bimbo — her attraction is exclusively sexual, and though she talks a great game, her character is no farther than Harlow's from a cheap brothel. The difference was that West knew it,

and saw the whole slummy scenario of her life as both hilarious and fitting. I've seen the sad future of bimbohood, West was saying, and she
is me.

Like Harlow and Todd, Lombard died tragically young, and by this
time one may wonder if having hair the color of sunshine genuinely ups
one's chances of buying the farm before you're 35. (Other contestants
in the sweepstakes: failed starlet/infamous HOLLYWOODLAND sign
jumper Peg Entwhistle, dead at the foot of the last "D" in 1933, and
grade B starlet-turned-posthumous gay icon Carole Landis, ODed in
1948.) It's a syndrome that saw its culmination in Marilyn Monroe,
Blondedom's greatest martyr. It's a short leap from the mountainside
Lombard's plane slammed into to the America that glimpsed Marilyn in
All About Eve and decided to worship her ivory emptiness until, like a
true sleeping beauty, she escaped from their gaze into neverending
slumber. In between were bright-eyed sexpot Betty Grable (such a
wholesome girl, if it weren't for that here's-my-ass pinup and the oceans
of GI spunk expended in its honor), lazy barroom tootsie Veronica Lake
and glossy girltoy Lana Turner, who may have possessed the Blondest
personality the movies have ever known. Hitchcock maidens Tippi
Hedren, Kim Novak and Grace Kelly demanded attention for a brief period, with varying success. But it was Marilyn who sanctified the Blonde
as an American archetype. She made bimbos, perhaps after the fact,
respectable; no one was ashamed to be a Marilynite, and yet no one
loved for her for the irony she didn't know from straight vodka. Forever
after bimbos received as much warm pity in pop culture as they did lust-
ful adoration. Her Blondeness was her halo and her destiny both. Her
myth, like Elvis' and James Dean's, may have been exactly what
America needed in the 50s — innocent, sexualized hubris chased right
into the nonsensical brick wall of movie star fame. She was most vivid in
photographs, in footage of her childishly singing "Happy Birthday" to
JFK, and in that skirt-over-the-subway-grate scene from *The Seven Year
Itch*; anything that smacked of gray matter — like acting — was significantly less interesting. Of course, the semi-seen movie of her real life
and death was the most vivid of all. Once she'd died, she embodied perfect Blondeness: a fantasy of pristine sexual satisfaction, forever young
and beautiful, curled up naked in linen sheets with one opalescent fore-

lock dangling over a cat-like eye.

You could tell it was an archetype, and would last as long as we do, once Marilyn's cartoonish doppelganger, Jayne Mansfield, emerged. Mansfield looked like Marilyn times five: a bushelful of bleached hair, fake eyelashes half a foot long, breasts the size of your head, and the voice of a cartoon kitten. Mansfield seemed factory-designed for sex; she was the grotesque, high-finned hot rod Lincoln to Monroe's sleek but demure Stingray. God knows what Mansfield was really like, because on-screen she's all artifice, a Robert Crumb sketch come to life. Whatever investment Monroe had in her own persona, Mansfield tripled the bet and let it ride.

Mansfield even went so far as to die young, too, not in a quiet, sedated slump but in a bloodcurdling, head-rolling car wreck. The atomic-chested hyperBlonde legacy trailed after her into the 60s, inching down into the mud with each passing incarnation: Mamie Van Doren, voluptuous star of numerous "Confidential" drive-in programmers and public exhibitionist even today, deep into her 60s; Lorna Maitland, who, in Russ Meyer's notorious *Lorna*, *Mudhoney* and *Mondo Topless*, redefined the scope of bimbo buxomness not only for Meyer's peculiar universe but for us all; the Gabor sisters, graduating quickly into middle-aged camp; and Barbie the Doll, whose wardrobe and lifestyle may have said Rodeo Drive, but whose proportions and vacant-eyed Blondeness said Skid Row. Of course, Barbie became a paradigm of barren sex appeal for generations of preadolescent girls, and was, ironically, the strongest indication to them that bimbohood is a state worth attaining. Most Marilyn imitators have been drag queens, but Barbie has helped spawn an entire nation of silicone-implanted, peroxided, buffed-out, thonged Aphrodites searching the safe-sex entertainment industry for wealthy husbands who won't mind the Harley Davidson logos tattooed on their shaved pubic mounds. Even from the mildest feminist perspective, her influence has not been healthy, and the Story of Blondeness runs a little deeper still, under the tide of feminist progress. Barbie's wholesale marketing of the bimbo ideal to the children of yesteryear inevitably raises a few questions today — as in, why in a world of Naomi Wolfs, Janet Renos and Tina Browns, did we buy and read Vanna White's autobiography by the millions? Why do we know anything about Pamela

Anderson's personal life? Why is there *TopModel*, period?

And make no mistake, Barbie lives on — check out your local Toys "R" Us, and you'll find an entire deep-deep pink aisle of Barbie accoutrements. There's no underestimating her clout in the culture; G.I. Joe, by comparison, was a lightweight. There wouldn't have been an Angie Dickinson or a Candice Bergen (both frosted, sexy tabula rasas in their youth) without her. Perhaps the actress who most closely resembled Barbie was Brigitte Bardot, down to the overteased hair, too-long legs and the dead eyes of a stuffed animal. (Bow, Harlow, Monroe, Bardot — you could write a song.) Bardot represented a new stage of sexual fantasy beyond even Mansfield — she wasn't physically exaggerated, but she was real, often nude and, most importantly, French. Bardot may have been the first bimbo you didn't feel even a little sorry for — there was no way she'd end up dead on a highway or in a hotel room with a bellyful of Percodans. She very often didn't even try to act, but merely posed, languishing nakedly in the sheets or gazing out through eyeliner like a giant, drugged cat. She wasn't smart — her sex was her power, it was all she had, and she may have been the first to realize it. You could never have her, but if you somehow could, there'd be nothing to talk about. There'd only be hay to make.

Imitators followed, of course: Monica Vitti, Anita Ekberg, Elke Sommer. Ursula Andress crawled out of the sea in *Dr. No*, with her huge forehead, garbled English and a puss that always seemed to be spoiling for a mud wrestle. She became Mrs. John Derek #1, paving a path of muscly cheekbones and sucked-in tummies for Linda Evans and Bo Derek to follow in turn. But the truest bimbos of the post-Bardot period were to be found on the tube. There was Barbara Eden on *I Dream of Jeannie*, whose bared midriff, hoisted boobs and subservient harem demeanor were closer to the archetypal image of sex slave than even movies usually dared to explore. Just as crude were the walking farmer's-daughter jokes of *Petticoat Junction*, the buckskin nympho Wrangler Jane in *F-Troop*, and all three of the mini-skirted Brady girls, bimbos in waiting. As the 70s pressed on, the prime-time Blonde became ubiquitous; just the most obvious were the all-hair-and-lip-gloss tag team of Farrah Fawcett-Majors and Cheryl Ladd in *Charlie's Angels*, both in their turn much more popular than their brunette co-stars; the stunning post-nuclear frontier of Blondeness as represented by Suzanne Somers in *Three's Company* (even Mamie Van Doren maintained a wisp more self-respect); and, later, the confounding mystery of Vanna White and the up-front warrior-woman physique of *WKRP in Cincinnati* star Loni Anderson, who actually played Jayne Mansfield in the TV movie *The Jayne Mansfield Story*, opposite Arnold Schwarzenegger, no less. The cosmic confluence of big hair, blind ambition and bottomless cleavage (and that's counting Arnold) was too much even for the hardiest bimbophile to take.

We should not overlook the role of the Blonde in the wonderful world of porn, which Marilyn Chambers revolutionized by virtue of sheer enthusiasm in *Behind the Green Door*. Of course, it's easy to be a brainless, bleached sex mink in porn — it's difficult to be much else with Ron Jeremy grinding away on top of you. To be convincingly ardent is the tough part, and Chambers mastered it by simply acting like a man; you never thought for a moment that she'd rather be doing something else. The Queen of Porn Blondes, however, was and still is for those with acute memories for utter sleaze, Traci Lords. Lords was, of course, underage for her entire adult film career (the scandal broke in 1986, after she'd turned 18), and so her adult oeuvre has been contraband ever since, but no one can be blamed for being fooled: featherheaded bitterness boiled out from behind her eyes, and few of her partners didn't seem intimidated. Lords had the scariest snarl in bimbo history. Her post-porn career, while remarkable, hardly lives up to her ravenous persona. By comparison, 80s porn superstar Savannah seemed too blank even to be bored with rote schtupping — passing thoughts have to be able to snag onto the brain like burrs to register, and you got the impression her cortex was Lucite-smooth. With Savannah, there was no need to imagine utterly brainless sex — there it was. Tattooed, peroxided to an exhausted frazzle and siliconed to the hilt, Savannah eventually blew her own brains out with a handgun after scratching her face in a fender-bender; you gotta wonder if sometimes movies, even porn movies, don't tell the gospel truth. No one mourned Marilyn-style for Savannah, though she may be the Saint Joan of bimbohood, the truest victim of her own Blondeness.

In the last 15 years, the Blonde has become a cultural institution,

warranting straight-faced press coverage and sociological consideration fit for a presidential caucus. Madonna has fashioned a hyperreal
career out of creating bimbo imagery for herself (including Monroe,
Novak and Bardot periods) that she craftily proceeds to deconstruct —
though by now we could all well wonder if the original bimbo shoe fits
the foot after all. Tippi Hedren's equally vacuous daughter Melanie
Griffith somehow graduated from nude-scene princess to respectable
leading lady, just as Kim Basinger hopscotched from deadeyed model to
Playboy nymph to movie star. Sharon Stone has enjoyed a Madonna-like
arc to her public life: she rose from the slimepit with one well-timed leg
spread, deconstructed in the press everything that made her famous,
and then, with her subsequent film roles, seemingly became aware that
she hadn't actually come that far at all. In real life, Blonde bimbos
reared their tawny, sheeny heads in a new and provocative context: as
scandal whores. Visions of Gary Hart schtupping Donna Rice ended his
presidential bid, Marla Maples (she and Barbie could be twins) wrecked
and rebuilt the Trump household, and, best of all, Gennifer Flowers, with
her roots glowering darkly at the press conference TV cameras,
announced she and Bill Clinton had been rutting like weasels for years.
She came forth, she said, for the national interest, but that was baloney
and everyone knew it. She came forth because she's a bimbo; if you
were the aging, bleached bed-trinket of the next president, what would
you do? To tie a huge, snow-white ribbon on the deal, Flowers (a Blonder,
more deliriously bimboish name I can't imagine) spread nude for
Penthouse, the soft focus working overtime, the soap suds conveniently hiding her middle-aged spread, the captions quoting her as saying "I
dare Hillary to bare her butt in any magazine. They don't have a page
that broad!" She might as well have written BIMBO on her ass, but we
didn't need clues to see her in the Jean Harlow role, yipping about being
the passed-over tramp, and waiting for her Gable to come to his senses.

He never would, and that's why he was elected not once but twice.
For all of that, perhaps nothing represents the new Bimbo Culture clear-
er than the celebrity of models. Whether they're blonde or brunette, the
phenomena itself is as Blonde as Savannah's split ends. Vanna White is
a Rhodes scholar by comparison. ("Well," she said once in an interview,
"you *do* have to know all the letters.") Elle MacPherson, Christy

Turlington, Kate Moss, ad infinitum: there are TV shows, magazines and books devoted to their personal lives, grooming habits and career moves; their desolate stares radiate from every media outlet available to us, cyberspace included. There's nowhere to hide — bimbos have reached a place of true eminence in our world, and they did it without compromising any of the marvelous hollowness that make them bimbos. The most vivid proof can be found in the bustier and bikini thong, respectively, of Anna Nicole Smith and Pamela Anderson. Both models first, skin magazine superstars second and multimedia lust objects last but not least, Smith and Anderson together have achieved a new level of respectability for bimbos everywhere, never for a moment mitigating their own beauty, voluptuousness or moral vacuum. The second coming of Mansfield (she was born, in fact, almost a year to the day after Mansfield's death), Smith even married a decrepit millionaire who died a few years later, after which she appeared on the Howard Stern Show sounding so drunk at 7:30 AM you could hear the whiskey boiling up in her throat, slurring every word. At the height of her notoriety, the waxen and curvaceous Anderson appeared in *Penthouse* performing fellatio on her new husband, Motley Crue drummer Tommy Lee. What might embarrass a normal human doesn't faze a bimbo queen. Both women are holograms of sexual need, projected fifty-feet tall against a neon web of advertising, skin mags and beauty worship. Neither is pitied or looked down upon by the masses, for whom they need only exist, and undress. Blondness has become a genuine commodity, and the bimbo a certifiable citizen. Harlow's dead-end universe of pantyless, drunken sex is long gone. Today, if Pamela Anderson wanted to run for president, I bet there'd be a few hundred thousand voters who'd think, why not. If she doesn't seem, well, *awake*, so what, neither did Reagan. At least with Anderson, there'd be no shortage of scandals.

(*Detour*, November 1995)

THE END OF NEW YORK, OR IS IT?

However over-anthologized and patronizing, Susan Sontag's "The Imagination of Disaster," flatly pegged what George Pal had known all along: that watching fantastic forces lay waste to a modern city is as much rank fun as we can have at the movies with the actors' clothes still on. Confining her primary argument to the Japanese rubber-suit epics of the original Godzilla heyday and the atomic-giant-bug cheesers of the 50s, Sontag's lordly ruminations have virtually nothing to do with sci-fi (there's no room in her liturgy for psycho/social staples like *Metropolis*, *Things to Come*, *Forbidden Planet*, et al.) and everything to do with pure disasters. Sometimes sci-fi but just as often pointless freeway pileups, disaster movies are nothing if not opportunities for us to see starkly what we fear in our bones might come as a result of our ceaseless progress and commerce. Should we build skyscrapers at all if they can be crumpled so easily by dinosaurs? It's the superstitious peasant in all of us wondering if too much knowledge and architectural ambition might be an affront to the gods.

We don't quake very readily at the sight of a small town mowed by a cyclone (*Twister*) or slagged by lava (*Dante's Peak*). But you fuck with a city, and you're fucking with the hopes and values of the culture. (You can't, after all, just get the neighbors together, *Witness*-style, to raise another UN building.) That's why barking-mad images of urban apocalypse make the dream police break out the riot gear: gargantuan tidal waves charging down a main artery, alien lasers blithely cutting iconic landmarks in half, GRMs (Giant Rubber Monsters) decimating moneyed neighborhoods with a massive sweep of tail, nuclear firewalls reducing entire midtowns to ash. Then there's the afters, the seductive, semi-animated matte paintings of the famous city's smoldering, half-standing skyline and, best of all, the post-Doomsday daydream of wandering alone in a megalopolis emptied of life. Rubbernecking at Ragnarok, we sweat only the big stuff, luxuriating in exactly how trifling our own deaths and taxes suddenly seem.

Sontag's right about one thing — movies' "sensual elaboration" of turmoil beats out fiction and art by a magma-slide. The 1998 summer slew of fortyplex calamities will only be measured in the long run by how convincingly they put our metropoli in jeopardy. But some cities are more sensual than others, and if you tally the urban centers that have been cinematically targeted for the atomic dustbin, New York rules. Where else should cosmic rack and ruin strike? London, never seeming quite ripe for full-on atomic holocaust, has only had a few buildings and buses trounced in *The Lost World* ('25), *The Giant Behemoth* ('59) and *Gorgo* (60). Similarly, Paris is a garden spot no self-respecting disaster would touch, the obliteration of the Eiffel Tower in 1923's *La Cite Foudroyee* notwithstanding. Plagued by nuclear ghosts, Tokyo would seem to have seen its fair share of cinematic assaults, but too many actually take place in the outskirts amid high-tension wires and old tile-roof temples. Chicago has weathered only the giant locust in *Beginning of the End* ('57), upping the ante on the genre's natural tendency toward Biblism. Philadelphia, no one's idea of a first strike zone, was barely identifiable under the ice age decay and roaming wildlife in *12 Monkeys* ('95). L.A. is no slouch, catching extraterrestrial hell in the transplanted *War of the Worlds* ('53), evacuated by plague in *The Omega Man* ('71), falling to pieces from beneath in *Earthquake* ('74 — there goes the Capitol Records building!), suffering hair-raising radioactive heat-death in *Terminator 2* ('91), and oceans of lava in *Volcano* ('96). But L.A. is at the same time too self-referential, devoid of resonant iconography (the HOLLYWOOD sign has always seemed on the verge of toppling over on its own), and finally somewhat suburban, and therefore not as distressingly vulnerable. And if it weren't for a few ostentatious public monuments, each scotched in *Earth vs. the Flying Saucers* ('56), *Mars Attacks!* ('96) and *Independence Day* ('96), D.C. wouldn't be worth a second look.

No question, Manhattan is ground zero if you're a massive, lurking cosmic or terrestrial force looking to generate the maximum frisson for your demolition dollar. Every culture has an end myth, and ours is Times Square flushed by a tsunami or crunched by a sauropod. (That Hollywood has secretly enjoyed watching New York burn, drown and die is undeniable, if chin-deep in irony given that in the wake of a real disaster — the last west coast earthquake — many of the studio barons have relocated eastward.) Probably the first movie to will Genesis-style mayhem upon Gotham was *Deluge* ('33), whose quaintly spectacular footage of the flooding of a model New York was reused later in *SOS Tidal Wave* ('38) and many serials since. Though not exactly lost, *Deluge* has gone virtually unseen, whereas the haphazard trashing of midtown perpetrated by *King Kong* ('33) is so primally familiar it's nearly a matter of recorded history — the then-brand new Empire State Building became forever afterward a locus of woe and awe, while Kong's decimation of the Third Avenue El has become, in many of our movie-soaked subconsciouses, at least, how the tracks actually disappeared. Comparatively, the 1976 Kong's conga 'round the World Trade Center shrivels in shame, leaving even fewer paradigmatic traces on our collective memory than, say, the thawed 'saur in 1953's *The Beast from 20,000 Fathoms*, who ruined not much more than a few dozen cars and a Coney Island rollercoaster on its way to extinction.

Meteorological disaster is another story: however graphic *Deep Impact* and *Armageddon* are about wasting an asphalt jungle or two (and the former is hair-raisingly graphic), their kneejerk use of goosey digital effects hardly measure up to the sprawling, grainy shots of a drowned New York, half-sunk ocean liners floating between the high-rises, in Pal's *When Worlds Collide* ('51), or the image of a blasted midtown skyline — the Empire State Building skeletonized — an aeon after atomic war in *Captive Women* ('52). The degraded quality of these matted images lends them a we-interrupt-this-program validity that computer-generated images, because they are so liquidly, clear and bruisingly ubiquitous, can never have. The experiences they provide are viscerally contradistinct: if today we are promised a propulsive theme park ride through Disaster Mountain, then we were stunned by a jittery glimpse of the earth's last on-location evening news report just before civilization signed off the air for good.

The desolation-row image-bank of impossibly barren, silent city streets stalked by the Last Man on Earth is particularly affecting, representing at the same time a manifestation of juvenile discontent — a scenario described by critic Philip Strick as "the disappearance of millions of one's fellow-men, leaving the advantage of their accomplishments unencumbered by the disadvantage of their presence." Adult phobia and childhood utopia both, it's a modern end-myth that generates its most monumental frisson from the Manhattan landscape. It's a principle of New York existence that *nothing* could actually empty the island of people except a genuine Armageddon, giving the images a circumstantial authenticity. A shotgun-carrying Harry Belafonte footing it through a chilly, unpeopled Times Square in *The World, the Flesh & the Devil* ('59) remains the archetype (how *did* they do it?), so much more phenomenally disastrous than Charlton Heston tooling around the barren streets of Santa Monica in *The Omega Man*, or the not-at-all-unusual shabbiness of wrecked Australian urbanity in *The Quiet Earth* ('85).

But the petrified scraps of old New York uncovered in *Planet of the Apes* ('68) and *Beneath the Planet of the Apes* ('70) cannot be matched for post-apoc heebie-jeebies, from the driftwood Statue of Liberty to the Public Library lions. Outside of the rather quixotic suggestion that Miss Liberty, especially her fragile right arm, is a great deal more resilient than we had thought, and the rest of the city's now-underground erections are a good deal less, the Apes movies are otherwise unique in their acute sense of geologic time, recognizing the sedimentary fact that to find St. Patrick's in the wasteland of the future, you're going to have to dig. (*Beneath* has an otherwise disorientating notion of plate tectonics, having frazzled chrononaut James Franciscus discover the remains of a non-existent underground Queensboro Plaza subway stop, Radio City Music Hall and the Stock Exchange all piled up in the same underground cavern.) Will James Cameron, if he ever ends up actually remaking the Apes saga, fathom that in thousands of atom-blasted years even his *Titanic* Oscars will be fossils?

But perhaps because Manhattan is in reality self-decimating, perpetually in the process of falling apart and being rebuilt, we masochistically find the sight of midtown being fireballed — portrayed with such uninhibited aggro in the galvanizing New York scene in *Independence Day* ('96), when the Empire State Building, as viewed down a fictional four-lane cross street, is blasted from the inside out, the resultant wave of flame tossing cars into the air like leaves — deathlessly alluring, a meditative release of self-loathing and wish-fulfillment, a testing of the doom waters. Look at it as the sociocultural equivalent of a schizophrenic teenager putting cigarettes out on her arm. The emotional currency of cataclysm is as old as star signs, but the exponential frenzy of our capitalist machinery gives the impulse a whole new tank of gas. The moral is as plain as the char-marks on Fifth Avenue concrete: the more we build, the more we have to lose when the Weird Sisters come to call.

(*The Village Voice*, May 19, 1998)

STRAIGHT TO HELL:
THE HIGHWAYS OF ALEX COX

Straddling the borderlands between surreal satire and social commentary, Brechtian disjunction and punk anarchy, Peter Brook and Johnny Rotten, Alex Cox is an authentic agent provocateur, the manic surveyor of a landscape marked by low-rent devastations: deserts (either natural, man-made or simply ideological), junkyards, atemporal urban Zones (in the Pynchonian sense) and proverbial back alleys of rabid authoritarianism, lunatic absurdism, hockey stick-wielding schoolgirls, cartoonish carnage, coffee-addicted gunslingers, highways littered with car crash detritus. You can read the mythopoeic collapse of civilization in the Cox oeuvre the same way you can chart the rise and fall of the Industrial Age with the real-life ghost factory towns and mountains of rusting debris left in its wake from Pittsburgh to Portland, America becoming in effect its own Century of Progress Museum. In *Sid & Nancy*, his best film, Cox's personalized wilderness is traveled in a purely psychosexual manner, while *Repo Man*, *Walker*, *Straight to Hell*, *Highway Patrolman* and the BBC version of Borges' *Death and the Compass*, taken together scan like a traveling roadshow through the jittery outskirts of an American proto-world After the Fall.

Still, the cliches of decimated Americana haven't been Cox's primary topos since *Repo Man*, which served both as obligatory novice work and arguably the most entertaining movie-movie to come out of the punk era. Rather, Cox has been more entranced by less powerful, and less suspect, territories as they weather the reverb from American culture shocks: Mexico, Nicaragua, McLaren-era London. (For a Brit, the bellicose repo underground of Cox's first film may have been conceived as an alternative territory, but, as we all learn sooner or later, the more underground you get, the more American things seem.) In fact, *Repo Man*'s Reagan-era razoring of popular culture constitutes Cox's first step toward fashioning his special brand of postmodern magical realism, a broadly comic sphere where people eat out of cans labeled FOOD and 19th-century colonialists make the cover of *Newsweek*. More than gags, Cox's satiric riffs define his films as both mutations of modern life and products of it, with as much of a stylistic stake in trash culture as a textual one. (Of no film is this more true than *Straight to Hell*, which comes dangerously close to becoming the trash it lampoons.) The hilarious mock-Peckinpah gore-poetry and shrill, Pythonesque gallows cackle running throughout *Walker* makes Cox, for me, the optimum director of choice for historical films. (He's reportedly written *Che Guevara* for Canal+.) For Cox, realism is decidedly moot — though, perhaps, to work under such an assumption is inherently more realistic, isn't it? The appearance of combat helicopters in *Walker* signals an historical impossibility as it becomes a cinematic imperative; in the country of the film's needs, arguing for historical fidelity is tantamount to extolling patriotism, to keeping faith with Manifest Destiny. If Cox's anachronisms seem sledgehammer heavy, it's because the stake he's pounding hasn't budged an inch since the actual Immortals took Nicaragua from its natives in 1855.

The rubber-room excesses of *Walker* were obviously not what Universal had in mind, so consequently Cox has spent years scrounging for funds and suffering project implosion (a co-writing credit, and WGA hassle, on Dennis Hopper's *Backtrack*, being booted after completing preproduction on *Let Him Have It*), as well as shooting the Iggy Pop/Deborah Harry video for the AIDS charity *Red, Hot + Blue*, and hosting BBC's independent showcase *Moviedrome* for seven years, where Cox has presented films like *The Honeymoon Killers, Diabolique, Kiss Me Deadly* and *The Big Silence*. Five years since his last finished film, Cox's *Highway Patrolman* (*La Patrullero*, debuting at Cannes '92), returns to the desert, but with a difference: the terrain is less comically metaphorical than tragicomically picaresque. What scans like realism at first blush is merely the plain clothes of Cox's savage god; working in a dusty, hyperventilating now, *Highway Patrolman* shrugs off overt surrealism for the deranged knotting of outlaw life into pockets of semi-surreal chaos. A cheap, Spanish-language Bildungsfilm furiously entangled in its own ethical netting (according to producer/screenwriter Lorenzo O'Brien, the film's modest budget was made available after *Straight to Hell* had a smash opening in Japan), Cox's movie adds significant totems to the mad bordergrounds of his earlier films. Most significantly, an Everyman representing if not exactly the best in us, then the most balanced of human aspects, something that couldn't be said for repo punk Otto, Sid Vicious or William Walker, all of whom lurked along the edges of sociopathy. At the outset, Pedro (Roberto Sosa), the young stripling of a career officer fresh out of the Academy, is sugar-sweet and squeaky-clean, an idealistic professional tyro of the sort we're used to seeing learn the ropes the hard way — indeed, he could be Harry Callahan's newest disposable partner. Plagued by a longing for his dismissive father's love, and a Manichean love for the law that is soon mangled beyond repair by his experiences on the job, Pedro is assigned to isolated stretches of Durango highway, and quickly adapts to the fluctuating morality of the Mexican road. Even so, his essential ordinariness makes him unfit for the job, and we're waiting for his implosion right from the start. (The script was true-to-life by the real Mexican patrol's standards, who thought an ex-patrolman had a hand in it.) Almost immediately Pedro finds himself accepting bribes from small businesspeople instead of stopping their livelihood dead by enforcing petty laws; in a rather Coxian flourish, his first true bribe, from a pig trucker with rotting cargo, is accompanied by the butchering of a diseased carcass by starving locals. Pedro subsequently gets piss-drunk, dallies with a local whore and staggers home to confront his crazed, knife-wielding wife, who is only placated from cutting her husband's throat by the wad of dirty cash he waves in her face.

It's part of the film's unpredictable charm that this claustrophobically-shot scene of connubial horror never defines Pedro's marriage, merely the worst moment of it. (Later scenes are, shockingly, quite tranquil.) As much as Cox's characters all entertain both kind and vicious tendencies, *Highway Patrolman*'s geography is pure road movie outland, the requisite American roadside attractions replaced by their more desolate Mexican brethren: children selling iguanas on the highway shoulder, Day of the Dead iconography, drug dealer's helicopters, dead pigs. The prehistoric mesas and outlying scrubwood divide *la patrullero*'s world even more sharply between civilization and primal violence, the endless two-lane highways running a thin edge of technocratic will through the cutthroat backcountry. Cox captures this in one brutal shot — a slow pan up the asphalt to a car wreck, the first sign of which we see is an entire severed leg lying in the road — and from therein lets Pedro's story do the talking.

Shot in protracted, handheld single takes, Cox's film appropriates the demi-doc ambience of Nick Gomez's *Laws of Gravity*, and the filmmaker's sinister urges toward the surreal find instead a home in the spirit world. Gunned down by a drunken driver, lying wounded and frustrated on the highway, Pedro is visited mysteriously by his estranged father, who begs him to give up his career. Unsurprisingly, once Pedro is recuperating at home, he finds out his father died the very hour Pedro lay prone on the highway bleeding. That the decidedly un-*Hamlet*-like ghost offers only bitter admonishments to its son comes as little surprise either, under the circumstances; rather more unsettling is Pedro's required visit to a psychiatrist's office, where at first the center of the room is filled with a skull-topped, Day-of-the-Dead shrine (actually a discarded miniature from a Mexican horror film), which quickly, via a simple jump cut, becomes a coffee table. This bizarre apparition is Cox's way of trafficking with ordinary Mexican mysticism while again testing the surface tension of the viewer's belief in realistic cinema, as when Werner Herzog, in *Where the Green Ants Dream*, deliberately didn't show the audience an Aboriginal totem that, if viewed by anyone, would reportedly end the world. Both instances are cinematic Gordian knots — what does "seeing" mean within each movie? How does a formal faith in paranormal myths affect the movie we're watching? How many realities are there?

Cox is alone in his ability to employ suprarational images to scathe social injustice, an agenda that might otherwise grow tiresome. Few films are as vicious in their attack of colonialism as *Walker* (who else would've dared to have Ed Harris grinningly snack on an organ meat yanked from a living Nicaraguan?), and *Highway Patrolman* is similarly anti-authoritarian while confessing the dead end helplessness of radical ideals. Fight the law, and the law always wins; however odd it may initially seem, Cox's tale of law enforcement is simply the same saga in another tongue. Pedro is far from an authority figure. He's a tool, the reluctant club of government, and he learns quickly he has much more in common with the people he's arresting than with his chief, his father, his governor or even his contemporaries on the force. After being reassigned to a shitty route for not writing enough tickets, being shot (endowing him with a permanent limp), and totaling his patrol car and having it replaced with a dilapidated heap, Pedro begins to come apart at the seams, finally exercising his authoritarian right of force on an insubordinative kid driver who turns out to be the Governor's son. "You fucked up," he's told by nearly everyone, and he knows it, but by this time he's thinking of everything but that rich brat he coldcocked.

The film hits a nightmarish crest in one late scene, when Pedro in his heap spots a suspicious truck speeding by during a routine stop, and radios ahead to Anibal, his best friend on the force. Moments later Anibal radios in a desperate SOS, and Pedro takes off to help him. Neither we nor Pedro can see Anibal, just hear him; as the gunfire rages on the other end of the radio, Pedro's panic mounts out of control until, fatefully, his car belches a cloud of black smoke and dies. Wired, exhausted and hysterical, Pedro grabs his gun, abandons his car and begins limping, torturously, up the highway. Cox follows him low to the ground, the soundtrack empty but for his hoarse panting, and this prolix tracking shot, embodying every forlorn road movie urge, every wounded ideal, every Sisyphean frustration with powers hurtling out of our control, is *Highway Patrolman*'s most expressive moment. The desperate limping seems to go on forever, leading Pedro eventually to Anibal's empty car and a trail of blood that leads, again, almost endlessly, into the brush where Anibal's gore-spattered corpse lies. The landscape and how it's crossed in this scene serves as an ideogram for *Highway Patrolman* as well as Cox's whole career (both on-screen and off), while at the same time being perhaps the most compassionate sequence he's ever shot.

Unlike more prosaic entries in its unlikely subgenre (*Electra Glide in Blue*, *The Border*), *Highway Patrolman* concludes with neither carpet nihilism nor redemptive happy ending, but with self-empowerment outside the boundaries of the law. Pedro ends up quitting the patrol when everyone least expects it, managing his in-laws' ranch and supporting the junkie whore he frequents throughout the film — in effect, unashamedly joining the common herd he'd previously been instructed to control.

On the other hand, as if manufactured by the right side of his brain as *Highway Patrolman* sprang from his left, Cox's one-hour BBC version of Borges' *Death and the Compass*, which aired in August '92 and shows no signs of surfacing stateside, is a return to the free-for-all irreverence of *Repo Man* and *Walker*, albeit lashed to Borges' self-consuming maze of a mini-plot. Cox's alterations to the classic story are few, although he clutters its passageways with a wealth of sardonic detail and berserk vaudevillian fantasias right out of Alfred Jarry: a madhouse police station where surgery is performed openly in the lobby, gun-toting harlequins, masked Mexican wrestlers playing poker, etc. Many of Cox's extrapolations have a superbly Borgesian flair, as when a witness describes the murderer as having "sharp features...no, not really sharp, sort of... nebulous." Also shot in Mexico, constructed of long unbroken traveling takes and populated by the usual suspects (including Peter Boyle, Roberto Sosa, longtime Cox affiliate Miguel Sandoval, and Christopher Eccleston, who Cox had cast in *Let Him Have It*), *Death and the Compass* free-associatively creates a political context for its central mystery and detective hero, Erik Lonnrot (Boyle): he's perceived as a shamanistic public leader who makes frequent TV appearances, wading through the rubble of a small nation torn by an unspecified civil disturbance. His antagonist, Red Scharlach, (a mere arch-criminal in Borges) is characterized here as an underground rebel leader whose TV broadcasts electronically obscure his face and voice. Lonnrot's unraveling of Borges' absurd Hasid-inspired murders creates its own menacing buzz, but Cox's mise-en-scene is something else: the handheld tour of the

Kafkaesque police station, punctuated by lulling announcements like "Police officers are reminded that the torture section must be kept tidy; use of the torture section is a privilege, not a right," is a wicked romp, while in other scenes Cox literally uses theatrical lighting on a single set to shoot both participants in a telephone call. The gates to Lonnrot's Picabian terminal beach, Triste-le-Roy, which in Borges swung open with a "laborious passivity," falls dead off its hinges for Cox. (And yet the politically incorrect Borgesian remark about Hasids literally performing human sacrifices is prefaced by Cox as being patently false.) The nutso milieu Cox erects around the story's framework is in outrageous contrast to Borges' dry, mock-academic prose, while seeming somehow more Borgesian than even Bertolucci's *La Strategia del Ragno*. "The world is a labyrinth," Borges says through Scharlach in the story, and Cox has made the labyrinth palpable; only Otto, escaping into the spaceship at the end of *Repo Man*, has found a way out. ("I know of one Greek labyrinth which is a single straight line," Lonnrot says moments before his execution, and it's the best definition of a movie I've ever heard.) *Highway Patrolman* and *Death and the Compass* share the same architecture — both are labyrinths whose centers, once discovered, simply stare abyss-like back at their captives.

(*Film Comment*, January – February 1994)

KIRBYOTICS: LIVE-ACTION CARTOONS

As children, when we first saw a lusty Tex Avery wolf's eyes explode out of his skull to the soundtrack blare of a car horn, it was like a window on the world we'd sensed was there but could never see had suddenly been thrown open. Cartoons, and their outlaw blood relatives comics, were better than drugs ever were because we could trust our senses even as human heads took the shape of frying pans and Bugs Bunny needed only to reach beyond the outskirts of the frame to find an anvil, a sledge, a banana cream pie. It's a landscape of raw human will, unfettered by morality or physics. If comics and cartoons have a ruling principle, it's the mandate of our most chaotic impulses, all the way from *Krazy Kat* to *Ren & Stimpy*. Fittingly, the relationship between cartoons/comics and actuality has always been antagonistic, even when considered outside the tiresome debate over whether juvenile minds have been warped by E.C. Comics, Wolverine or Beavis and Butt-head. Comics' stylized forms and eye-stretching compositions were devised to express motion where there wasn't any; frame by frame, they're restless metamovies that never stop trying to burst free into a continuous third dimension. Likewise, cartoons have always struggled, often deliriously, to bridge the imaginative gap between what we feel and what live-action movies can ordinarily show us. Both are Fudd-like, as it were, in their blind determination to stand in mid-air over a yawning chasm of visual possibility.

Perhaps this is why, as a source of trash culture recyclables, comics and cartoons have always been highly prized, though never quite so much as now: following major studio releases like *Dennis the Menace*, *The Flintstones*, *The Mask*, *The Crow*, *The Shadow*, *Timecop*, *Richie Rich*, *Tank Girl*, *Judge Dredd*, the ongoing Addams Family and Batman sagas, *Mortal Kombat*, *Casper*, *The Phantom*, *101 Dalmations*, *Mars Attacks!*, *George of the Jungle*, *Spawn*, etc., live-action transcriptions of 2-D have become a Hollywood phenomena. Struggling to emerge from preproduction are film versions of *Catwoman*, *Black Panther*, *Spiderman*, *Dr. Octopus*, *Prince Valiant*, *Speed Racer* and *Sgt. Rock*; flesh-and-blood versions of *Daredevil*, *Magilla Gorilla*, *Betty Boop* and *Green Lantern* cannot be far behind.

Familiar and unexamined both, it's an odd meeting of medias, one that goes as far back as *Ella Cinders* (1922). Purloining the flotsam of daily comic strips, periodic comic books or intentionally ephemeral cartoon shorts is a time-honored tradition for the concept-hungry movie industry. For the bulk of the century, live-action comics were adaptable fodder for cheap programmers — *Joe Palooka*, *Gasoline Alley*, *Blondie*, *Barney Google*, *Ace Drummond*, *Little Iodine* — and even cheaper serials: *Dick Tracy*, *Red Ryder*, *Flash Gordon*, *Chandu*, *The Phantom*, *Terry & the Pirates*, *Tailspin Tommy*, *Superman*, *Captain Marvel* et al. Live-action comic movies were for the most part too constricted by budget and time to even attempt recreating the comics' dense, propulsive mise-en-scene. Today, the impulse to fondly resurrect and reinvent the childhood hours wasted reading *Silver Surfer* and watching Bullwinkle reruns runs to the looney tune of $50-70 million a pop; whereas Hollywood could previously afford to make 28 *Blondie* films (sometimes four in one year), in the 90s one *Flintstones*, with its avalanche of merchandising tie-ins, could nearly make or break a studio all by itself.

More vitally, hyperbolic comic/cartoon imagery is an established movie aesthetic today — a berserk kind of ironic pop-art expressionism we could call Kirbyotics (or Texism, or Herrimantics, depending on who you consider to be the Delacroix of graphic storytelling). Back in the days of *Blackhawk* and *Congo Bill*, a nylon costume and a few undressed backlots were enough. Today, the crux of all 3-D cartoon movies is the manner by which they appropriate the Caligarian intensity of comic/cartoon visuals. Because the armor-plated, turbo-charged panels of a Jack Kirby or Steve Ditko comic, or the protean physical madness of a Tex Avery cartoon, can only be approximated with actors and real settings, the resulting gestalt becomes entangled in formal incongruities and often plummets right down the rabbit hole. Via extravagant lighting, clownshow-bright color schemes, aggressively unreal decors, models that hardly try to disguise their model-ness, and make-up designs meant, in effect, to look drawn, recent movies have struggled back across the dimensional equator that comics and cartoons have always tried to breach by their very nature. The irony in this transmedia do-si-do is obvious, but what's rarely considered is the universe that live-action cartoon movies engender, and how its laws are rooted in the incongruity of stepping stylistically back toward handrawn art. This way lies madness, of course, but their schizophrenic frisson makes films from *Popeye* to *The Mask* and *Mars Attacks!* fascinating in ways normal movies, or comics, can never be.

2-D pop culture is a world of both desolate and chaotic landscapes, where art styles (Arcimboldo, Rousseau, De Chirico, pop, op, surrealism, futurism, cubism, etc., etc.) are simultaneously amplified out of control and folded into the batter, where they are often found again and reconstituted as art (witness Roy Lichtenstein's Ben Day-dotted, comic panel versions of classical paintings). Whereas on one hand you could characterize cartoon stylistics as graphic compensation for a lost dimension, on the other you could acknowledge that flatness can be the form's trump card: the illusion of depth can be manipulated or discarded altogether, the suspension of movement becomes a compositional modus operandi, raw shape and texture take on a primal significance. Settings can vanish in the whorl of the moment, or warp in accordance with the protagonist's worldview, all without camera tricks or in any way jarring the viewer/reader from his narrative trance. After all, drawn two-dimensionality implies the whims of an artist just as cinema implies the intractability of photographed "reality." It's this ripple in the continuum that distinguishes the 3-D foray into the 2-D territories. The rainbow colors, acute angles and Basil Wolverton freakishness of Warren Beatty's *Dick Tracy* bear no logical relation to the film's narrative or worldview, which is essentially kiddie noir. Rather, the film's changeling visuals are meant only to invoke, outside the context of the film's self-knowledge, the simple, pop-cult beauty of the Chester Gould strip, and 2-D-ness in general. Taken literally, the vivid, dreamlike designs and mutant villains (especially William Forsythe's Flattop) are free-floating concepts, disoriented from either realism or the bare-bones resourcefulness of tabloid comics. The stylizations of noir, say, or musicals, create an unreal universe reflective of its characters' inner life; in the live-action cartoon, the films' characters are oblivious, and the inner life reflected really belongs to us, a collective inner life hypnotized by and tripping out on the maximized junk phantasia of two-way wrist radios, Batmobiles and Acme Atomic Bombs.

Though most pre-80s examples of the genre ignored style altogether, there were pioneering, albeit campily dated, efforts: the 1966 *Batman*, and its accompanying TV series, punched up its pre-postmod genre satire with lurid lighting, camera tilts and on-screen exclamations ("KA-POW!"), while Roger Vadim's version of Jean-Claude Forest's sketchy *Barbarella* played like a Haight-Ashbury Halloween party, complete with play-acting, glitter drag and let's-put-on-a-show set clutter. But it wasn't until Robert Altman's *Popeye* (1980) that the phantom tollbooth between comics and flesh-and-bone saw any real traffic. (Precedents, such as the expensive *Superman*, and cheap made-for-TV takes on *Captain America*, *The Hulk*, *Wonder Woman* and *Spiderman*, were relatively prosaic.) So thoroughly incongruous is *Popeye*'s universe — as if it had been halted midway through metamorphosing from solidity to eccentric caricature — that anyone unfamiliar with the original cartoons would find it utterly incomprehensible. Bringing a Max Fleischer scenario to life is unquestionably daring; not significantly retooling it, so it makes sense in three dimensions and with living actors, is almost Dada in its denial of aesthetic integrity. Robin Williams is Popeye with one eye unexplainably squinted shut, and with huge, foam-rubber forearms that look tumorous; the landscape around him is equal parts Boys Own bric-a-brac and jolly-roger jungle gym. The idiosyncratic aura of Popeye's milieu, which worked in the comic strip and cartoons, hardly "works" here because its raison d'être exists far outside of the film experience. This is hardly a new predicament in a world of neo-neo-noirs and instant decade revivalism; Altman's film simply places it front and center. Far from the film's governing flaw, the disjunctive ontology of *Popeye* is its most beguiling feature. Somewhere in the co-opted chaos you can see the melancholy rituals of pop culture run like clockwork, and hear their songs of desire for a world better, and simpler, than the one we've got — one where Olive Oyl is the prettiest girl in town, and where spinach will make us strong.

In their transmutation into 3-D environments, fundamental texts like *Popeye* can acquire the mystery of glyphs. But while Altman's film seems surreal and poignant, the similarly esoteric 3-D world of *The Flintstones* is merely counterfeit cartoon, aping its relatively jejune source's most popular tropes ("Cha-a-a-arge it!") and remaining ignorant of what makes either cartoons or live-action movies similar and discordant both. *The Flintstones* is too nakedly engineered for culture sponging to display anything but a deep ignorance of cartoons, movies and the void between them. What finally differentiates *Popeye* from *The Flintstones* is that its failure is one of desiderata, not greed.

It can be rather Gordian as textual knots go, and, unsurprisingly, most films' attempts at confronting the vision of their graphic source material have been half-hearted: *Conan the Barbarian* and *Brenda Starr* make few concessions but nevertheless achieve a degree of synthesis via fortuitous casting. Like *The Incredible Hulk*'s Lou Ferrigno, Arnold Schwarzenegger and Brooke Shields are both ideally two-dimensional and physically grandiloquent as comic characters come to life — the Kirby-like Schwarzenegger is actually quite a bit more cartoonish than artist Barry Smith's gritty Conan. *Howard the Duck* and *Teenage Mutant Ninja Turtles*, both based on semi-subversive underground comics, crashed and burned by inserting obvious animatronic creatures into otherwise ordinary milieus — in comics, *everything* is real, and of a piece. *Sheena*, *The Rocketeer*, *Swamp Thing*, *The Punisher* and *The Fantastic Four* have only their ad art to recommend them; Stephen King and George Romero's *Creepshow*, while not based on an extant comic, went so far in adopting comics' formal outfitting that one might reconsider calling it a movie (not a problem with the dull E.C. retreads of

Amicus' *Tales from the Crypt* or *Vault of Horror*).

Tim Burton's *Batman* and *Batman Returns* established, for all intents and purposes, the 2-D-into-3-D paradigm for some time to come, and he did it without leavening the artifice with an overdose of winking irony — although Jack Nicholson's conspicuously Jack-like Joker does often crash out of the movie's macrocosm and into our laps. Burton's films, like *The Crow*, erects a fully integrated urban nightmare in which Dr. Mabuse himself would have felt perfectly at home, where it is always night and heroes and criminals alike are so tortured by bitterness and hate they're edged into nocturnal sociopathy and fetishism. It's no mistake that a large part of both *Batman* movies takes place on the roofs and in the sewers of Gotham City, and even the ghoulish mutant pathology of the Penguin is believable given his history and habitat. Less effort is spent trying to replicate the iconography of the comics — Danny DeVito's sleazoid Penguin is hardly the monocled, top-hatted gadfly the 2-D Batman originally battled, while Catwoman and Batman are both dark angels with far messier psyches than their drawn counterparts — than reconceive it all within a context that's simultaneously fantastic, crowded with childhood fears and scrupulously adult-directed. One needn't know the comic books, or wax nostalgic for them, to grasp the chill and dark disquietude of Burton's cityscape. Among their other triumphs, and despite their narrative clodishness, the *Batman* films' German Expressionistic schema proved the viability, formally and economically, of big-budget Hollywood films indulging in visual stylization and creating their own hermetic cosmos. Joel Schumacher's *Batman Forever* and *Batman and Robin*, however less inspired visually than Burton's films and however dependent on the elastic presence of Jim Carrey (a man whose genre has truly come) or mountainous glares of Schwarzenegger, proves that the strategy will outlive Burton's interest in it as long as scene-stealing villains are available. (My choice: Jeremy Irons as the Bookworm.) A close cousin graphically and narratively, *The Crow* takes the Langian bitterness several steps further into monochromatic rack and ruin, approximating the arcing perspectives of comic visuals by ceaselessly scanning the alleys and pinnacles of its proto-Gothic city miniatures as no film has done since the 1930 mystery *The Bat Whispers*.

Perhaps merely a measure of respect for the 2-D mediums is required, and respect for Bob Kane's (and Frank Miller's) Batman is admittedly easier to come by than for late Hanna-Barbera. After a century of cinema, cartoon environments have become a way of life, and cannot be underestimated. After all, the predominant cultural persona of 20th Century America is a cartoon rodent's (Mickey, not, alas, Bugs), and his passage into hyperreality was as easy as building DisneyLand/World, autonomous city-states we can only visit and where native citizens Mickey, Goofy, Donald et al. roam freely. The country of Disney even has its own high-flying Union Jack, a silhouetted Mickey on a white field. What could be more of a live-action cartoon? The baroque, shadowless, faerie grotesquerie of Disney World's architecture, structural and otherwise, is as close to an ideological 2-D secret garden as we may ever have. Strolling through its faux byways, it seems to lack the mysteries of a 3-D world, and yet the apparent lack of depth comes to seem the greatest mystery of all. Hitchcock, had he lived forever, would've certainly wanted to set a thriller within Disney World's (or EuroDisney's) deranged perimeter; that the city elders would've forbade such a tourist-tapering project further indicates a certain nationalistic sanctity, motivated as much by the idolatry of the cartoon ideal as by money. It may not seem as crackpot as the Toontown of *Who Framed Roger Rabbit*, but because it's real, it's stranger still.

Who Framed Roger Rabbit itself, though originating not with an existing cartoon or comic but a novel, owes more than any film to the current of cartoon life. Here, the mixture of the depthless and the deep co-exist without cross pollination, a touchy situation reflected in the ghettoized nature of Toontown. The film's proposition — a parallel world in which cartoon characters are a real race relegated to particular social roles and their own Chinatown, otherwise mixing uncomfortably with a noirishly stylized human society — becomes a hall of mirrors once we see Mickey, Bugs, Betty Boop and Koko the Clown all as Toontown denizens. The talent-duel between Donald and Daffy Ducks is more than just a coalescence of opposing matinee memories: it cordons off an imaginative territory for them more chaotically democratic than Disney World, and ratifies their germaneness in the cultural forebrain. If they can't come to us (that is, become 3-D), we'll go to Toontown, and meet them on their own terms.

It's a concept filled with genuine affection, but *Who Framed Roger Rabbit* also straddles possibly the most disquieting domain between the two realms — the tooning of the body. Somewhere between the flat, exaggerated, endlessly malleable figure of a cartoon specimen and the breathing physique of an actor (even Arnold) lies an undeniable anxiety the prosthetic forearms of *Popeye* only barely suggested. The dynamic freedom of 2-D systems represents a kind of wishful thinking, and it would be a peril to our collective sanity if the fearless cruelty of a Daffy Duck cartoon entered our world or ourselves. When Christopher Lloyd's black-robed ur-villain peels himself off the floor after being bulldozed, reinflates himself with helium and takes off his hand to reveal a looming, hand-drawn buzzsaw, it's a profoundly befuddling sight — we're getting what we wanted, and at the same time realizing we were wrong, please send him back to Toontown before it's too late. Call it depth supremacy if you will, but although Toontown is a sly comment on socialized racism, it's as necessary as a leper colony. Throughout *Roger Rabbit*'s climactic scene Lloyd's blood-red eyes fibrillate and bulge in a lurid animated whorl, and especially for kids, who have seen eyes like his a zillion times before in pure cartoons, the effect can be outright terrifying. The impulse to ghettoize is, under the circumstances, understandable.

In this sense, *Roger Rabbit*'s finale is to *The Mask* and *Casper* what *Steamboat Willie* was to *Pinocchio*. What was suggested by Lloyd's seething cartoon body parts becomes wholesale bedlam in *The Mask*. Thanks to computer animation, Jim Carrey explodes like a big bad Avery wolf but in three solid dimensions: his eyes fly out of their sockets like solid glass fastballs, his lusty heart bursts out of his chest and nearly tears his shirt open, etc. In *Casper*, based on the utterly guileless Harvey comic and TV series, and which does in fact boast "more" visual effects than any movie ever made, the ghosts themselves are 3-D and transparent both, and capable of anything; computerized and bursting with cartoon hubris, they retain as much visual integrity as co-stars Cathy Moriarty or Eric Idle. One of the film's cleverest subtexts is the very characterization of ghosts as cartoon-like beings — when Moriarty and Bill Pullman pass beyond the veil, their animated spirits are "drawn" caricatures of their fleshy selves. We even get to see the live boy Casper once was, and he's real — that is, uncartoonish. More subtly than *The Mask*'s MacGuffinish artifact, this simple metaphysical observation rationalizes *Casper*'s entire universe. No more incongruities: given a rationale and a raw moment of state-of-the-art F/X, we have no reason not to believe our eyes.

Now, if someone decides that Bruce Willis should run out of the film's frame and past the sprocket holes, or Meg Ryan should get sucked into a vacuum cleaner, there's no holding them back. There's little remaining reason why Silver Surfer or the Road Runner or Pogo cannot be perfectly realized as live movie phenomena. Finally, with the troublesome yet undeniably hellzapoppin potentialities of digital imagery, the dementia of 2-D art has genuinely entered the third dimension, and anything is possible. Except, perhaps, the certainty of realism and the continuing segregation of cartoon imagery from cinema as a whole. The gates of Toontown are now open. Finally, and forever, the creatures are free.

(*Sight & Sound*, July 1995)

OUT OF THE NURSERY, INTO THE NIGHT:
FILM BLANC

If so compelled, you may search for Shakespeare amid the incandescent ignis fatuus and silvery costume-shop foofaraw of Max Reinhardt and William Dieterle's long-ignored *A Midsummer Night's Dream* ('35) at your own dubious expense. Whatever is Shakespearean in this odds-bodkins Hollywood capriccio (outside of a few early German silents, theatrical legendmaker Reinhardt's sole contribution to the medium) is not at all what makes it unique and indelible. That would be the simultaneously chintzy and cosmic visions of dancing faerie children ascending a circular stairway of mist (roping around a giant elm) straight into the Milky Way, of goblins parading through the moonlit birches, of forest flora shot through glittered silk and haloed by soft-focus starbursts, of a satyr carrying a swooning sprite into the night sky and submerging into it as if into a lake of oil, only her arms left swaying amid the stars. Who misses the text (cut by half, at least) that isn't there? Many times more seductive than Edwardian comedy or iambic pentameter, this imagery seems simultaneously freshly born and incalculably antiquated, like our memories of ourselves as children — were we ever that young?, and where, precisely, did all that time go?

A golden-era freak that may be the most particularly designed film since *The Cabinet of Dr. Caligari*, *A Midsummer Night's Dream* represents merely the most thoroughgoingly zealous incarnation of a cultural tradition embodied not only in movies, but in faerie tales, nursery rhymes, painting, children's books, garden walks, distracted Victorian imaginings, daydreams, stories our grandparents read by oilight long after bedtime. The secrets of this style, of why it is so mysteriously hypnotic and entrancing, particularly in movies, may rest more directly with our sublimated desires as a society in this century than does any other; if this has been the century of cinema, then films like Reinhardt's and Dieterle's are its manifest dream-work. Indeed, the moving transgression of the veil between spirit and flesh, artifice and reason, in films from Méliès' *Le Voyage a Travers L'Impossible* ('04) to 1995's *A Little Princess*, remains a ravishing and eloquent allegory of the experiential flux between film and reality. When the disjoined lovers of *Peter Ibbetson* ('35) meet in the misty meadows of their dreams, they are escaping into an expressly cinematic realm, and even *The Wizard of Oz* ('39) knew the difference between staying home in stormy old Kansas and going to the Oz movie palace for a Technicolor matinee. But reflexivity is merely the vehicle, while the manifestation and reacquisition of a child's worldview is the cargo. Because it's childlike and asks us to be that as well, this is a heretofore uncategorized film genre defined in its stories and often purposefully archaic style by the sacredness of possibility, or rather the meaninglessness of impossibility, the prepubescent sense that if we can imagine it, it will happen, that love and innocence and truth can transcend time and space and death. Children will talk with stars, melancholic snow will suddenly fall in empathy for a doomed woman, lovelorn ghosts will haunt the storm-battered moors, the barren clipper headed for rocks, the shadowy Central Park bench. There are orphanages shaped like castles, castles shaped like dozing men, cities like forests and forests like mazes only an answered wish can rescue you from. Sometimes there are only paper moons and toadstool rings, and the vine-enrobed columns may be, and perhaps should be, painted on the nursery wall, the wildwood's oaks made of cardboard, and the distant ramparts built of toy blocks. Trying to distinguish between dreams and verity is like telling between twilight and morningbreak by measuring the length of your shadow.

Call them "romances" (in the 14th century, Pearl Poet sense), child-ly film, romanticist films, nursery films, *film enchante, film argente* (since it could be argued that *A Midsummer Night's Dream* and *Peter Ibbetson* are the penultimate expressions of silver nitrate splendor), or, why not, *film blanc*, since if film noir is typified by its lack of light and hope, then *film blanc* can be characterized by its starlight, reflection and metaphysical luster. (A garbage-can moniker like "fantasy" is wholly inadequate, encompassing everything from *The Thief of Baghdad* to *Splash* to any film involving a superhero.) Simply defined, the nursery film as we know it is a product of the contemporary popular imagination as it waxes upon and moons over its own extraordinary childhood: 19th century romanticism and the accompanying emergence of children's mass culture. (The notion of childhood as a freestanding life phase deserving of its own rights, media and exemptions was, of course, a cru-cial Victorian creation.) For the most part Anglo-Saxon and set either in the 1800s or in a present thrumming with spiritual nostalgia for the old century, these films are like ghost images of a premodernist, pre-WWI sensibility we long for and idealize just as we might our dimly remem-bered preadolescent selves.

At the same time, Victorian morality is all but ignored. Blithely meta-physical, these films commix the Christian, Freudian, mythic, transcen-dental, pagan and occult however they see fit (try to unsnarl the other-wordly dynamic within Walter Lang's *The Blue Bird* ('40) or Wenders' *Wings of Desire* ('88)), although often they fabricate their holy systems from scratch, reinventing the dynamics of natural/supernatural exis-tence as they go, and freely engaging in flabbergasting storybook absurdism as randomly as trees dropping their apples. At their most fervent, nursery films' visual essence incorporates equal parts celestial awe, theatrical chintz, sorcerous iconography and a kind of exquisite toychest expressionism, a dizzy, unironic confluence of heavenly visi-tors, flying trains, Yorkshire glades, painted planets and shamelessly transparent and therefore strangely ravishing optical flimflam. *A Midsummer Night's Dream* is nothing if not a masterpiece of obviously affected kitsch so doped up on celestial tchotchke-ism that the will to irony is buried under the deluge of all-trusting, starry-eyed optimism.

It's a sensibility that runs from Méliès (especially 1907's *L'Eclipse du Soleil en Pleine Lune*) and Biograph fantasias a la *The Golden Beetle* ('07) through to Enyedi's *My Twentieth Century* ('88) and beyond; Clair, Vigo, Borzage, Cocteau, Demy, Gilliam and Maddin all made their critical fortunes variously trafficking in the *film blanc* aesthetic, and any version at all of *Alice in Wonderland, The Secret Garden, Baron Munchausen* and L. Frank Baum's Oz stories, including (or especially) his own aeruginous whoppers *His Majesty, the Scarecrow of Oz* ('14) and *The Magic Cloak of Oz* ('15), can be considered genre cornerstones. There are scores more, some of which qualify simply by glimmering occasionally with stylized Victorian imagery, i.e. *History Is Made at Night* ('37), *The Night of the Hunter* ('55), *Bram Stoker's Dracula* ('92), etc.; some of which prosaically traffic in romantic spiritualism, i.e. *Here Comes Mr. Jordan* ('41), *The Ghost and Mrs. Muir* ('47), *Portrait of Jennie* ('48), etc.; some which chronicle the faerie-tale aesthetic's lyrical crossbreeding with the substance and anxieties of industrialization (*A Nous la Liberté* ('31), *Brazil* ('85)), an embracing of a struggle otherwise often expressed as horrified dystopianism. Sometimes, a mere visual whisper of Victorian toy-ness can salvage utter tommyrot: the lamentable Chris Elliott comedy *Cabin Boy* ('93) takes place wholly in an oilpaint-&-cardboard universe, while the recent *FairyTale: A True Story* ('97) is rescued from oblivion by the infrequent glisk of sprite-haunted countryside, candle-lit nursery and Lost Boy innocence.

You can virtually count the entirety of Victorian pop culture as the genre's antecedents, but the influences run back to various Celtic myth traditions and faerie lore, Mother Goose, Grimm, Spenser, Gainsborough and particularly the children's literature of Baum, Barrie, Carroll, Potter, Grahame, et al., and the illustrative art of Randolph Caldecott, Kate Greenaway, Arthur Rackham, Jessie Wilcox Smith, Edmund Dulac, Maxfield Parrish, et al. It was a visual and narrative aesthetic, however unformalized, that invaded the theater (where *Peter Pan*, a seminal pathmark that has yet to be filmed satisfactorily, first placed its stamp on the cultural template), bookmaking, advertising, interior design and, more or less permanently, our dreams. Like noir, *film blanc* has its roots in the peat of naturally occurring Euro-expressionism, and so the genre has always stood directly across the yard from gothic — the philosophical and stylistic difference between them is the Blakean difference between innocence and experience (wonder and menace, child and adult). Being a kind of nostalgic magical realism eternally exploring the dynamic of passion over materiality, *film blanc* also shares interfaces with the woman's film (Geoffrey O'Brien in *The Phantom Empire* inadvertently conjures up the former while describing the latter: "It was the end of religion, and the filmmakers must have almost known it as they crafted their humorous afterlives, their bumbling or bureaucratic angels. They designed a soft death for the children to enter without terror, a welcoming and interminable Oz."), as well as surrealism, miracle literature and Dickensian melodrama.

What distinguishes *film blanc* from its numerous nexuses and junctions is their distinctive juvenescence, their ceremony of innocence. To a child, a movie can literally be a heaven, and is no farther from her grasp for that; what happens in heaven — immortality, freedom from the reigns of space and time, union with the divine, reunion with loved ones — can happen in movies, and happens commonly in the nursery film, where the only criteria is the sweet will and enraptured flight of an innocent consciousness. Or the filmmakers' fabricated simulacra of such, of course, a scrim of ambiguous formal tension that may account for the genre's penchant for often spellbindingly affected visual humbuggery, a la the luminescent studio forestscapes of *A Midsummer Night's Dream* (in which a 4-year-old Kenneth Anger, quixotic dabbler in film enchante himself, played the Changeling), the crazed ramshackle artifice of *Babes in Toyland* ('34), the fake forests of *The Wizard of Oz*, *The Blue Bird* and *The Company of Wolves* ('84), the storytime tableaux of the river journey in *The Night of the Hunter*, the carefree use of paintings and etchings as scenery in Karel Zeman's *Baron Munchausen* ('61), and the enchanted junkyard set design of Guy Maddin. Compare this bewitching poppycock with the ostentatious concoctions of *The Dark Crystal* ('83), *The Neverending Story* ('84), and *Legend* ('86) — these triumphs of post-Tolkien gargantuanism fail to capture the charm of the genre precisely because of their expensive completeness, their dogged devotion to approximating a freestanding universe. The stardust-carpeted vistas of the Reinhardt/Dieterle film blaze so brightly with mysterious glamour *because* we are not compelled to believe them to be real but to be the flimsy, handmade and therefore beautiful walls of a dream.

Herein lies, too, a romance with antiquation — the moon is better painted onto the sky, and even better painted on so long ago that the gesso cracks deepen its smile. The further a film's style purports to be pretechnological — innocent, pre-cinematic — the more ambiguous and child-like the film becomes. It's hard to imagine *The Golden Beetle* or *A Midsummer Night's Dream* ever belonging to the contemporary moments they surely had, just as it is nearly impossible to place Maddin's furiously antiqued movies in any historical "now." (Twenty-five years from now, will the ironic absurdism of *Archangel* tarnish into an everlasting romanticism?) To a child the world begins with his or her first eye-opening, and every cultural artifact, every movie and story-book, belongs to an ancient foretime, be it the pre-Christian epoch of faerie lore or Shakespeare's day or 1935. (And in which does *A Midsummer Night's Dream* take place, exactly?) So, the inherent nostalgia and self-apparent handcraftiness of the genre directly reflects onto the life experience of children, as perceived by adults. But how does one articulate the aesthetic's unquestionable allure? How can I explain why I find the rendered plankboard futurisms of Méliès, the dreamishly fraudulent frond gardens of *Zoo in Budapest* ('33) the window-view of snow falling past the darkened painting of moorland in *Wuthering Heights* ('39), the haloed backyard dreamtime of *Curse of the Cat People* ('44), the aluminum foil knight's armor in Rohmer's *Perceval* ('78), the conversational stars swirling overhead in *My Twentieth Century*, so gorgeous, indeed, so lavishly mundane they border on the cosmic?

It may be that, at least for this century and for those of us who spend much our of time looking backward (as cinephiles must), the nursery film style is explicitly evocative of the raptures and sufferings of childhood, *our* childhood. The unrealistic visuals confirm our distance, reward our guilelessness, stylize our remembrance. Here, the child and the heavens are deceptively intimate, as if nothing of any great consequence could ever happen anywhere between them. But because it is a fantastic, idealized universe, *film blanc* might well suggest to us not what we've lost in our younger selves, but what we could never have at all, the safe, unfenced, fabulistic world we never knew, where death is meaningless, love is steadfast, brave children can master their own fate alone, and the caring and the cruel are always separate and recognizable. Buried not very deeply in these films is the raw knowledge that a child's life can be a masque of trauma and elation that would wither an adult. The plight of children as they, with such inadequate tools, attempt to survive under the oblivious wheels of the adult world is a titanic subject movies rarely tackle (*The 400 Blows, Empire of the Sun, Landscape in the Mist, Il Ladro di Bambini* and *Ponette* are a few notable exceptions); it constitutes emotional material so overwhelming and dangerous (especially for parents) that perhaps as a culture we require it to be sublimated into mythopoeia. Thus, the archetypal victimization scenarios of *Zero de Conduite, The Blue Bird, The Night of the Hunter* and *A Little Princess* are objectified into, respectively, magical anarchy, symbolist bedtime story, Caligari-esque morality tale, and anthemic, what-little-girls-are-made-of passion play.

For either children or adults, this mode can surely be characterized as "escapist," but perhaps only Stan Brakhage would argue anything except that movies are escapist by nature. Escapism is the taste and mouth-feel of the cinema we consume — it is why we consume it — and can be read as simply another word for a universal demi-religious and artistic impulse: sanctuary. (It's no coincidence that film blanc enjoyed its heyday during the Depression.) But is it very many doors down from the metaphoric lyricism of what we ordinarily (and profitlessly) consider "art film"? Take, for example, the gimcrack fairy-tale use of snow in *The Wizard of Oz, It's a Wonderful Life* ('46) (talk about cosmic — the implication stands that George Bailey's existence determines the weather), *Edward Scissorhands* ('88) and *A Little Princess* — is it such a commute from the poetic rapture imparted onto sudden snowfalls in Tarkovsky and Angelopoulos? Don't they possess the same generous, rhapsodic frisson, and inaugurate the same breath-holding enchantment? Why a common phenomena like snow should resonate with such mysterious import is another question; the genre's rampant symbology awaits a fixated semiotician. But the point remains that there's little ground lost between escaping and re-experiencing a sentience long lost to age. Understood as an emotional cultural project in fathoming and celebrating that most elusive and powerful of life periods, *film blanc* becomes a document of pure self-imagining, and a key to what Rimbaud called the magic study of our happiness.

Common Freudian symbolism notwithstanding, the unmappable, terrifying country of sexuality is itself converted into an abstracted, cosmic mystery, a romantic matter upon which angels and moons ponder, and which can, seemingly for mystic reasons all its own, penetrate the veil between life and death. It's not sex, not in any meaningful manner, that compels Cathy's ghost to return to Heathcliff or Jean the barge captain in *L'Atalante* ('34) to dive underwater looking for the dream-image of his lost wife — it's a lyrical sense that if a crucial emotional justice is not done, the stars themselves would start flickering out. It's the power of sex transmogrified into quaint, workaday grandeur by a consciousness that doesn't understand its banalities.

Movies, again by their nature, reduce us to the rapt, trusting attention of children, a universal impact that seems on the face of it to be the flip-side to the well-accepted critical notion of cinema as an exercise in sexual attention, a form of mass voyeurism. Or if it remains a sexualized gaze, then it is sex, perhaps, as it eventually comes to fulfill for us the cosmic longing we had as children, rather than an infantile impulse awaiting pubertal fulfillment. Perhaps religious faith and sexual gratification are what in time answer childhood's question, long after the truth we sought dangled neverendingly out of reach in a starry azure sky. In either case, movies return us to our first looking upward, and if the nursery film has any validity as a socioculturally reflective style, like noir, then it may be that this simple blast of cinematic consciousness is its primary theme. What is visualized, via the Victorian battery of icons, is the very distance between our present and our lost past, the tiresomely ironic now and the richly innocent then.

My own childhood experience may be typical, but like everyone's has acquired the personal nimbus of legend: the first film I ever remember seeing — I may have been four — was Wyler's *Wuthering Heights*, and for me it still holds a seminal position in the history of experience. Merle Oberon's round, softly Oriental face; the mysterious connotations attached to the word "gypsy"; Cathy's thunderstruck (and thoroughly enigmatic, for a kid) realization, "I *am* Heathcliff"; Heathcliff's deathbed pleading, "Do not leave me alone in this dark where I cannot find you";

Alfred Newman's melancholy score (which has the lamenting force of a death memory now); the final vision of the two lovers' ghosts walking away into the snowy matte painting — this somewhat prototypical and often ungraceful Classics Illustrated Hollywood movie burned and continues to burn like a comet in my life's self-regarding eye. Because it struck me young, I'll never get over it. Otherwise floating happily upon a sea of black-&-white reruns and trash culture as I grew, and dutifully digesting along the way the barbed roughage of alcoholic parents, my preadolescent 60s self further fed the fire by spending vast amounts of time wandering through the northeastern forests I was fortunate enough to be born within yards of. I lived so thoroughly and with such concentration in the woods that though I was a skeptical kid and declared my atheism long before secondary school, I could've, had I'd been adequately schooled in my Irish roots, believed wholeheartedly in trolls and wood sprites. If there seemed little difference between the movies and the forest then, it's because they both meant sanctuary, and both expressed my deeply private sense that the outside world as it spread itself out before me wasn't quite up to my aching hopes.

Of course, it isn't still. The seductive grip of this sanctuary as it occurs in *film blanc* — say, the glowing wilderness, Shetland unicorn and bridal veil made of spider webs in *A Midsummer Night's Dream* — can make me dizzy today. The genre remains as much a catalogue of *objets* as it is a narrative convention or visual style, and in that can often only be cherished, like an old-country totem or fading family photograph. Equally, it doesn't traffic in mere utopianism or anxiety, unlike many genres — like a vintage portrait of your grandfather standing on a lawn in his best Sunday suit, *film blanc* acknowledges the anxiety of time and loss, then cascades blissfully beyond it.

(*Film Comment*, November – December 1998)

TERRA PARANOIA: *AEON FLUX*

Twin Peaks, Wild Palms, The X Files, Nowhere Man, The Kingdom, Millennium, The Invaders, Aeon Flux, The Maxx, Sliders, The Burning Zone — television in the 90s has become a Pynchonian ground zero, where the anxious engines of alternate universes are fueled by an unshakable sense of technophobia, dislocation and powerlessness. It's as if healthy world views are instantly warped into paranoid qualm by the convex window of television itself, a rupturous notion in the commodity/consumer telescape not lost over a decade ago on David Cronenberg or Don DeLillo, as seen in *Videodrome* and *White Noise*. Is television finally recognizing itself in its own shivery reflection, queasily acknowledging its own instinct for control? Has the invasive intimations of cyberculture helped expose the true message of the medium — essentially, the frantic pursuit of individuation within inescapable patterns of force? Are we seeing television express even the crazed, invisible electronic reality of its own airwaves, transmissions and pickups?

MTV's *Aeon Flux* is the purest distillation of the new teleconsciousness, an utterly arcane, visually relentless, narratively hermetic vision of a superhero futureworld after the rain. Anyone who has happened on it while channel-dancing knows the suck of its vertiginous perspectives, the puzzling lure of its ambiguous nexuses. Shoplifting from every post-mod source imaginable, most notably *Metal Hurlant* comics, Japanimation, J.G. Ballard, Samuel R. Delaney and Cronenberg himself, series creator/director/story writer Peter Chung gluts his pioneering cartoon epic with so much strange, irrational *stuff* you can go ape-shit trying to keep it all collated. Which is not, apparently, one of our intended tasks — the furious contradictions and unexplained intercourses of *Aeon Flux* work like koans, and we're supposed to let the menacing enigmas flow over us like a red tide.

In its initial incarnation, as five-minute, no-dialogue bites of *Liquid Television*, *Aeon Flux* was pure terra incognita, introducing us to a barren, ocean-logged dystopia clogged with endless post-industrialization, constant and impregnable apocalyptic portent, hyper-viral infections and conspiracies, deranged sex, appalling mutations, and addictions that cross over Burroughs territory and into unspeakable waters. Espionage was its m.o., however undecipherable the relationships involved. Each episode was an island of pointless action, covert creeps and microscopic happenstance. Aeon herself, a spellbindingly all-powerful, supersexed action heroine reborn from old Drulliet/Moebius/ Caza comics by way of Egon Schiele (Chung's endless narrative corridor owes much to Moebius' *The Airtight Garage of Jerry Cornelius*), was just as much of a mystery: we rarely understood what she was seeking (or escaping from), and her alliances with other characters were endlessly mutable. Sometimes armies fell under her machine gun fire, sometimes she'd trip and fall to an undramatic death. Either way, with the next segment we'd be back to square one.

Graphically, *Aeon Flux* was and still is as sophisticated as anything on TV; the consistent, disarming excellence of the animation, especially once the series was upgraded to weekly half-hour segments, is a feat unto itself. Now, with dialogue, semi-recognizable motifs and reoccurring characters (though their significance and relatedness often change in mid-episode), Chung's funny car derby of colliding narrative clues seems at first blush more civilized, less haywire. Actually, *Aeon Flux* has come into its own in the extended format, deepening its enigmas as it imbues them with melancholy and wry satire. Politics are discussed, motivations are bared, but the grand scheme is no less ambiguous; even so, the storytelling is so brisk you're *sure* it can be deciphered, reorganized, linearized. Chung has referred to it as "psychodrama disguised as action adventure," but if so, the psyche involved is hardly Aeon's, or even Chung's — it is the visual text's, as it struggles against cohesion and cartwheels toward entropy. "Flux" indeed; every stainless steel cleft and damp body orifice can become a secret chamber for imprisoned enemies, habit-forming larvae, insidious mechanisms, you name it. Aeon has been cloned, betrayed, seduced, killed and born again. At one point, an artificially impregnated man (one of many dastardly, body-corrupting experiments performed for unclear and unsavory reasons) gives birth to a four-eyed infant god. At another, the torso of a kidnapped political figure is opened up and turned into a visceral hallway leading to a fetishized, Lynchian antechamber and, beyond that, to the Ernst-like edge of the world.

Whatever its other thematic claims — and they could be extensive — *Aeon Flux*'s primary issue is cinematic narrative itself; by utilizing complex narrative praxis but denying them any form of coalescence, Chung baits out into the light our thirst for connections, for principles of order. More than just a puzzle with no solution, the show is a nearly abstracted viewing experience, a living comic book whose pages have been jumbled, maimed by chance and lost in the wind. Like desperate cave-dwellers instinctively conjuring myths to explain the chaos of the night sky, we try to find morals, filiations, meanings in what is, finally, an act of pure seeing.

(*Film Comment*, January – February 1996)

IT'S OFF TO WORK WE GO:
LABOR IN MOVIES

Seen through the reality-bites lens of class economics, movies are largely the construct of Hollywood's ersatz aristocracy, born of ego, greed and the absurd cultural coin called showmanship. And it shows: from the beginning, stars and players have been regarded as Renaissance royalty, and the movies themselves, hoping to subsidize the myth and privilege of sovereignty, traffic in images of idle affluence. It's a paradigm endemic to Hollywood, to be sure, but inevitable wherever visual media has found a substantial audience. Dream machines manufactured for the great unwashed, movies — from *Gone With the Wind* to *My Best Friend's Wedding*, and *The Birth of a Nation* to *Titanic* — spend much of their screentime selling us real estate porn, thrilling us with the travails of the recumbent rich, dazzling us with demonstrations of leisure.

But even when films ostensibly address the non-wealthy majority, their characters seldom seem to have a job, or spend much time doing it. (In Hollywood terms, this would mean taking time off from the plot to make a living.) Think of the last film you saw in which somebody actually worked. Often, an off-camera trade like architect (*Fearless,*

Intersection, Til There Was You, etc.) or sculptor (*Before and After, The Juror, Stealing Beauty,* etc.) is offered as the source of wealth. When active professions are used in a movie's gearwork, they're used as heroic, fact-finding means-to-a-plot — lawyer, reporter, detective, psychiatrist. There are too many films to count that merely dawdle on criminals. Rarely does anyone *work.*

Work, as in labor, is the lost tongue of pop culture, the movies' single most overlooked aspect of human life. (What lawyers and cops do in movies isn't work, because real lawyer and cop work — waiting, negotiating, reading — is unwatchably dull.) Even the few films that allege to take on working-class subjects rarely spend any screentime showing us what it means to work. Rather, an atrocity like *Hoffa* illustrates its empathy for laborers by having them heave brickbats rather than actively engage in the livelihood they're fighting for. *Rob Roy* is ostensibly about farmer's rights, but no one does a stitch of farming. The setting of *Legends of the Fall* is a hard-working ranch on which no one ever goes to work. *Short Cuts, Nobody's Fool, Sling Blade* and *Brassed Off* all involve blue collar characters we never see do anything but kill time. In *Swing Shift, Norma Rae* and *Silkwood*, semi-skilled factory work — crucial to the stories of each movie — is reduced for the most part to breaks and off-time.

It's a crime, because work is an intrinsically spellbinding and profound cinematic act. Whenever someone is involved in concentrated, honest labor on film, it's as if the movie we're watching has suddenly become infused with the fiery juice of reality, a dynamic charge that no masquerading as a white-collar intellect or neurotic aristocrat can provide. (Of course, the visual representation of work is subject to finagling, a point made in Wajda's *Man of Marble* and *Man of Iron.*) Whether it be a dazzling skill or a mundane chore, work *happens,* in front of us and often in real time, and therefore carries the veracity of truth.

In John Turturro's *Mac,* the homilies about labor were stopped dead for half a minute by a bricklayer neatly, rhythmically laying bricks. *Jude* (contrast it to the luxuriously inert *Sense and Sensibility* and *The Portrait of a Lady*) casts an unblinking eye on working as a stonemason and upon laboriously slaughtering a pig for pork. *Germinal* spent serious attention on the actual toil of mining. Building a barn in *Witness,* growing tobacco in *Sommersby*, picking cotton in *Places in the Heart*, cleaning a medieval church organ in *Brother of Sleep* — in each instance, mediocrity blazed briefly with authenticity. *Like Water for Chocolate*, *Eat Drink Man Woman*, *Heavy* and *Big Night* all involve us in the praxis of cooking — in the last, the one-take sequence of Stanley Tucci simply scrambling and serving eggs is pure life-in-motion. (Was anything in *The Godfather Part III* as remotely enthralling as Andy Garcia teaching Sofia Coppola how to make gnocchi?) Robert M. Young's *Caught* glories in the proper cleaning of shad, and Benoit Jacquot's *A Single Girl* makes the rounds of a room service waitress hypnotic and suspenseful. Even the ridiculous technical craftwork of moviemaking — capturing and analyzing recorded sound in *Blow-Out*, laying down foley tracks in Albert Brooks's *Modern Romance* — exudes an enthralling buzz. In Victor Nunez's *Ulee's Gold*, the film's dry story often idles quietly as we breathlessly watch the hands-on business of beekeeping.

Of course, movie work has a forgotten history — a century's worth of industrial and training films that capture the process of labor in the objective manner of primary flickers like "Carmaux: Drawing Out the Coke" (1897), in which we can see French workers extracting a massive load of distilled coal coke. (Most early Lumiere, Edison and Biograph shorts, however, depict leisure, landscape and vaudeville — which is to say, little has changed since.) The Soviets made sure to balance their revolutionary agitprop with visions of serious mass labor, culminating in the eye-popping, step-by-step casting of the giant church bell in *Andrei Rublev*. (Like Antonioni and Bergman before him, Tarkovsky quickly lost any interest in working-class contexts.)

The Italian realists, for the most part, kept their promise to the peasant class, a tradition leading to the agrarian toil of Olmi's *The Tree of Wooden Clogs*. Robert Bresson knew the exact value, and spiritual import, of watching an act perfectly performed — see *A Man Escaped*. Zhang Yimou and Chen Kaige were, for a time, keenly aware of the work process (*Red Sorghum*, *Yellow Earth*) before settling for melodrama and stasis.

Many of the best labor-class films are testaments of crisis — Ken Loach and Mike Leigh both make films in which prole lives are left dangling in a post-industrial vacuum, where meaningful blue-collar work is an outmoded ideal and where new info-age anti-professions, formed wholly of communication, persuasion and appearance, are becoming the status quo. (Loach's *Land and Freedom*, though work-free, heeded the testimony of the peasant class like no English-language film since *Salt of the Earth*.) It's one of the great unspoken conflicts in movie culture: how to give expression to labor as a vital human reality in a century when labor itself is no longer a highly prized, reliably honorable or inherently essential enterprise. Films as disparate as *Taxi Driver*, *The Conversation*, *Repo Man*, *The Rapture* and *Do the Right Thing* all hum with the lost pain of irrelevant, unproductive, parasitic employment; the aimless horror and rueful wit of each film corresponds directly to its protagonist's ambivalent and hopeless relationship with the service-related and/or cruelly exploitive occupation he or she performs. So little of contemporary employment can be literally termed "work" that it's little wonder that films bothering to consider Noam Chomsky's "restless many" are seeing working-class lives as imbued with a fresh strain of nihilistic futility. Unsettling documents like *Safe*, *Lamerica* and *Trainspotting* can be seen as responses to the abject lack of authentic late-20th century work.

Perhaps the American century's romance with movies — which will tarry on non-laboring lifestyles for as long as audiences characterize movies as an "escape," meaning for the medium's lifetime and not one second sooner — is in part a struggle to adjust to the disappearance of work. What are we escaping, exactly, and why does it feel so much like emptiness?

(*The Village Voice*, July 8, 1997)

PETER JACKSON'S EARTHLY CREATURES

After a full century now, it's no wonder we're doped up on the torque of a life with movies: no other human creation ever has let us step through a window into the rag-and-bone-shop of others' hearts, has allowed us to *see* ancient Rome or Satan or a man shake hands with himself or change into a wolf and back again, has changed the government of our dreams and the manner by which we view the passage of our own lives. Perhaps most of all, movies are sensory dynamos, hurricanes of compressed experience. Whatever chaos there is in life there is in movies tenfold; the simplest, stupidest action movie can become sublime through the choreography of extraordinary commotion, and any argument against it is an argument against cinema. Formally, movies can make our perspectives their warped own in the passing of a frame, make nonsense of body tissue, space and time, use visual momentum itself as a bludgeon. Sometimes we are made to feel that we're choking on our own hearts, frozen on the dark brink of complete bedlam, and it's that taste of burnt nerves and raw pleasure that is one of movies' primal selves.

It's an excessive mind state, one predicated on vertiginous risk and the queasy comedy of catastrophe, and Peter Jackson has made it his own. Just as Busby Berkeley trucked in the utopian geometrics of success and love, Jackson contemplates in a similarly absurd fashion the texture of disaster, albeit on a personal level that in *Braindead* (titled *Dead Alive* in the U.S. thanks to a copyright tiff; Jackson considered calling it *Everlasting Rot*) exceeds and violates any notion of physical intimacy movies may still keep faith with. Hapless ruin, be it visualized as the gargantuan horror of *Akira*, the amusement park thrill machines of *T2*, *Speed* and *True Lies*, or the miniature mano a mano nightmares of *Tetsuo*, *Evil Dead II* and Jackson's films, has a seductive charm that suckles the sadist in all of us. (And this includes *Heavenly Creatures*, visually conceived as it is like a fever-dream, and constructed so intimately around the heroines' obsessions that we, too, begin to look forward to the liberation of bloodshed.) Make no mistake, it's a time-honored sensibility — the "sick joke" midnight between farce and savagery can be traced, *pace* pop cult maven David J. Skal, to Jacobean death jokes like Cyril Tourneur's *The Revenger's Tragedy* (1606). Of course, what makes Jackson stand alone in this killing field is hardly *Braindead*'s passionate devotion to out-helter-skeltering the competition; it's *Heavenly Creatures*, a masterpiece that simultaneously marks a quantum leap from the crude emotional syntax of zombie comedies, and expresses Jackson's topos even more eloquently. For Jackson's earlier films are freshmanic, take-no-prisoners taboo-busters, built for shock and speed, fueled by a very real and reckonable will to power and punkish hunger to usurp authority — they make trouble like a smart, bitter 16-year-old anarchist dizzy with his/her new sense of misunderstood self, of independence, of subversion and fearlessness. They're films the girls of *Heavenly Creatures*, in another time and perhaps gender, might've made themselves. Jackson simply transferred his furious instinct for Dada thumb-nosing onto his Christchurch teenagers. In this way, and especially regarding the matricidal imagery of Jackson's earlier work, *Heavenly Creatures* can be read as autobio, New Zealand punk style.

Jackson's first film, *Bad Taste* (1988), is a clumsy, cheap and sometimes hilarious shotgun wedding between an alien takeover film and a cannibal farce, and is notable for little beyond its intermittent Three Stooges riffs and seminal use of explosive birth/womb jokes. The type of movie that's often financed by the crew's frequent trips to the blood-bank, *Bad Taste* was actually shot over three years, and it looks it; still, Jackson's consistent fondness for fish-eye compositions, loopy land-scapes and biocombustability is unmistakably present. It's apprentice work, and indicative of where a subversive spirit can lead you if you haven't developed the legerdemain and style necessary to speed the profane imagery across the screen like bullets out of a hundred guns. From the first, *Bad Taste* quite apparently interfaced with the gory post-Stooge sensibility of Sam Raimi — Jackson's filthy blood-chuckles are the direct progeny of Raimi's first two *Evil Dead* movies, which simply carried the work of Herschel Gordon Lewis, Paul Morrissey, George Romero and Frank Henenlotter to its logical extreme. What Raimi intro-duced to the subsubgenre of body assault comedy was a breathless degree of formal dementia, often abandoning his stories altogether for giggly jags of jet-propelled visual fury. That, and his deep understanding of physical comedy (the outer limits of which are represented by, of course, Moe, Larry, Curly & Co.) and its proximity to pain. (Note that all Raimi movies, even *The Quick and the Dead*, have cast credits for one or more "Fake Shemps," homage to the decidedly un-Shemp-like dummies that often got hurled out windows in the aging Stooge's stead.) Comparisons between Raimi and Jackson are unavoidable; coopting the protean charge and pacing of Raimi's films while maintaining a particu-larly NZ trashiness, Jackson had attempted to outgrue Raimi from the gitgo (consider Jackson's Curly to Raimi's Moe, reacting in frantic fury to every eyepoke and brickbat), and after *Braindead* even Raimi has implicitly admitted that cannibal slapstick has seen its *Intolerance*.

Their careers have counterpointed from the moment brain matter began falling comically out the back of one of *Bad Taste*'s protagonist's skulls, and although Raimi is the pioneer, and technically the more polished moviemaker, Jackson has proven to be the more imaginative, and the least genre-constricted. Whereas Raimi ascended to the exhila-rating comic-book hyperbole of *Darkman* (his best), Jackson tangoed into savage media parody with *Meet The Feebles* (1989), an enthusias-tically bloodthirsty rip through the Muppets and showbiz fables in general. That there are no humans in the film doesn't prevent Jackson from studying the arc of viscera, vomit and disease as it invades a preposterous TV fantasy world. *The Muppet Show* per se may be an easy target, and the subjection of puppets to the foulest of human inequities a one-note joke born of a film majors' beer-flooded dorm caucus, but Jackson hits every comic note and never takes his foot off the insult-throttle: the various felt-&-vinyl bottomfeeders inhabiting this particular theater of cruelty include a satyric rabbit dying slowly of a sex disease, a knifethrowing junkie frog given to 'Nam flashbacks (the cruelest and funniest puppet persona), a big-boss walrus caught more than once screwing a cat on his desktop, a huge, drug-dealing wild boar, an elephant saddled by a chicken with a paternity suit (he insists the child isn't his, but it *is* half chicken, half elephant), a toilet-loitering fly reporter who patrols the theater for scandal, a rat who shoots S&M porn loops in the sewers with an udder-ringed cow and a cockroach, etc. Most of the ensuing madness is seen through the wide eyes of a method-acting, lispy hedgehog new to the Feebles and caught perfectly between cuddly and mortified, especially once the obese and much-abused hippo starlet picks up a machine gun and plows through the company like a postal worker on the first day of unemployment. The pure excess of crude invention, devastating character assassination and wicked visual vaudeville (the shivering frog's brutal POW nightmare, a la *The Deer Hunter* and complete with Vietcong gophers arguing Marxism around the campfire, is breathtakingly ballsy) are formidable and exhausting, as is Jackson's mise-en-scene, which makes hay out of the Muppets' below-the-belt neverland by emphasizing the Feebles' sexual and excretionary activities. Indeed, it seems the paradox of hand-up-the-ass puppet architecture, from Mortimer Snerd to Svankmajer's Punch & Judy to Alf, may have been what stimulated Jackson in the first place. Despite so much suffering (the AIDS-haunted rabbit's final on-the-air vomit fit is the outer limit), the nasty anthropomorphism never graduates onto a sober *Maus*-like plateau, and good thing: excessive anti-authoritarian stances like Jackson's are always built on the most delicate and treacherous of aesthetic urges. Pussyfoot, and it collapses into a lie; as in a good bar brawl, if you wonder where the door is, you've already lost the fight.

Jackson never lets us up for air, and so *Meet the Feebles* can seem relentless and unkind, an observation Jackson would surely have taken as a rave. (Jackson is as far as a filmmaker can get from wanting to involve us in a group hug.) In this way Jackson's first three films carry an unmistakably Sadean attitude: we crave narrative balance, and so triumphant disrespect for the vox populi is often best expressed as ceaseless, irrational battering. Sade, Lautréamont, Jarry, Celine, Genet and Burroughs, the Dadaists, Surrealists and Lettrists, acid rock, punk and rap; Jackson's lineage runs back to Bosch (especially in *Braindead*), and through every college room, postered hideaway and teen hangout in the land, ringing with derisive laughter over an adult world constructed of safety, duty and sense.

Indeed, *Braindead* (1992) laughs louder at death than any movie ever has, and the titanic scope of dismemberment and butcher-shop slapstick pales all other attempts at blood humor, no matter the medium. (Yet it seems more human than Raimi's films; clocking in at this point with *Army of Darkness*, the slight, cartoony coda to his *Evil Dead* trilogy, Raimi was at once out-Raimied and past his prime.) Truly, Jackson's is the most hemophiliac of movies — once it begins geysering plasma it just can't stop. (Beware renting the cut, R-rated version on video.) Still, this bloodshot bouillabaisse comes off as buoyant and invigorated with its own reckless nerve — before the zombies attack the Norman Bates-ish hero's house en masse in a Spike Jones replay of *Night of the Living Dead*, we're treated to the hero's zombie Mom obliviously eating her own detached ear and spitting out the earring, the same Mom rising from her grave just in time to bite a gang thug in the crotch (yes, while he's pissing on her grave), a kung fu-fighting priest slamming his foot right through undead torsos ("I kick ass for the Lord!"), two drugged zombies copulating (those Gothic ultimates, death and sex, finally meet) and speedily generating a purebred zombie toddler, who descends on the local playground, and much more. In terms of filmmaking chutzpah, it's like watching someone walk out onto the wing of an airplane. Once the climactic attack gets under way, the walls are literally painted red with movie blood (watch out for the self-ambulating pile of intestines, complete with farting anus), and it's the movieness that's the crucial issue: Jackson is crazy in love with bad taste, and his elan compounds every frame. For anyone with eyes, the wit and ocular tumult of *Braindead* proved that Jackson had more than visions of exploding tissue in his heart — compare it to the equally ghoulish but insipid and lugubrious rot-fests of Jorg Buttgereit (*Nekromantik*, etc.). *Braindead* is a delirious hootenanny celebrating the rush of movies themselves, their potential for realizing unimaginable imagery, their subversive spirit, their ability to bring breathless joy to the most harrowing and scatological material, their mad hubris and scorched-earth defiance. It's a wild-eyed party movie, and cinephiliacs everywhere are invited.

Viewed this way, the Tasman Sea-sized leap to the comparatively restrained and sober *Heavenly Creatures* doesn't seem so huge, though it shouldn't for other reasons: for one thing, *Heavenly Creatures* is, objectively, hardly a restrained or sober work — indeed, its portrait of l'amour fou is brilliantly eccentric, passionate and risky. For another, the rebel-yell authorial dynamics of Jackson's earlier movies are sublimated as *HC*'s heroines' warped and frustrated world-view — the amphetaminic escalade of rage and manic humor belongs to the girls, coming from the inside out, not so much to Jackson's film. The infamous 1954 New Zealand murder of Honora Parker by her daughter Pauline and her schoolmate Juliet Hulme (real-life mystery author Anne Perry as a youngster) must have been a magnet to Jackson's particular penchant for psychosexual damage and mother horror (*Braindead* climaxes with a hellish primal scene, as the hero's Mum transforms into a giant Moloch and swallows him up her uterine canal — cinema's most graphic episode of vagina dentata). Hulme and Parker are half-lost in the hermetic, mock-medieval world of their own gland-powered reveries, an extreme intimacy (not unlike Jackson's fondness for the hidden interiors of body works) that's taken as overtly sexual (Jackson's, too?) by the girls' unlucky parents. Jackson clearly identifies with his misunderstood teenagers, and what may have seemed to some simply devilish japes in his previous films are used here to detail a deeply felt inner life. If you're as loathe as I am to shrug off Jackson's earlier films as merely vicious yock tantrums, then it must be admitted that gore comedy is not, in the end, a particularly challenging mode. Jackson knew he had run that jalopy right into a brick wall, which is where it belonged. So, in one lovely, graceful twist, he abandoned the company of Raimi, Henenlotter & Co. and expatriated to the country of earnest art films, style trumps and Oscar nominations. (Raimi's contemporaneous genre defection, *The Quick and the Dead*, merely transfers the same *Evil Dead* heehaws to a static frontier farce.) *Heavenly Creatures* displays good taste no one had the right to expect from Jackson, but it still crackles with a try-anything overload of visual ideas: the girls' fantasy world is filled with life-sized clay figures, distant castles, unicorns and ordinary Christchurch landscapes that morph into flamboyant storybook gardens (the most creative use of morphing I've ever seen); adults are shot like matinee villains, but remain sympathetic; the camera's careening flights and suffocating closeness to things evokes a swollen, pubertal angst the true story can only half-express. What may be more of a surprise is Jackson's handling of the actors, conducting laurel-ready performances, in two tough roles, from nonvets Melanie Lynskey and Kate Winslet, as is the purple, righteous, painfully desperate entries from Pauline's real diary, read as narration. To imagine for a moment the naked, expressive anguish and ardor that *Heavenly Creatures* contains bursting from an American movie is to glimpse an unknown, unrealized and probably impossible Hollywood.

As a treatment of a real murder case, Jackson's film is uniquely empathic and fleshy — compare the crude shortcomings of the nevertheless fascinating Leopold and Loeb trilogy, *Rope*, *Compulsion* and *Swoon*, and Jackson positively glows with humanism. *Heavenly Creatures* is many things to many people: a docudrama on microdots, a hellzapoppin opening of old wounds and plumbing of mad love, a valentine to all of us run over by the ten thousand cruel stories of youth, but it's never less than a crazed and earnest testament to how movies can express emotions by the creation, and manipulation, of vision. As per Hitchcock's attestation of what makes great cinema, we would still know exactly what *Heavenly Creatures* is about, textually and viscerally, even if the soundtrack were dropped out. Jackson may be the artist to definitively film *Madame Bovary*, Henry Miller or *The Castle*. That Jackson can so adroitly use hot-diggity horror movie conventions to drench us so effortlessly in the sweaty madness of adolescent angst and matricide is an ordinary miracle not only for the filmmaker but of the medium itself. After a century, we may take cinema a bit for granted — in our placid thrall to a star's sexual aura or our routine expectation of plot zigzags, we may fail to fully grok the rare and momentous journey we're on, where a minute alteration of the focal plane can reveal a human truth, and where a camera swirling over the heads of schoolgirls can speak to us of their giddy hungers and precarious grip on reality. We live with this second language everyday, and are encouraged to think of it as "information." Jackson's right: we should think of it instead as rapture, as sorrow, as flight.

(*Film Comment*, May – June 1995)

MICHAEL WINTERBOTTOM:
CINEMA AS HEART ATTACK

Narratively, the scene is inconsequential: two English journalists gaze down a hallway at a patiently sitting Bosnian child we've never seen before and never see again. Both her parents have been killed, one whispers to the other, what can we do? We've got to tell her, the other says. Cut to a 90-degree change in perspective, looking straight on at the journalists and a few caregivers as they huddle around the girl, who is helplessly sobbing. The crying is real enough to make you recoil; the journalists, living and working in a corpse-littered Sarajevo, are sympathetic but unaffected. With abrupt resolve the girl stands and walks away from the adults, and suddenly the camera becomes mobile and follows behind her, walking and weeping alone down the hall. She's about to disappear into the world forever, and the journalists know it — the camera knows it, too, and tries to keep track of her for at least a few moments longer. But as if realizing the hopelessness of the gesture (a hopelessness the semi-true story as a whole struggles to refute), the film cuts away from her, and she is gone.

Suddenly we are flushed and breathless with horrified heartbreak, purely by way of the unexpected, rigorously restrained camera movement. In virtually every frame of Michael Winterbottom's *Welcome to Sarajevo*, the camera functions as an independent, keen, empathic consciousness, moving of its own discerning will around the city and through the anarchical day-to-day nightmare lives of its citizens. Plot and character surface slowly, like divers who have cut their weights, from the Moloch's mouth of irrational hate, paralyzing fear, raining death and mourning. The inexhaustible textures achieved, the literal depth of its visual experience, the exposed-nerve immediacy and doubtless strength of its compositions, the ceaseless, unforecastable motions of its vision — it's more than merely a hot-topic movie, a humanist tract, even a searing melodrama of child rescue (though it is assuredly all three), it's an act of visual intervention, scorched earth imagemaking, a purifying needfire in the dark fields of the human republic. It is intended to rip your gaze free and drop it into the pit.

With only three acidic, uncompromising, disparate but strangely congruous features on his resume, Michael Winterbottom might just be that rarest creature, a British visionary. Each of his three theatrical films — *Butterfly Kiss*, *Jude* and *Welcome to Sarajevo* — is a model in how to attack three over-familiar genres (homicidal buddy road movie, Classics Illustrated costume drama, journalist-in-a-wartorn-country agitprop) and make them seem so new you feel as if you're inventing them with your eyes, right now. But no one could follow them as models, because they are shot and cut like a heart attack, because their identities are so essentially untrackable, associative and imbued with the sense of immediate and unstoppable experience. (His shots often approximate the swivel of the head looking over a room or a landscape, and few living directors can so quickly and clearly map out in-frame *and* off-frame territory.) Filmmakers are so often celebrated for sunsets, for florid Steadicam maneuvers, for all-this-and-*Terminator-2* property destruction, and particularly for dialogue they didn't write, that it almost seems pedagogic to claim greatness for Winterbottom on the basis of formal rigor. But rigor is as precious this late in the American century as unmoneyed integrity, and as rare in films as logically located source light. A descendent of Lang and Pontecorvo, Winterbottom never blinks when he should sit and stare, and never shoots action to seem more spectacular or uncanny than it truly is. The films move expressively, ambiguously, through their subjects, via unorthodox (but never look-Ma) compositional ideas, a galvanizing sense of off-screen space, razor-sharp leap cuts and a handheld temper so spontaneous and yet intense that you're never unaware of each film unfolding before you as a raw vision and not a prefabricated text.

Winterbottom's shots do real work — there's earned muscle behind them, and a bridgemaker's grip of moral priority. (He knows when to cut loose the safety net of sound, too, in *Jude* when the children's bodies are discovered and frantically rearranged by the hero, and in *Sarajevo* during the very real footage of the Bosnian concentration camps.) Winterbottom is frequently bleak, but never in an expressionistic, metaphoric manner; the epic trauma of the films is concrete, human, inevitable, spattered in real blood and revelation. He's a humanist, but so unsentimental he approaches being a Stoic, and living the truth of Kierkegaard's "dread and freedom."

Winterbottom began as an Oxford grad and television editor, making his first mark, perhaps fortuitously, directing no less than two documentaries about Ingmar Bergman. Dramatic and serial work followed, including the first episodes of "Cracker," and the searing four-part Roddy Doyle mini-series "Family" (a condensed version of which saw some festival play). One of Winterbottom's BBC melodramas, *Go Now*, starring Robert Carlyle as a plaster worker suddenly stricken with multiple sclerosis, has been expanded and set for release later this year in the wake of *The Full Monty*; though cold evidence of Winterbottom's energetic naturalism and grace with actors, the film is strictly journeyman work, bridled by the narrow interests and formulaic sensibility of television.

1995 is also when Winterbottom crept into features with *Butterfly Kiss*, written by Frank Cottrell Boyce (after "an idea" by both of them), a dry-eyed, wicked exploration of abusive relationships and working-class dislocation. We first see Eunice (a grating Amanda Plummer, delivering her lines like relentless left hooks) in pieces — her feet, head, disheveled clothes — walking along a busy English highway, muttering furiously, the film just as skittish and distracted as its subject. (Immediately it was evident that Winterbottom had overpowered the chokehold of television ratios.) When she enters a roadside convenience store and roves through it ranting about a record she's looking for, the camera can barely keep up with her, perpetually jostling for a clear shot. Gradually Eunice is revealed to be an abject psycho wandering the gray British hinterlands and leaving an inexplicable wake of corpses; Saskia Reeves, as Miriam (Mi, for short), is a blandly accepting, disaffected clerk she meets and seduces. Mi and Eu (a tiresome suggestion that the entire tale, as narrated by Mi from prison in lovely b/w cutaways, is a delusion) hit the road together, coming upon no wide open American road movie roads but one dreary Brit dead-end after another. We only realize how far gone Eunice is once she strips and reveals a self-lacerating battery of chains, cuffs, locks, piercings, tats and bruises. (Winterbottom's oeuvre is filthy with Holy Shit scenes.) It's only a matter of time until she melts down altogether, taking as much of the world with her as possible. Of his three films, *Butterfly Kiss* is the one in which the material isn't quite up to the shrewd formal zeal Winterbottom applies to it; the scenario affords little ambiguity, depth and resonance, and is comprised too overwhelmingly of cheesy elements common to low-budget resume movies. All the same, Winterbottom gives the saga of Eu and Mi a disquieting visual originality: from convenience stores to truck interiors to off-road lostlands, every scene's environment is shot as if it had just been discovered on Io. (He favors compressed visuals with many layers of realistic action, his heroines caught haplessly somewhere in the middle.) Mi's baptism by burial in a silent forest, bathed with blue magic hour half-light, is breathtaking, as are the final, traumatized images of Mi, shot in a slow, darkening flutter right off the editing flatbed. But watch how Winterbottom composes the pair's first lovemaking session — from the foot of the bed, gazing up at Eu's hunched, naked form as she licks an astonished Mi, whose hands come around to tentatively, blindly caress Eu's chain-and-bruise-covered back. Winterbottom holds this image just long enough to conjure rogue associations of the dark, saintly waters between penitent flesh and barking mad spirit, and long enough for us to realize it's an epiphanic moment for the characters, without ever seeing their faces. It's a quintessentially cinematic image, the sort unobtainable in any other form, and the sort that most filmmakers seem to no longer be capable of capturing with any dependability.

Doing Hardy as your second film sounds like an unadventurous bet on an even money horse for a Brit director, except that *Jude* has the impact of a cosmic action. Visually assaultive, unpredictable and thorny, *Jude* offers no succor amid the pre-industrial equipage and provides no thrill to the real estate porn sensitive. (From the first b/w shot of the cloud-shadowed hill, the landscapes look as if they've been painted with a steel bristle brush.) As modern, sinewy and seriously stuck in the bog of poverty as recent adaptations of Austen, Forster, James and Wharton have been nervelessly romantic and entranced with the leisure of wealth, Winterbottom's movie basks in the clean truth of catastrophe. But more importantly in filming Hardy's tale of love among the ruins, he shoots the action as if the two lovers (Christopher Eccleston and Kate Winslet) are the vital axis of all that is happening in the world around them, and are simultaneously a pair of mere pilgrims desperately gripping the speeding planet's husk as it threatens to throw them off. From the very first scene (of Jude as a child chasing crows from a massive plowed field, struck dumb by a cross of lynched crow bodies hanging in the wind), the movie places Jude either at the roiling heart of chaos or at the empty fringes; he often has to struggle for a foothold in the frame. As injustice and ill-fortune pound away on the couple, leading them eventually to outright Hardyesque tragedy and a peculiarly passionate, unHardyesque climax (courtesy of screenwriter Hossein Amini), Winterbottom's visual choices get riskier — the aforementioned Holy Shit scene, when Jude discovers the suffocated bodies of his three children, is overcome suddenly by a panicky, silent hand-held-ness, knocking the wind out of us before the story data even reaches our brains.

Jude's dominating aura, as it is of *Sarajevo*, is one of tougher-than-leather grownup regard for the plight of the innocent. Set, like *Sarajevo*, in a place and time when death, particularly for children, is brutally common, *Jude* throbs with the heartbreak and resilience of a mother who must have ten children so six will live. Winterbottom never withers before the terrible, or stoops to sensationalize, melodramatize or spectacle-ize the tragic. Rather, his visual choices reveal an almost extrahuman strength in containing extraordinary and deeply considered outrage, which you can still sense like strained veins through the skin of a bricklayer's arm. Again, it's rigor — *Jude* is the skilled, calloused laborer to the Ivory school's bloodless fop. Though he suffers for the victims, Winterbottom's more interested in those strong enough to survive.

On all levels, the three films are about struggle — every man for himself and God against all — not conclusions. *Welcome to Sarajevo* (also written by Cottrell Boyce, based the memoir by journalist Michael Nicholson) struggles to understand, visually as well as narratively, the unfathomable, a civilian civil war wherein butchery matter-of-factly replaced neighborliness. Winterbottom pushes his formal inquiry even further, into a terrifying, clear-the-decks combat zone of shifting mock-doc POVs, real news footage, jump cuts, home movies and ironic audio-visual slams (even the layering in of "Don't Worry, Be Happy" over shots of wounded toddlers seems sharp and apt). Since the film is about tele-journalists, its entire perspective is both ethically tainted and enlightened by witnessing the action through video cameras. Sometimes you can't tell where the real video begins and the fictional ends — just as the found footage folded into Werner Herzog docs like *Echoes of a Somber Empire* can seem the most Herzogian, often *Sarajevo's* many pre-existing news shots of the Bosnian carnage seem to epitomize Winterbottom's aesthetic. (Long glimpses of wounds and corpses are unmistakably real, but footage of the torched National Library is a vision out of Dante.)

Never allowing the ever-present and ambiguous ideas of "seeing" and media-directed gaze to overwhelm the crisis (which would succeed, and has succeeded in lesser films, in focusing all of a film's energy on the journalist), the filmmaker sees the war through the helpless journalists' eyes, which are perpetually on the edge of tearing up and breaking down. (The journalists are necessarily cynics, but are constantly being emotionally overhauled by what they see — even Woody Harrelson's opportunistic American star reporter has become, by the end, a humble crusader for peace.) When a hairy Serb Chetnik patrol halts a bus of orphans American aid workers are trying to get out of the country, we're not worried for the journalist hero Henderson (Stephen Dillane) but for the children, several of which the Serbs grab and take by gunpoint. Children are *Sarajevo's* relentless focus; couple it with *Jude* (and even the nervewracking scene in *Butterfly Kiss* when it seems that

Eu might kill an 8-year-old) and you can read a strong current of parental anguish invading Winterbottom's conscious filmscape.

Opening with scenes from the 1984 Olympics, *Sarajevo* takes no prisoners: you've never seen so many dead babies in your life, particularly not in U.S. coverage of Bosnia. Which is a dilemma the film's journalists constantly face — how to make the ongoing conflict sexy over and over again for primetime news? The amoral vagaries of public attention is merely one of *Sarajevo*'s many thrumming piques. But outrage is cheap, and Winterbottom prioritizes instead the visual environment he dumps us into, making sure the action cascades across the restless frame (and beyond) without signs of jerryrigging, dramatic setups/rewards, emphatic emotional engineering or cheap structural ideas like redemption or "character arc." The film's primary story, of Henderson/Nicholson deciding to smuggle a young orphan girl out of Bosnia and bring her home to England with him, arises out of the Ernst-like rubble with no forewarning — it's just something merciful that happened, naturally and humanely, somewhere in the funhouse urban horror of the U.N.-designated "14th worst place on Earth."

Although I think Winterbottom's film may have to stand in the shadow of Angelopoulos's *Ulysses' Gaze* and Kusturica's *Underground* as a fictional attempt to plumb the millennial essence of Bosnia (even as Winterbottom's climactic cello performance, a re-enactment of a very real incident, scans like a miniature of Angelopoulos's orchestral maneuver in the ruins), it is easily the most crucial and riveting film of its perhaps dubious genre, certainly running roughshod over, say, *Salvador*, *Under Fire*, *The Year of Living Dangerously* or *The Killing Fields*. If that says little in the end, let it be recognized that Winterbottom is one of the very few filmmakers working in English who seems to be incapable of a boring shot, and keeps his imagery alive not through pyrotechnics or stylized design but via a dazzling fidelity to the nature of intense experience. He may well be the only commercial director to whom a "moral cinema" is possible.

(*Film Comment*, January – February 1998)

STOP-MOTION JIMJAMS: RAY HARRYHAUSEN

For me it was the harpies. At 10 already my medulla throbbed with images of appalling, haywire lunacy — dinosaurs stalking the streets of Tribeca, 30-foot fiddler crabs, two-headed Roc hatchlings, alien saucers crash landing into the Capitol dome, gargantuan octopi ripping down the Golden Gate Bridge, hydras and cyclopes and platoons of sword-brandishing skeletons. At least I could sleep, for the most part, through the lurching, proportion-screwing dreams it all spawned. But the harpies, bluish, leathery and creepy as a cold spot in a strange cellar, kept fluttering over me, *picking* at me, and I couldn't sleep peaceably for weeks.

Revisiting the berserk stop-motion worlds of Ray Harryhausen, after a childhood spent retrieving my eyeballs from under the TV and slapping them back in my head in time for the next centaur to gallop across the screen, is like picking through old toys you'd thought the Salvation Army had carted away long ago. Ridiculous, sublime and sadly antiquated by industry standards ever since the body-snatching infestation of digital animation (which places us somewhere in the mid-80s; even the *Star Wars* films, in their original versions, relied on Harryhausenish frame-by-frame figure movement), Harryhausen's is the most literal mythopoeic cinema ever constructed. He reigned supreme for three decades as the single most accomplished F/X wizard in the world, running from his apprenticeship to Willis O'Brien on *Mighty Joe Young* (1946) to *Clash of the Titans* (1981), his official swansong. Nearly anyone whose home harbored a TV in the 60s and 70s has the familiar Harryhausen topos imbedded on his or her alpha waves: the lizard-hipped postures, roiling reptilian tails and many-armed sabre-fights, the disturbing flexibility of stone and bronze colossi, the skeletons come to life in the ancient-Greek noonlight, the warping of scale perspectives, the in-our-face manifestations of nightmarish mythic archetypes, the weird, jittery sharpness of impossible entities, etc. There could have been no casual dalliance with fable, Biblical or otherwise, in the Indy Jones movies, nor the theropodian thrills of *Jurassic Park*, without Harryhausen's precedent. If there is a Jungian collective unconscious that can indeed be glimpsed through the looking-glass of primitive myth, then Harryhausen alone gave its archetypes cinematic life. If movies are indeed universal, then Harryhausen's images are their bete noires, the shuddery daydreams of ancient man terrorized on the plain by the new idea of half-man/half-anything monsters and godly whim.

Though they do literally belong to an exclusively preadolescent universe — these are the best *toys*, after all; who didn't want an 18-inch-high, fully posable latex cyclops to play with? — Harryhausen's movies opt less for Joseph Campbell's heroic brand of mythmania than for the mythic image's hellzapoppin expression of disquiet and horror. Only rarely did a Harryhausen critter's breach of the reality web not tap into a primal fear — the tiny Eohippus in *The Valley of Gwangi*, the R2D2-ish owl in *Clash of the Titans*, for two. Otherwise, welcome to the jungle: the pterodactyl lifting a cowboy off his horse and flying away in *Gwangi*, humans trapped in a giant honeycomb by a 20-foot honeybee in *Mysterious Island*, the seven skeletons ("the children of Hydra's teeth") rising swords-first from the dirt and falling en masse into battle stances (squa tront! as the old E.C. Comics used to say) in Harryhausen's premier achievement, *Jason and the Argonauts*. The dynamic of human-meets-leviathan is perpetual, hopeless combat. *Jason* also features the unsettling vision of the bronze giant Talos, tottering across a Greek beach before Jason unplugs his heel and lets the water out, as well as those harpies, which still plague me. Maybe they embody, like much of Harryhausen's work, a deathless instinct for superstitious loathing within that collective unconscious; maybe they're just fucking scary.

Archetypal anxiety had always been Harryhausen's basic text, whether he knew it or not; his first full-length films were classic Cold War expressions of atomic unease, Otherliness and cosmocentric hate. *The Beast from 20,000 Fathoms* is a seminally American take on primeval chaos visiting death upon the modern metropolis (and, eventually, Coney Island), and the freeway-decimating octopus in *It Came From Beneath the Sea* abstracted that idea further, into pure aquarium jimjams. *Earth vs. the Flying Saucers* remains one of the era's most rabid UFO movies, whose aliens display unbridled, even unreasonable, hostility toward the old U.S. of A.; though the film remains a template for any reading you'd care to give, the emphasis on military confrontation and federal icons is targeted directly at Moscow. After Hiroshima, America imagined anything could happen, and in a Harryhausen movie it certainly, dependably would, preferably in or around a familiar and disposable landmark. (And the films were his; the credited directors were as negligible as the actors.)

His move to ancient myth, Raquel Welch dinosaur sagas and Jules Verne seemed prescient, as the tense and placid Cold War segued into the more complicated 60s, but his shuddery world-gone-mad scenarios just got buggier. All the same, the primitive allure of their frame-by-laborious-frame F/X was just as fascinating — we all knew how the effects were managed, and the subtechnological beauty of the tarnished Talos or the manacled dragon in *The 7th Voyage of Sinbad* seemed, well, myth-like in its own right. Whether it be Méliès, the German Expressionists, the cheaply contrived monster insects of the 50s, or the contemporary junky retro-designs of Gilliam, Caro/Jeunet and Guy Maddin, the *artificialia* of fantastic imagery — the zipper on the monster suit, as it were — has a distinctive, instantly antiquated lustre that seamless visual effects cannot match. The fantastic tangibility of Harryhausen's creations is what made them memorable — unlike computer animated figures, which move with an unnatural yet unthreatening fluidity, Harryhausen's homely behemoths obey the same laws of movement that constrain the actors, and inhabit the same space, turf and sunlight. Their three-dimensionality is not illusory, and their hesitant, unblurred motions are strangely poignant.

Sinbad's cyclops or Jason's Talos aren't real, after all, and yet their liberation from the rush-hour time tunnel at the back of each kid's skull made reality a dubious quantity. More literal than Bosch or Giotto, Méliès or De Mille, Harryhausen's images take the possibility of phantasmata seriously, without once succumbing to showbiz tricksterism or even expressionistic riffs. At all times, the dinosaurs and griffins obey physical laws, mythic prescriptions and the logic of magic. (Who knew that you could raze a 100-foot bronze titan by unplugging his heel? It seemed to make perfect sense.) Indeed, Harryhausen's world became truly timeless once his Cold War sci-fi days were over; his submersion into myth and Mesozoic tarpits was complete, never acknowledging current fashions or cultural obsessions, never referencing anything outside the hermetic demands of his ancient sources. When his filmmaking methods approached obsolescence, he retired rather than pollute his deranged, pantheistic biosphere with slicker technology. He'd already shown us a cyclops and dragon fighting to the death — even if it's filmed again with the liquidiest computer visuals megabucks can buy, we've already seen it, for *real*. As F/X capabilities accelerate, I can easily imagine Harryhausen's rough-hewn images taking on the raw, gritty integrity of news footage. Perhaps that's what Ray had in mind all along.

Studies in an alternate physical truth of a kind only cinema can muster, movies like *Jason, Mysterious Island, It Came from Beneath the Sea* and the Sinbad epics could be read as an audiovisual library of mythic experience — the jolt of seeing those harpies for the first time can't help but approximate the funky disquiet of a B.C. plebe hearing about them around the pre-European cave fire. At the very least, the films should be required viewing for anyone under 12, the soil of whose brainpans have dampened and grown moldy in recent times with the vigorous polishing playing Sega provides. One three-fingered, many-headed Harryhausen monster chasing real people through a torchlit cavern could set the mud on fire.

(*The Village Voice*, April 18, 1994)

INDEX